D0489199

The Child and Family in Context

Developing Ecological Practice in Disadvantaged Communities

Owen Gill and Gordon Jack

RHP

Russell House Publishing

Barnardo's

Published in 2007 by:
Russell House Publishing Ltd
4 St. George's House
Uplyme Road
Lyme Regis
Dorset DT7 3LS

Tel: 01297-443948
Fax: 01297-442722
e-mail: help@russellhouse.co.uk
www.russellhouse.co.uk

© Owen Gill and Gordon Jack

British Library Cataloguing-in-publication Data:

A catalogue record for this book is available from the British Library.

ISBN: 978-1-905541-15-7

Typeset by TW Typesetting, Plymouth, Devon

Printed by Biddles Ltd, King's Lynn

Contents

Preface

In this book we examine the implications for the practice of a wide range of child welfare agencies and practitioners of the relationships between the personal characteristics of children, young people and families who come to their attention, and the disadvantaged communities and neighbourhoods in which most of them live. We do this by exploring the ways in which practice, underpinned by ecological theory can help to safeguard children and young people and promote their welfare, considering the issues and challenges presented by this way of working.

It has long been recognised that the environmental circumstances in which children and young people grow up play an important role in shaping their development. The child psychiatrist Donald Winnicott, for example, wrote about the connections between the child, the family and the outside world over 50 years ago (1964). However, it was Uri Bronfenbrenner who was the first to directly apply ecological theory to human development (Bronfenbrenner, 1979). Since then, the main area in which ecological theory has influenced child welfare practice in the UK is through official guidance on the assessment of children's needs, which requires that child development is considered within the context of their family and community environments (DoH, 2000). However, even within this ecological approach to the assessment of children's needs, mainstream child welfare agencies have followed long established practice in continuing to place major emphasis on the development of children and young people *within* their families. With only a few exceptions, for example in work with disabled children and some approaches to youth work (Westcott and Cross, 1996; Beresford et al, 1996; Jack and Jack, 2000; Holman, 2000), consideration of the interactions between these family systems and the wider communities and society in which they are located continue to be relegated to a secondary position (Jack, 2000).

We were sufficiently concerned about this narrow focus on the internal dynamics of family life at the expense of a proper consideration of the influence of factors external to the family, to write a book, *The Missing Side of the Triangle*, which challenged this imbalance (Jack and Gill, 2003). Drawing on our practice experience of working in local authority children's services and voluntary agency anti-poverty programmes over many years, as well as social work and community work education and research, the book combined research findings with practice examples that emphasised the central importance of the voices and experiences of children, young people, their parents and carers, and demonstrated the role played by community-level influences in their lives. In doing this, we aimed to provide professionals working with children and young people, and their families, with information and practice tools required to undertake more holistic ecological assessments. By focusing attention on the community and society level influences on children and families, and the inter-connections between these factors and different aspects of child development and parenting capacity, the book attempted to rectify some of the shortcomings in the official guidance.

This volume takes the process of using our knowledge and experience of applying ecological theory to work with children and families a stage further. Employing a similar combination of research findings and practice examples, we aim to explain and illustrate important aspects of what we have termed 'ecological practice'. As far as we know, this term has not been used before in relation to social welfare work with children and families.

In essence, we see ecological practice as a synthesis of existing but largely disconnected forms of practice. At one end of the current spectrum of approaches there is the *individually-oriented practice* typical of mainstream children's services in health, education and social work, which often gives only limited consideration to the influences of community and society level factors on the development and behaviour of individuals. At the other end of the spectrum there is *community-oriented practice*, common in the fields of housing and neighbourhood regeneration, which takes as its primary concern groups and communities, but often with fairly limited consideration of their impact on the lives of individual children and families. Even when attempts have been made to combine various aspects of these contrasting approaches, as in some recent preventive and early intervention initiatives such as Sure Start and the Children's Fund, there has been little evidence that the often complex and fluctuating boundaries and interactions between the internal and external worlds of children, young people, their families and carers have been properly understood or explored. Our aim, therefore, is to outline a form of practice which is systematically underpinned by ecological theory, developing holistic and integrated approaches which are capable of simultaneously understanding and address-ing all of the significant influences in the lives of children and their families.

We have organised the material in the book into three sections, the first of which deals with the **research and policy background to ecological practice**. This section begins by providing a general introduction to developing ecological practice with children and families (Chapter 1). An analysis of the context for ecological practice in disadvantaged communities in the UK comes next (Chapter 2), followed by a review of the research evidence about the impact on children and families of living in these circumstances (Chapter 3). The first section of the book concludes with an examination of some of the main ecological processes that operate in disadvantaged communities (Chapter 4).

The second section of the book considers the **practice implications** of systematically applying ecological theory in work with children, young people and families. It begins by looking at the development of practice approaches to the connections between the child, the family and the community (Chapter 5). This is followed by descriptions of ecological practice in the four community settings that provide the source of many of the other practice examples included in the book (Chapter 6). We then consider three different but related facets of contemporary practice: community approaches to safeguarding children (Chapter 7); capacity building with parents and children (Chapter 8); and regenerating neighbourhoods and improving community safety (Chapter 9).

The final section considers some of the main **challenges of ecological practice**, including the development of evaluation for ecological practice (Chapter 10), and the challenges facing organisations and practitioners in the development of this form of practice, particularly in relation to the delivery of more integrated preventive, early intervention and community-oriented services through children's centres and extended schools (Chapter 11).

Busy practitioners and service managers, looking for the quickest way to access information about ecological practice, may find it most helpful to start by reading the introductory chapter, before going straight to the practice section of the book, and finishing with the concluding chapter. The first section of the book, which considers the research and policy background to ecological practice, together with the evaluation chapter, can be used for reference purposes. Others, coming from more of an organisational or policy perspective, may choose to read the first section of the book and the concluding chapter in more detail, perhaps dipping in and out of the practice section to provide illustrations of ecological practice with different groups or in particular settings.

The research material and practice examples that we have included in the book attempt to cover not only the diverse range of different groups of children, young people and families resident in the UK, but also some of the main community contexts within which they are presently living. To this end, material is provided about a range of children and their families including disabled children and young people, children of different ages and genders, and children living within white, Black and minority ethnic, dual heritage and refugee families. Practice examples are also provided from a wide range of disadvantaged community contexts, including an inner-city neighbourhood, a rural market town, a peripheral housing estate, and a large coastal town. Issues relating to the participation of children and young people in decision-making are integrated throughout the book, but are given particular emphasis within Chapter 8, which addresses the wider issue of building the capacity of all community members. Throughout the book, all names and other identifying details included in the practice examples have been changed to maintain confidentiality.

In developing the idea of ecological practice we are aware that we draw from ideas of community practice and community development. We are also aware that, over many years, other practitioners, working in a range of child welfare settings, have implicitly approached their work in this way. But we think it is important to present mainstream practitioners with a more holistic theoretical approach to their work which links the internal world of the family to the external world of the community, and assists them to work creatively with these connections.

About the Authors

Owen Gill has been involved for more than thirty years, both as a researcher and practitioner, with the connections between children and their communities. Research for his PhD investigated the links between housing provision and patterns of adolescent delinquency. As a practitioner, he has worked with families in a wide range of different settings, including rural and inner city communities. He is currently anti-poverty co-ordinator for Barnardo's South West, a post which involves managing community development work, and also researching the impact of poverty on children's lives. He has published widely on this work.

Gordon Jack, who is currently reader in social work at Durham University, has been involved in social work practice and research with children and families for the past thirty years. His research work has focused on the links between the well-being of children and young people and their wider family and community circumstances, highlighting in particular the influences of poverty and other forms of inequality and disadvantage. He has taught and published widely on these issues, including writing *The Missing Side of the Triangle* with Owen Gill (Barnardo's, 2003) about the importance of assessing the wider family and environmental factors in the lives of children and young people.

Acknowledgements

We are grateful for the help and advice of a number of friends and colleagues in the preparation of this book, including Bill Jordan, Delia Jack, Deena Haydon, and Helen Donnellan. Colleagues in Barnardo's have also given us valuable support and helped with case examples. They include Jane Stacey, Pat Wiltshire, Kalif Noor, Helen Dunn, Sadie Hall, Sue Sharps, Rhiannon Prys-Owen, Hilary Horan, Sara Tibbs and Jenny Lewis.

We would also like to thank Geoffrey Mann, of Russell House Publishing, who has provided us with invaluable guidance and support throughout the writing of the book.

Chapter 1. **Introduction: Developing Ecological Practice With Children and Families in Disadvantaged Communities**

This chapter will consider:
- The limitations of individually-oriented approaches to the welfare of children and young people.
- The application of ecological theory in work with children and families.
- The current policy context for ecological practice.
- Measuring and mapping the well-being of children and young people.
- Some of the challenges involved in developing ecological practice.
- The main elements of ecological practice.

Introduction

Current approaches to welfare work with children in the UK typically focus on their immediate family circumstances, often failing to adequately address the way that children's development is also influenced by the wider community contexts in which their development is taking place.

In order to illustrate some of the consequences of focusing attention on the individual and family aspects of children's welfare, at the expense of the neighbourhood and community influences that are also invariably of significance, we start with a practice example from a study of child abuse networks by one of our research students (Monk, 2004):

A primary school teacher was concerned about the sexualised behaviour of several children in her class. Further enquiries revealed that many of the children's parents had concerns about a man working in the local newsagents, who lived in the same cul-de-sac of social housing occupied by many of the children about whom the teacher was concerned. On further investigation it was revealed that this man had previous criminal convictions for sexual offences against children and that he had used similar employment in the past to gain access to children. It subsequently emerged that his brother-in-law, who lived with him, and another male friend, who was a frequent visitor to the household, also had convictions for sexual offences involving children.

Examination of the records held by the local health, education and social services revealed that there were child protection concerns about children living in nearly half of the households in this single cul-de-sac, consisting of 40 dwellings. However, up to this point, none of the individual professionals or agencies involved had been aware of the extent of one another's involvement with other families living there, nor had they identified any neighbourhood-level concerns about the welfare of children in this area. This ignorance was evident in what happened in two other households in the cul-de-sac. One involved a family who had recently been rehoused, on the advice of a judge, to move the children away from a previous sexual abuser. The other concerned local authority foster carers who were looking after a child recently placed with them in ignorance of the fact that their next door neighbours, on one side, were being investigated for their possible involvement in a serious intergenerational child sexual abuse network, and on the other side the household included a six year-old boy who had recently been discovered taking part in inappropriate sexual play with other boys at the local school.

This example graphically illustrates some of the serious shortcomings of children's safeguarding policies that rely exclusively on individual referrals. Whilst we are not arguing that such individual approaches are not important, it seems evident to us that they are often not sufficient to effectively safeguard children and promote their well-being. Taking an optimistic view of the future, in which more integrated children's services are delivered via children's trusts under the policy umbrella of *Every Child Matters*, improved information sharing between the various agencies involved *might* reveal situations like this at an earlier stage. However, it is difficult to see how these changes, on their own, will help agencies and practitioners to develop practice approaches that have the potential to address the combined effects of individual, family and community level factors on children's well-being simultaneously, in a way that would have been appropriate in the above practice example. Instead of relying entirely on individual referrals as the basis for meeting their duties to safeguard children and promote their well-being, it seems clear to us that mainstream children's services need to integrate these with more community-focused processes, capable of identifying and pro-actively responding to neighbourhood-level problems, like the ones that are evident in the above practice example. Conversely, agencies that traditionally rely primarily on a community-orientation also need to develop and integrate into their practice more individually-oriented perspectives, considering in greater depth the specific ways in which their interventions impact on the lives of particular children and families.

Applying ecological theory in work with children, young people and families

We believe that ecological theory is of central importance in the development of holistic approaches to safeguarding children and young people, and promoting their well-being. Within ecological theory, children's developmental outcomes are understood to be dependent on the interplay between strengths and risk factors in their personal and family circumstances, their friendship networks and situation at school, and the wider communities and society of which they are a part. These factors are in a constant state of flux and children, with their evolving understanding and capacities, shape their well-being by mediating all of these factors in their lives (Bronfenbrenner and Morris, 1998). Ecological theory therefore proposes that the development of children and young people can only be understood properly by viewing it as taking place within the context of a number of overlapping and interacting social systems. The child or young person is directly present within some of these social systems, such as their household, school and immediate neighbourhood, whilst there are others in which they are not directly represented but which impinge on their development, including their siblings' social networks and their parents' or carers' friendship, leisure and workplace relationships. Ecological theory also requires that the influences of wider social systems are taken into account, including the cultures, political systems, social institutions, and values that exist in the society in which they are growing up (Bronfenbrenner, 1979). The influences and experiences that result from the interactions between these different social systems play a key role in determining the extent to which children and young people either thrive and reach their full potential, or experience difficulties in their development which can have lasting detrimental effects on their well-being and future life chances. Within ecological theory, the development of children and young people is therefore understood to be inextricably linked with the characteristics of these social systems, and the way in which they interact with one another.

The ecological theory of human development already underpins much current theorising and research in the field of child and family welfare, either explicitly or implicitly, both in the UK and elsewhere. There is an increasing focus on illuminating the connections and mutual influences between the different social systems in which the child's evolving life is set. However, there is a significant disparity between this ecological framework and most current welfare practice in the UK and elsewhere. The dominant culture within mainstream child welfare agencies, for example, is primarily concerned with identifying and managing 'dangerous adults', and the provision of services to help to meet the needs of vulnerable individual children and their families. This means that the allocation of resources and the attention of practitioners are concentrated on what are essentially reactive responses to the conditions that exist *within* families.

The work of a wide range of professionals, including social workers, health visitors, family support workers, child and adolescent psychiatrists and child psychologists, therefore focuses on addressing problems identified as being primarily internal to the child or their family, such as sibling relationships, and parental capacity to keep children and young people safe and provide them with a secure and stimulating home environment. At the same time, another distinct group of practitioners, including community workers, neighbourhood regeneration workers, community safety officers, and housing workers, if they have a focus on the lives of children at all, tend to view them as a sub-group of residents within the wider contexts of community and neighbourhood. In our experience, very few professionals focus much of their attention on examining the *connections* between the well-being of individual children and young people, and the external factors that help to shape that well-being, such as the wider social networks and community resources available to local people, and there is little practice literature to help them to do so.

In many ways it is understandable that we do not have an established knowledge base for putting ecological theory into practice. There is a close relationship between the development of practice knowledge and the power of individual professional groups and organisations to determine the boundaries within which that knowledge is developed. In the UK especially, practice knowledge in the field of child welfare has largely been generated within the context of strictly demarcated professional and organisational boundaries, and there have been few groups or agencies with a remit to take a holistic view of children's lives, working at the interface of the different social systems that impact on their development. Processes of what Moss and Petrie (2002: 65) have referred to as 'atomisation' and 'compartmentalism' have occurred, within which:

> . . . *services together with the practitioners who staff them and the departments who have oversight for them, target certain groups of children, see certain parts of the child, bring certain understandings of the child, want certain outcomes from the child, have certain rationalities which shape how they think about legitimate intervention with children.*

We consider these processes to be damaging to the welfare of children and young people and our aim, in the remainder of this volume, is to outline a more holistic and integrated form of what we have termed 'ecological practice'. Based on ecological theory, this approach focuses particular attention on the links between community and neighbour-hood conditions, on the one hand, and children's everyday experiences and development, on the other.

We think it is important that information about ecological practice is accessible to a wide range of professionals whose actions and decisions impact on the lives of children and their families in one way or another. It is likely to be of most relevance to professionals working under the umbrella of children's trusts, including social workers, family support workers, youth workers and youth justice workers, education welfare officers, child and adolescent psychiatrists, child psychologists, health visitors and school nurses. However, it is also intended to be accessible and relevant to a wide range of other professional workers, including those in the fields of public health, education, housing, planning, community work and regeneration.

The current policy context for ecological practice

Developments in national policies relating to the organisation and delivery of services for children and young people in the UK, for example under the government's *Every Child Matters* and *Youth Matters* agendas in England, make this a particularly auspicious time to be exploring the main components of ecological practice.

In recent years there have been a number of initiatives in the UK that, either explicitly or implicitly, have included recognisable elements of an ecological approach. These include the Sure Start and Children's Fund programmes developed in England which were designed to improve prevention and early intervention services to reduce poverty and social exclusion amongst disadvantaged children and families, and the On Track and Communities that Care programmes directed at reducing youth offending and other aspects of problematic or anti-social behaviour amongst young people. To a greater or lesser extent, all of these initiatives have been introduced with the links between children and their communities as a central concern, and the requirement that different child welfare agencies work more closely together in the delivery of 'community-based' services. These attempts to develop more holistic approaches to addressing the problems in children's lives have also been incorporated into legislation with, for example, the implementation of the Children Act 2004 and the policy developments that accompanied it heralding major changes in the organisation and delivery of services for children and young people in England.

The background to these changes included the independent inquiry into the death of Victoria Climbié (Laming, 2003) and *Safeguarding Children*, the Joint Chief Inspectors' report about the overall child protection system (DoH, 2002). Both reports highlighted major shortcomings in the organisational and professional arrangements for safeguarding children, including the perennial problems of effective multi-agency working and confusion about the accountability of different agencies and professionals. *Keeping Children Safe*, the government's response to these reports, concluded that the existing legal framework for safeguarding children, the Children Act 1989, remained basically sound. However, the report identified serious weaknesses in the way that it was being interpreted, resourced and implemented (DfES et al., 2003).

The government set out its proposals to address these problems in a Green Paper on the future of children's services, *Every Child Matters*, which proposed wide-ranging reforms designed to improve inter-professional working and accountability, and to tackle staff training, recruitment and retention problems. Central to these reforms was the acknowledgement that 'child protection cannot be separated from policies to improve children's lives as a whole'. The Green Paper argued that everyone in society has a responsibility for securing children's well-being, through the achievement of five key outcomes: 'being healthy, staying safe, enjoying and achieving, making a positive contribution and economic well-being' (HM Treasury, 2003: 5). However, it recognised that the achievement of these outcomes would require long-term changes in organisational and professional cultures and ways of working.

The government's overall approach to the restructuring of children's services was encapsulated in the statement made at the time of the Green Paper's publication by the Secretary of State, Alan Milburn, who said that the only way to break down the barriers between services was to 'remove the barriers altogether'. At a national level this involved integrating responsibility for children's education and social services under the new post of Minister for Children within the Department for Education and Skills, establishing the post of Children's Commissioner for England to act as an independent champion for children, and developing an integrated inspection system for children's services. At local authority level, *Every Child Matters* proposed the appointment of directors of children's services, with combined responsibility for education and social services for children, and the development of children's trusts to bring together the overall planning and commissioning of children's services. Within these new organisational arrangements, to be in place in all local authorities by 2008, targeted services for children with particular needs are to be provided within the context of universal services for all children. There is also an emphasis on meeting the five *Every Child Matters* outcomes, outlined above, through early intervention, information-sharing and multi-professional working.

Whilst the organisational changes outlined above are clearly of major proportions, arguably the most radical aspects of the new arrangements lie in the duties placed on children's services authorities to safeguard and promote the well-being of *all* children living in their area (Children Act 2004, ss. 10–14). Three main mechanisms are identified to achieve this ambitious objective, the first of which is the duty placed on local authorities to promote co-operation between all of the relevant agencies, including the possibility of pooling their resources. The second is the development of databases, covering each local authority area, containing information about all children and young people living there and identifying children who have particular needs. And the third involves the establishment of Local Safeguarding Children Boards in each authority (to replace the previous Area Child Protection Committees), on which all key partners are represented, with responsibility for ensuring co-ordinated and effective strategies to safeguard and promote the welfare of children in their area.

In our view, these mechanisms are not sufficient to achieve the objective of safeguarding and promoting the well-being of all children without other significant changes, particularly in relation to the existing cultures and practice approaches of mainstream children's services organisations, and the professionals who work within them. In fact, we think that these new arrangements are more likely to be used to reinforce the existing focus on vulnerable, 'high-risk', individual children, than to develop the type of ecological practice which we consider is essential for the effective safeguarding of all children and young people, and the promotion of their well-being.

Although the UK government has recognised the need for changes in the cultures and ways of working within mainstream services, their primary focus is on breaking down inter-agency barriers and developing earlier interventions. There is virtually no acknowledgement of the need to develop more holistic practice approaches to safeguarding and promoting well-being. Nowhere is this more evident than in the guidance published to aid multi-disciplinary working, which identifies over 150 different areas of knowledge and skills required by the new children's workforce, only one of which makes even passing reference to the influence of the wider social context of children and young people's lives on their development (Department for Education and Skills, 2005a: 11).

Measuring and mapping the well-being of children and young people

Despite the entrenched focus on vulnerable individual children, young people and families within welfare practice in the UK, at a policy level there is increasing interest in measuring and mapping the well-being of *all* children and young people, at both national and local levels. New datasets, including the 2001 Census, the Family and Child Study, the Millennium Cohort Study, the British Household Panel Survey, and the English Indices of Deprivation are beginning to provide information about different aspects of child well-being across the UK. Similar information is also increasingly becoming available in other countries, enabling researchers and policy makers to develop international league tables of children's well-being (Ben-Arieh and Goerge, 2006). For example, Bradshaw and colleagues (2006) have constructed a league table of children's well-being across the European Union, using existing datasets, and combining an ecological framework with a children's rights perspective. The overall index is based on the average rating of children's well-being in each of 23 domains (incorporating a total of 51 indicators), which are grouped into eight clusters, as set out below:

- *Material situation* (child poverty; child deprivation; and parental worklessness).
- *Housing and environment* (overcrowding; local environment and space; housing problems).
- *Health* (child health at birth; immunisation; health behaviour).
- *Subjective well-being* (self-defined health; personal well-being; well-being at school).

- *Education* (attainment; participation; youth labour market outcomes).
- *Relationships* (family structure; relationships with parents; relationships with peers).
- *Civic participation* (participation in civic activities; political interest).
- *Risk and safety* (child mortality; risky behaviour; experience of violence).

It can be seen from the summary league table (Table 1), that Cyprus, the Netherlands, Sweden and Denmark are at the top of the child well-being league, with the Slovak Republic, Latvia, Estonia and Lithuania at the bottom.

The researchers note that, although there is some relationship between child well-being and the level of wealth of a country, this does not explain the presence of, for example, Spain and Slovenia in the top third of the table, or of the UK near the bottom (Bradshaw et al., 2006). On closer inspection it can be seen that distinct groups of countries, from particular regions of the EU, are doing better or worse than others. For instance, the Scandinavian and Mediterranean countries are doing well, whilst the Baltic States and the Slovak Republic are doing poorly. The explanation for these trends provides a clear illustration of ecological theory, with better overall child well-being attributable to different combinations of factors within different countries, including relatively low inequality (Slovenia, the Netherlands, Scandinavia), better inter-personal and community relationships (Spain, Slovenia), strong welfare state provision of family benefits and social services (Scandinavia, the Netherlands) and an emphasis on children's rights (Scandinavia). The poorer overall ratings found in the Baltic States and the Slovak Republic are attributable to a combination of high levels of absolute poverty and inequality together with major gaps in their social infrastructure.

However, of most interest to us in this book is the lowly position of the UK, the fifth richest nation in the world, in relation to children's well-being. This is explained by the relatively high levels of inequality that exist in the UK (that are discussed in the next chapter), combined with the absence of the sort of socially unifying mechanisms operating in other countries, based on either the welfare state (Scandinavia) or the family (Mediterranean), which help to promote community cohesion and inclusion. This is evident in the UK's poor performance in relation to a range of measures of inter-personal relationships and community participation, coming either bottom or second bottom out of all EU countries on each of the measures of 'children's relationships', as well as performing very poorly on the 'civic participation' and 'subjective well-being' measures. These findings are of major significance at a time when personal and social skills are emerging as increasingly important in determining relative life chances. This was starkly illustrated in a study carried out by the Institute for Public Policy Research which revealed that, for young people born between 1958 and 1970; these 'softer' skills became over thirty times more important in determining their life chances, with young people from less affluent backgrounds being less likely to develop these skills than their more fortunate peers:

> *For those born in 1958, the connection between family background, personal and social skills, and success later in life was barely discernible. But for a significant proportion of those born in 1970, social mobility – the passing on of disadvantage through families – was clearly due to the connection between family background and personal and social skills.*

> (Margo and Dixon, 2006: viii)

Table 1 Child well-being in the European Union (Bradshaw et al., 2006)

Country	Average rank	Health	Subjective well-being	Children's relationships	Material	Risk and Safety	Education	Civic Participation	Housing
Cyprus	4.6	5			1	2		1	14
Netherlands	5.1	2	1	5	10	5	6		7
Sweden	5.8	1	6	15	2	3	2	14	3
Denmark	6.5	3	9	10	6	15	3	4	2
Spain	8.9	13	3	9	8	1	15		13
Finland	9.8	7	12	17	3	7	4	18	10
Germany	10.0	10	7	12	12	12	9	10	8
Slovenia	10.4	15	8	3	4	18		13	12
Belgium	10.8	20	15	6	18	16	1	5	5
Ireland	12.4	19	5	8	19	20	7		9
Greece	12.5	25	4	11	17	8	16	2	17
Italy	12.5	16	11	4	15	6	19	11	18
Austria	12.6	21	2	16	7	19	17		6
Luxembourg	12.6	11	20	19	5	9	20		4
Hungary	12.9	22	10	7	14	14	12	3	21
Poland	12.9	6	19	13	23	11	5	6	20
France	13.0	14	13	14	11	10	14		15
Portugal	13.0	9	16	2	13	17	18	7	22
Malta	13.5	24	17	1	24	4			11
Czech Reb	14.1	4	14	22	9	21	10	17	16
UK	16.0	23	18	23	20	22	13	8	1
Slovak Reb	16.6	17	22		25	13	11	9	19
Latvia	17.5	18	21	18	16	23	8	12	24
Estonia	19.9	12	23	21	21	24		15	23
Lithuania	20.0	8	24	20	22	25		16	25

As we will go on to illustrate in the next chapter, the UK has become an increasingly divided society over the past 35 years. In this context, the IPPR researchers go on to note that rising family incomes for many, since the 1970s, have created a set of more affluent parents who are increasingly able to purchase constructive, organised or educational activities and access to institutions that facilitate their children's personal and social development. However, those in poorer groups are unable to provide similar benefits for their children, leaving them to spend more of their time 'hanging out' with friends and watching TV, activities associated with poorer personal and social development, which places them at an increasing developmental disadvantage.

Whilst the basis of this particular piece of research has been questioned by some commentators (e.g. Williamson, 2006) the significance of the low levels of child well-being that exist in the UK at the present time, and the increasingly important role played by personal and social skills in the modern world, can hardly be overestimated. Evidence like this, that so clearly demonstrates the connections between factors at different levels of children's lives – individual, family, peer, school, community and society – in shaping their development and well-being, provides strong justification for the development of social policies capable of addressing these issues, alongside the sort of holistic ecological practice that we outline in the rest of this volume.

Some of the challenges involved in developing ecological practice

Whilst never explicitly acknowledged, it can be argued that the aspiration to safeguard and promote the well-being of all children that underpins both *Every Child Matters* (ECM) and the Children Act 2004 is based on ecological theory. However, as already noted, ECM does acknowledge that the achievement of its five key child well-being indicators will require major changes in organisational and professional cultures and ways of working including, we would argue, the development of more ecological practice. However, this will inevitably involve addressing a number of key challenges. In terms of the relationship between the child (or young person) and family, on the one hand, and their neighbourhood and community contexts, on the other, we think that the following are some of the most important challenges:

- Developing a practice theory of the relationship between the child (or young person) and family, and their neighbourhood and community, which is accessible to the range of different professional workers whose actions and policies impact on the lives of children and young people.
- Developing the knowledge and skills of practitioners, so that they can understand and map the complexities of neighbourhood and community factors in relation to the well-being of individual children and young people.
- Developing ways of working that can successfully *combine* neighbourhood and community level interventions with individual child and family interventions.
- Developing effective multi-agency partnership working, between different organisations and different practitioners, which supports ecological practice.

Underlying all of these challenges, there is a further very important challenge related to issues of empowerment. Working in neighbourhoods and with different communities inevitably raises issues about power and control. There have been many examples, over recent years, of both large and small scale initiatives which have tried unsuccessfully to impose externally-generated solutions onto disadvantaged neighbourhoods and communities. A key aspect of ecological theory, which we have not discussed so far, is its emphasis on a phenomenological perspective, in which the subjective views and experiences of children and other family members are understood to be of central importance in shaping their behaviour and development, and the subsequent course of their lives (Bronfenbrenner, 1979). As a consequence, ecological practice (like neighbourhood and community work) has to operate within a framework in which power is shared, with an emphasis on listening to and acting upon what individuals and groups of people think is important in their lives and may want to change. This can sometimes sit uneasily with more traditional, individually-oriented ways of working with disadvantaged families, where the professional is often deemed to be the expert, offering solutions and ways forward, which can be experienced as profoundly disempowering by individual family members.

Some of the main elements of ecological practice

In Section two of this volume we provide a number of detailed examples of the way that ecological practice can be developed in different settings and with different groups of children, young people and families. However, for the purposes of this introductory chapter, some of the main elements of ecological practice that emerge from this material are:

- Listening carefully to what children and young people, their families and carers say about the balance between the strengths and difficulties in their lives, paying particular attention to what they consider to be the origins of any difficulties and whether they view them as internal or external to the family.
- Working to make disadvantaged communities more supportive of the needs of all children, young people and families.
- Working to bring into play the physical and social resources of disadvantaged communities for the benefit of individual children, young people and families.
- Working with children and young people, their families and carers to enhance their skills in accessing the beneficial aspects of the communities to which they belong.
- Working to help children, young people and families identify the pressures and dangers of their community settings, developing their sources of support, personal resilience, and other coping resources.
- Acknowledging that children and young people, their families and carers are not the passive victims of the pressures of their situation, and recognising the ways that they actively engage with their environment and play a part in shaping it.

It can be seen that all of these elements of ecological practice are essentially about different facets of empowerment (Shera and Wells, 1999) and the links between the lives of children and young people at individual, family, group and community levels. These are issues that are explored in more depth at various points throughout the rest of the book.

Conclusion

We have identified that a fundamental aspect of ecological theory is the importance it places on the community and environmental contexts of children's lives, and the influence these factors have on their development and well-being. The reader will have noted in what has already been said, as well as in the title of the book, that our primary focus in this volume is on developing ecological practice in the context of disadvantaged communities. This is because these are the areas in which the greatest combination of difficulties affecting children's development and well-being are likely to be found. We recognise, of course, that some children and young people face difficulties and disadvantages even if they live in more affluent surroundings, or if their own families are relatively affluent. We also subscribe to one of the key principles underpinning *Every Child Matters*, that child protection and other services directed at vulnerable children cannot be separated from policies to improve children's lives as a whole. However, although we are confident that many of the ideas that we have developed about ecological practice in this volume have utility for work with all children, including those living in less disadvantaged circumstances, our experience to date limits the extent to which we can identify any significant differences that might exist.

It should be noted that when we use the term 'community' here, and throughout the rest of this volume, we are referring to both geographical communities and communities of interest, including the virtual communities, facilitated by the internet, that are playing an increasingly important role in many people's lives. We are, therefore, interested both in the influences related to where people live, and the different religious, ethnic, cultural, professional, leisure, and other identity and interest groups to which they belong. In adopting this definition, we are following the Standing Conference on Community Development, which views community as '. . . the web of personal relationships, groups, networks, traditions and patterns of behaviour that exist amongst those who share physical neighbourhoods, socio-economic conditions, or community understandings and interests' (SCCD, 2001). Also, for ease of reference, whenever we refer to 'children and families' in the rest of this volume this should be taken to mean children and young people, as well as their biological families and other carers, unless otherwise specified.

Overall, one of the key messages contained in the research into children's well-being and future life chances that has been discussed in this chapter is the central importance of issues of child poverty and other forms of disadvantage. As we now go on to examine, these issues provide a very important context for the development of ecological practice in the UK at the present time.

Chapter 2. **The Context for Ecological Practice: Poverty and Inequality in the UK**

This chapter will consider:
- How poverty is defined and measured and why the UK has such high levels of inequality.
- The effectiveness of current social policies in addressing the problems of poverty and inequality.
- The families and children most at risk of experiencing poverty and inequality.
- The concept of multiple deprivation, and the way that it is geographically distributed throughout the UK.
- The main implications of poverty and inequality for ecological practice with children and young people, their families and carers.

Introduction

Over the last quarter of a century or so, the UK has become one of the most unequal societies in the developed world (Hills, 2004). Although, overall, people in the UK are better off than in the past, across a range of measures, the benefits are spread very unequally (Office for National Statistics, 2004). Who you are and where you live are major factors in determining your chances of experiencing poverty and disadvantage, on the one hand, or affluence and privilege, on the other. However, the evidence from studies in the UK consistently indicates that social workers and other child welfare professionals tend to underplay the significance of these factors in children's lives, displaying what has been termed 'poverty blindness', and under-reporting other forms of disadvantage, such as poor housing conditions (Packman et al., 1986; Becker, 1997; Clark and Davis, 1997; Dowling, 1999).

In this chapter we look at poverty and disadvantage in the UK, focusing both on the historical development of high rates of inequality and the current position, particularly in relation to the spatial distribution of poverty and disadvantage. Our purpose in doing this is to understand the factors that contribute to the creation of the contexts in which children are living, a pre-condition for developing ecological practice and promoting well-being.

Defining and measuring inequalities in income and wealth

The first attempts to quantify the extent of poverty in particular areas of the UK were undertaken, over 100 years ago, by Charles Booth and Seebohm Rowntree, in London and York respectively (Glennerster et al., 2004). Rowntree drew a distinction between 'primary poverty', which was essentially an *absolute* measure of the minimum income required to keep body and soul together, and 'secondary poverty', which was a more *relative* concept, closer to Booth's notion of a 'line of poverty', below which people would be unable to sustain what was deemed to be a socially acceptable standard of living. Combining his two measures, Rowntree estimated that 28 per cent of the population of York were living in what he described as 'obvious want and squalor', slightly lower than the figure of 31 per cent judged to be living below Booth's 'line of poverty' in London at that time (Glennerster et al., 2004).

Following a series of similar local poverty surveys, carried out by different researchers across England in the first half of the twentieth century, Rowntree undertook two further studies in York (Rowntree, 1941; Rowntree and Lavers, 1950). The survey published in 1950, which was undertaken after the introduction of the Beveridge welfare state reforms, concluded that poverty had all but disappeared in York at that time. However, this was the smallest and least rigorous of his three York surveys and it seriously under-estimated the real extent of low income that existed at the time (Glennerster et al., 2004). This was revealed by studies undertaken in the late 1950s and 1960s using national data for the first time, which showed that poverty had, in fact, never gone away (Townsend, 1962; Wedderburn, 1962). For example, using a relative definition of poverty (set at 140 per cent of basic benefit rates), it was calculated that one in seven of the country's population were living in poverty in the early 1960s (Abel-Smith and Townsend, 1965).

Townsend subsequently developed his definition of relative poverty to include all people who 'lacked the resources to obtain the type of diet, participate in the activities and have the living conditions and amenities which are customary, or at least widely encouraged or approved in the societies to which they belong' (Townsend, 1979: 31). This definition of poverty is very similar to that which is used by the European Commission today, which includes all people 'whose resources (material, cultural and social) are so limited as to exclude them from the minimum acceptable way of life in the member states in which they live' (Commission of the European Communities, 1994).

The way that poverty is currently quantified within the EU involves defining anybody who lives in a household with an income (adjusted for family size and composition) of less than 60 per cent of their country's median, either before or after housing costs have been deducted, as living in poverty. Whilst many other ways of defining and measuring poverty have been developed, including the periodic 'Breadline Britain' surveys that identify the proportion of the population who lack items from a list of 'socially perceived necessities' (Mack and Lansley, 1985, 1991; Gordon et al., 2000) it is the relative poverty line approach that has been most widely adopted throughout Europe and the rest of the developed world. Although this approach has some significant limitations, it provides a convenient way of making comparisons of relative poverty rates across groups and geographical locations, at both national and international levels.

Rising poverty and inequality in the UK

Although poverty was not eradicated by the development of the post-war welfare state in the UK, by the late 1970s both income inequality and relative poverty in the UK were at historically low levels. However, under the policies of successive Conservative governments during the 1980s, which included the deregulation of economic markets, increased incentives to work, and reductions in spending on welfare benefits and public services, income inequality and relative poverty grew faster in the UK than in almost any other developed country in the world. Child poverty in the UK more than doubled during this period, whilst the disposable income of the top ten per cent of the population grew by 38 per cent, in real terms, which was more than five times the rise experienced by those in the bottom ten per cent of the population (Office for National Statistics, 2004). The proportion of households that lacked three or more 'socially perceived necessities', such as beds and bedding for all household members, two meals a day, and celebrations on special occasions like Christmas, also rose steeply, from 14 per cent in 1983 to 21 per cent in 1990 (Mack and Lansley, 1991).

The best way of measuring the distribution of income across whole populations is the Gini Coefficient, which uses a scale running from zero to one, representing the range from complete equality, where everyone in a country receives exactly the same income, to complete inequality, where one person receives all of a country's income. For developed countries, the Gini Coefficient is typically between 0.25, representing a relatively equal society, and 0.35, representing one that is relatively unequal. At the start of the 1980s, the Gini Coefficient in the UK was at the lower end of the normal range, reflecting the fact that it was a relatively equal society at that time. However, during the rest of that decade it rose rapidly, before flattening out during the early 1990s, and then rising further, to 0.35, in 2000/01, indicating that the UK had become a very unequal place to live in terms of disposable income. The poorest tenth of households at that time were taking home less than three per cent of national income after tax and benefits, compared to 28 per cent for the top tenth, a nine-fold difference (Department for Work and Pensions, 2005). These rising levels of inequality are also reflected in the fact that only the USA and Ireland had higher overall poverty rates amongst developed countries in 1999 (Glennerster et al., 2004), by which time child poverty affected one in three children in the UK, the highest rate among all EU countries (European Union, 2001).

On top of these inequalities in the distribution of income it is important to note that wealth, which includes assets such as savings, shares and property, is even more unequally distributed than income in the UK. For example, in 2001 it was estimated that the richest one per cent of the population in the UK held nearly a quarter of the nation's wealth, whilst the poorer half of the population held just one twentieth (Office for National Statistics, 2004). Home ownership is now the most important aspect of wealth held by individuals in the UK. Using a measure based on the amount of equity people have in their own property, a Shelter study found that 'housing wealth' in 2003 stood at an average of about £40,000 for every person in the country. However, due to regional variations in property values, households in the wealthiest areas of the country possessed over five times the housing wealth of those living in the poorest areas. Housing inequalities of this nature are growing almost exponentially and, if current trends continue, it is estimated that children living in the wealthiest areas will have access to more than one hundred times the housing wealth of children living in the poorest parts of the country in thirty years time (Thomas and Dorling, 2004).

The causes of rising poverty in the UK during the 1980s

The reasons for the rapid growth in poverty and inequality during the 1980s, to the levels that are still with us today, are now well understood and documented (Bradshaw, 2002; Hills, 2004). To begin with, there were major changes in the labour market which, together with the changing demographic characteristics of the population and the social policies implemented during this period, had a huge impact on levels of relative poverty, particularly in relation to families with children. In the labour market, which was subject to strong influences from globalisation, de-industrialisation and technological advances during this decade, there were periods of high unemployment in the early 1980s (as well as the early 1990s). Furthermore, an increasing proportion of the employment that did exist became insecure, part-time, and episodic. Jobs also became more concentrated in certain households so that, between 1983 and 1994, while the proportion of two-earner households in the UK grew from 54 per cent to 62 per cent, the proportion of workless households more than trebled, from 6 per cent to 19 per cent (Gregg et al., 2000). Work also increasingly provided more unequal returns, with a widening gap developing between the incomes of skilled and unskilled workers (Atkinson, 2000). The demographic characteristics of the population were also changing during this period. Most notably, the population was ageing and there was a significant rise in the number of lone parent families, which was accompanied by a fall in lone parents' employment, as the large birth cohort of the 1960s (the 'baby boomers') began to join what was already a crowded labour market.

Social policies can be directed towards reducing the inequalities that result from these sorts of changes in the labour market and the population characteristics. However, policy in the UK at this time, rather than combating rising levels of income inequality, actually reinforced them. For example, from 1981 benefits were only up-rated in line with prices rather than earnings, and the entitlement of 16–18 year-olds to claim benefits was withdrawn. The value of child benefit was also frozen, funding for public services was cut, and the tax system became significantly less redistributive, shifting towards more indirect taxes (paid at the same level by everyone, regardless of their income), coupled with a more regressive direct taxation regime. By comparison with many other European countries, social policies in the UK at this time were far less effective at protecting families with children from rising levels of poverty (Oxley et al., 2003).

A change of direction in social policy

The extent of relative poverty in the UK, and recognition of its damaging consequences for the economic and social development of the country, prompted the New Labour government elected in 1997 to prioritise policies to reduce poverty, particularly amongst families with children, as well as pensioners. This was most dramatically signalled, in 1999, when the Prime Minister, Tony Blair, made his historic pronouncement that the government intended to eradicate child poverty within a generation. The policies introduced to achieve this ambitious goal included a national minimum wage, and a range of 'New Deal' programmes designed to move targeted groups (young people; lone parents; long-term unemployed adults) off benefits and into work. A new system of tax credits was also introduced, initially targeted at supplementing the income of working families, as well as increases in the value of Child Benefit and the Income Support scales for children, alongside significant increases in spending on public services, particularly health and education.

These policies reduced the levels of relative poverty found in the UK at the start of the twenty-first century, particularly amongst targeted groups such as families with children, as well as having a much smaller influence on the overall levels of income inequality. For example, child poverty is currently on a downward trend, with the number of children living in households with an income below 60 per cent of the median, after housing costs have been deducted, having fallen by 700,000, from 4.2 million (33 per cent of the child population in England) in 1996/97 to 3.5 million (28 per cent) in 2003/04 (Department for Work and Pensions, 2005). Between 1997 and 2003 it has also been independently calculated that the net income (after housing costs) of a couple with two children on half average earnings rose by over 35 per cent, whilst that of a lone parent with one child on half average earnings went up by over 23 per cent. Overall, including increased spending on early years' services, the additional commitment of resources for children, between 1997 and 2003, was calculated to have amounted to an extra one per cent of the country's Gross Domestic Product (Stewart, 2005).

Unfortunately, the reductions in child poverty that have been achieved since 1997 have only succeeded, so far, in returning it to the levels that existed at the start of the 1990s, with the huge rise that occurred during the 1980s yet to be touched by recent reforms. Using the before housing costs measure, the government set itself the target of reducing child poverty from its 1998/99 level by a quarter by 2004/05, and a half by 2010, with the eventual aim of achieving levels of child poverty comparable with the best that exist in Europe by 2020, which currently stand at about six per cent. At the time of writing it is clear that the first of these targets has not been reached, and it is evident that the future targets will not be met under current policies, which rely too heavily upon employment as the main route out of poverty (Evans and Scarborough, 2006; Hirsch, 2006).

The problems with the current, employment-focused strategies for reducing child poverty include an increasingly polarised population in the UK, with a rising number of two-earner households existing alongside a smaller but significant proportion of households, about one in six, in which there is no working-age adult in paid employment (Department for Work and Pensions, 2005). Also, although paid work is identified as the most likely route out of poverty, low pay means that work is no guarantee of an end to poverty. In 2002/03 for instance, two-fifths of poor households contained someone in paid work (Palmer et al., 2004). These problems are hard to shift because, not only do low paid workers tend to remain low paid, but also their jobs are often insecure and short-term, leading to a cycle in which periods of low pay are interspersed with periods of unemployment (Kemp et al., 2004). This pattern tends to negate the benefits that the new tax credits regime and, to a lesser extent, the national minimum wage, have brought to many working families. Despite the help available to working parents through the tax credit system, the high cost of childcare in the UK can also act as a barrier to taking up paid work for many low income families, and can make them worse off in work than on benefits.

Furthermore, although there has been a very slight reduction in overall income inequality in recent years, differences in household income between those at the top and bottom ends of British society remain at historically high levels (Department for Work and Pensions, 2005). As we have already noted, disparities in wealth, particularly those related to home ownership, serve to reinforce income inequality in the UK at the present time, and the government have so far refused to acknowledge that such inequalities are a problem for society, let alone making any commitment to social justice policies designed to achieve more equality in the distribution of both income and wealth.

The risks and dynamics of poverty

From the evidence summarised above, it is clear that particular types of household are at increased risk of experiencing poverty. Longitudinal analyses of trends in poverty are beginning to shed more light on both *who* is most likely to experience poverty, and for *how long* they are likely to experience it.

Not only are the risks greater for households in which there are no adults in paid work, or which are headed by a lone parent, but they are also greater for households that include a young mother (aged less than 30 years) or young children, and larger families that have three or more children. Households headed by a member of a Black or minority ethnic community (especially of Pakistani or Bangladeshi origin), or with a disabled member (adult or child), are also more likely to have low incomes (Berthoud, 2002; Bradshaw, 2002; Department for Work and Pensions, 2005). For example, analysis of the *Households Below Average Income* data has revealed the extent of child poverty among some minority ethnic groups, with 69 per cent of Pakistani and Bangladeshi children found to be living in households with incomes below the poverty threshold (after housing costs), compared with 41 per cent of Black Caribbean children, 36 per cent of Indian children, and 27 per cent of white children at that time (Marsh and Perry, 2003).

As this analysis goes on to reveal, there are a number of explanations for the lower household incomes of the majority of Black and minority ethnic groups, including demographic factors and family structure, geographical location, housing, unemployment, low pay, educational background, and qualifications. However, it also reveals that in-group differences are becoming increasingly significant and complex. For example, although Indian children tend to live in households that have comparable income, on average, to white families, the existence of a minority of very affluent households tends to mask the fact that a significant group of Indian households are affected by low wages and unemployment. However, in contrast to the positive overall position of Indian families, children in Pakistani and Bangladeshi households, along with a smaller number in Black African families, tend to experience greatly heightened levels of disadvantage across the full range of measures, whereas Black Caribbean households present a more mixed picture. Higher rates of child poverty among Black Caribbean families appear to be associated with the greater proportion of households in which only one parent is resident, despite the fact that Caribbean lone parents are more likely to be in work than white lone parents (Marsh and Perry, 2003).

Whilst data of this kind indicates some fairly entrenched overall patterns of poverty risk for different groups, there is considerable movement at the individual level in both directions across the poverty threshold, from year to year. The people who are poor in any one year are not necessarily the same as those who are poor the next year. However, the UK is characterised by relatively limited social and economic mobility so that, although 'permanent poverty' is unusual, persistent or repeated episodes of poverty are not. For example, whilst only two per cent of the 5,600 or so adult respondents that make up the sample used for the annual British Household Panel Survey were poor every year between 1991 and 2000, over one in seven of them were poor in at least half of those years. In relation to child poverty, analysis of the first six waves of this survey (between 1991 and 1996) reveals that only 1.4 per cent of children lived in poor households in each of the six years. However, much higher proportions were living in poor households for at least three of the six years, with pre-school-aged children at the greatest risk (20.9 per cent lived in poor households for at least three of the six years), followed by primary-aged children (12.2 per cent) and secondary-aged children (7.2 per cent) (Hill and Jenkins, 2001).

Even when people move out of poverty, income mobility in the UK tends to be short-range, with the majority of people either staying in the same ten per cent of the income distribution, or only moving up or down to the immediately neighbouring deciles (Hills, 2004). This is a particular problem in the UK, which has seen inter-generational social mobility decline markedly during a time of rising income inequality, partly as a result of the increasingly close relationship between family income and factors such as social skills development and educational attainment (Margo and Dixon, 2006; Blanden et al., 2005).

The concept of multiple deprivation

Whilst the definitions of relative poverty that are now widely accepted incorporate aspects of inequality that go beyond low income, more recently terms such as 'social exclusion' and 'multiple deprivation' have emerged in an attempt to encapsulate the way that social problems such as low income, unemployment, lack of education and skills, high crime and poor housing, tend to co-exist. The New Labour government elected in 1997 acknowledged the multi-dimensional nature of disadvantage by establishing the cross-department Social Exclusion Unit (SEU) soon after it came into office. In 1998 the SEU reviewed the existing evidence about area deprivation, and concluded that there were up to 4,000 neighbourhoods that constituted 'pockets of deprivation where the problems of unemployment and crime are acute and hopelessly tangled up with poor health, housing and education' (SEU, 1998: 9). The government also introduced a new way of monitoring progress in tackling disadvantage and social exclusion on an annual basis, published under the title *Opportunity for All*, which uses a wide range of indicators across the different dimensions of deprivation (Department for Work and Pensions, 2004). The effectiveness of this approach is being independently monitored by a similar exercise, carried out by the New Policy Institute (Palmer et al., 2004).

Starting in the same year, the government also commissioned work on the development of *Indices of Multiple Deprivation*, the latest version of which were constructed by the Social Disadvantage Research Centre at the University of Oxford in 2004. They are based on the notion that distinct dimensions of deprivation, recognised and measured separately, can be combined into meaningful overall indices (ODPM, 2004a: 9).

The latest *Indices* combine seven domains of deprivation (income; employment; health and disability; education, skills and training; access to housing and services; living environment; and crime), drawing on a total of 37 separate indicators. The domains are 'weighted', according to their perceived level of influence, with income and employment considered to be of most significance (given a weighting of 22.5 per cent each), followed by health and education (13.5 per cent each), and then the other three domains (9.3 per cent each). Because of the problems associated with previous versions of the *Indices*, with wards varying considerably in size and ward-level data often masking significant within-ward variations in deprivation, they have now been produced using the smallest available geographical units. These are called Super Output Areas (SOAs), of which there are over 30,000 in England, consisting of an average of 1,500 people each. However, even within these relatively small areas, it must be recognised that the least deprived areas may still contain deprived individuals, just as the most deprived areas may contain some affluent individuals.

Of course, any combined measure of this kind has its strengths and weaknesses. For example, whilst the measures of income deprivation currently being used include some welfare benefits and tax credits, they exclude others, notably the main disability benefits. Also, the methodology used for deciding upon the weight to be assigned to each of the separate measures selected for inclusion, as well as the domains generated from them, will always be open to debate, and some of the domains are undoubtedly more robust than others. Nonetheless, it provides a relatively robust measure with which to identify regional variations in the levels of multiple deprivation, as we will now go on to consider.

The geographical distribution of multiple deprivation

We have already seen how personal and family characteristics affect the chances of experiencing poverty and other related forms of disadvantage. However, where people live can also be a major factor in determining their level of risk (Hirsch, 2004). The evidence indicates that spatial concentrations of poverty and wealth, in the UK and elsewhere, are nothing new (Tunstall and Lupton, 2003). Examination of Census data from 1971 to 2001, for instance, indicates that different groups of people were 'spatially sorting' into ever more homogeneous communities during that period, resulting in deepening concentrations of both poverty and wealth (Dorling and Rees, 2004). During the 1980s, these sorting processes accelerated, largely due to growing geographical differences in employment, wages and housing costs (Hills, 1995; Lee and Murie, 1997).

As we have already noted, the housing system in the UK underpins the geographical distribution of disadvantage, translating labour market and income inequalities into residential segregation (Fitzpatrick, 2004). Furthermore, differences between neighbourhoods were also reinforced during this period by changes in social policies that promoted the role of the market and restricted public spending, particularly in relation to housing. Most significantly, the 1980 Housing Act introduced the 'right to buy' policy, giving local authority tenants the opportunity to purchase their council accommodation at a discounted price. This led to a significant reduction in the number of council-owned properties, which fell from 6.5 million in 1979 to 4.5 million by 1996, representing a decline in the share of the total housing stock from 29 per cent to less than 19 per cent (ODPM, 2004b).

This privatisation programme not only reduced the number of social housing units available for rent, it also fundamentally changed the nature of the social rented sector. A process of residualisation occurred, in which better quality properties in more desirable areas were bought by those with the means to do so, leaving more disadvantaged tenants typically occupying poorer quality properties in less desirable areas. Subsequent analysis of households moving into and out of social housing has confirmed that the social and economic base of the sector has become much narrower since the 'right to buy' policy was introduced. For example, households entering the social rented sector in 1993–94 tended to be younger, and more likely to consist of either lone parents or unemployed members. Conversely, tenant households who moved house to become owner-occupiers were far more likely to consist of couples, and to be headed by someone older and economically active (Burrows, 1997). The privatisation of council housing has continued under the New Labour governments in office since 1997, with growing 'right to buy' sales being supplemented by the large-scale transfer of housing stock from local authorities to housing associations, a process which started in the early 1990s but has accelerated significantly since 1997 (Ginsberg, 2005).

Despite the introduction of new neighbourhood renewal policies, designed to help meet a government pledge that 'within 10 to 20 years nobody should be seriously disadvantaged by where they live' (Social Exclusion Unit, 2001), processes of social and economic differentiation appear set, if anything, to widen further in the future (Burrows et al., 2005). One of the drivers behind these processes is the growth in internet-based neighbourhood information systems, many of which have been developed by marketing companies. These web sites provide information at individual post-code level, allowing individuals with access to the internet and the financial means to act on their choices, to select their preferred type of neighbourhood, facilitating ever more sophisticated sorting of populations according to such factors as income, educational level and aspiration, the quality of local services and facilities, and lifestyles.

The latest version of the *Indices of Multiple Deprivation* reveals just how complex the geographical distribution of multiple deprivation has now become (ODPM, 2004a: 52). Whilst the most deprived areas are spread throughout all regions of the country, every region also contains SOAs that are among the least deprived in England. Furthermore, many deprived areas are in close proximity to less deprived areas, leading to considerable heterogeneity within certain regions or local authority districts. For example, Swindon contains eight of the least deprived SOAs, but it also contains seven of the most deprived areas, and Dudley, which has nine of the least deprived SOAs in the country, also has thirteen of the most deprived areas. However, in these more mixed urban areas, a range of strategies can be used to create social distance where geographical separation is limited (Fitzpatrick, 2004). These local differences in the relative socio-economic circumstances of often adjoining populations can have major implications for those who experience them, as we will go on to consider at various points throughout the rest of this volume.

Patterns of multiple deprivation in England

An overview of the regional patterns of multiple deprivation across England is presented in Table 2. It can be seen that most major centres of population contain SOAs with high levels of multiple deprivation. Concentrations of deprived areas are particularly noticeable in parts of London, Manchester, Liverpool, Newcastle, and the conurbations in Yorkshire and the Humber, and the West Midlands. Some smaller centres of population also contain very deprived SOAs, including former mining areas in the North East and Cornwall, along with various ports and large seaside towns, such as Plymouth, Kingston-upon-Hull, Bristol, Great Yarmouth, Margate, Hastings, and Skegness.

Although there is considerable heterogeneity and complexity in the distribution of multiple deprivation across England, nonetheless certain regions also present fairly distinct profiles. For example, the South East region overall is the least deprived, whilst the North East region contains very few of the least deprived SOAs and, along with the North West region, has the highest proportion of the most deprived areas.

Table 2. Regional variations in multiple deprivation in England, 2004 (ODPM, 2004)

Region	Number of SOAs	Number of SOAs in the 10% most deprived (%)	Concentrations of most deprived SOAs
North East	1,656	362 (22%)	Newcastle-upon-Tyne; South Tyneside; Sunderland; Gateshead; and former steel, ship-building and mining areas (Easington, Middlesbrough, Hartlepool, Redcar and Cleveland, and Stockton-on-Tees).
North West	4,459	936 (21%)	Liverpool; Manchester; and surrounding towns (St. Helens, Wigan, Bolton, Salford and Oldham).
Yorkshire and the Humber	3,293	523 (16%)	Kingston-upon-Hull; Sheffield; Leeds; Bradford; Kirklees; Rotherham; and former coalfield areas (Doncaster, Wakefield, and Barnsley).
West Midlands	3,482	476 (14%)	Birmingham area (including Wolverhampton, Walsall and Sandwell); Coventry; Stoke-on-Trent.
London	4,765	458 (10%)	Inner London Boroughs (Tower Hamlets, Newham, Hackney, Islington, Haringey, Camden, Westminster, Brent, Southwark, Greenwich and Lambeth).
East Midlands	2,732	238 (9%)	Leicester; Derby; Nottingham; and former coalfield areas (Ashfield, Bassetlaw, Chesterfield and Bolsover).
South West	3,226	98 (3%)	Plymouth; Bristol; parts of Cornwall; Weston-super-Mare.
East	3,550	74 (2%)	Norwich; Great Yarmouth.
South East	5,319	83 (2%)	Coastal towns (Brighton and Hove; Hastings; Thanet).

The supplementary *Index of Multiple Deprivation Affecting Children* reflects the complexity of the regional distribution of overall deprivation. For example, there are over 6,000 SOAs where more than a third of children live in 'income deprived' households, and almost as many in which fewer than five per cent of children do so. The South East region has the lowest proportion of children living in income deprived households (14 per cent), with the East (15 per cent), the South West (16 per cent), and the East Midlands regions (18 per cent) not far behind. By contrast, the London region has the highest proportion of children living in income deprived households by this measure (28 per cent) followed by the North East (26 per cent) and the North West (23 per cent), and then Yorkshire and the Humber, and the West Midlands regions (both 21 per cent). These regional patterns in the distribution of child poverty closely match those for overall multiple deprivation, with the exception of London, which has the highest proportion of children living in poverty, but comes roughly in the middle of the regional distribution of overall multiple deprivation across England.

Conclusion

Amongst the conclusions that can be drawn from the evidence about poverty and inequality summarised in this chapter, which have implications for ecological practice as well as national social policies, perhaps the most important is the fact that an individual's chances of experiencing poverty and disadvantage are the result of a combination of a wide range of inter-related factors. Whilst these factors include their personal characteristics and the structure of the households and wider family networks to which they belong, they also include factors that are largely determined by the way that society is structured and organised, including where people live and the social and economic circumstances and social policies of the country to which they belong.

Throughout the rest of this volume, the ecological theory of human development will be used to examine the way that these different factors, at individual, group, community and society levels, interact with one another to shape the health and well-being of children and adults, as well as the functioning of the families and communities to which they belong (Bronfenbrenner, 1979). The evidence considered so far confirms what has been known for a long time, that patterns of inequality within disadvantaged areas are largely determined by national factors, but that local circumstances play an important role in determining the impact that these inequalities have upon individuals and families (Townsend, 1979; Jack, 2005). It is clear, therefore, that action to effectively tackle the high levels of inequality and pockets of multiple deprivation that currently exist in the UK requires a combination of national policies, designed to improve the circumstances of disadvantaged individuals relative to the rest of the population, wherever they live, and ecologically-based social welfare practice that can address some of the compounding effects of the neighbourhood environment (Lupton, 2003; Jack, 2005). It is the second part of this equation which is the main subject of the rest of this volume.

Chapter 3. **The Impact on Children and Families of Living in Disadvantaged Communities**

This chapter will consider:
- The importance of community for disadvantaged children and families.
- Research evidence about the impact of living in disadvantaged communities on families and children.
- Levels of child density and the age structure of disadvantaged communities.
- The influence of geographical location.
- Transience and community.
- Vulnerability and resilience in the lives of children.

Introduction: The importance of community for disadvantaged children and families

Having explored the reasons for the high levels of child poverty and other forms of inequality in the UK at the present time, and some of its spatial dimensions, we now move on to look directly at the impact of community-level factors in disadvantaged communities on the lives of children and their families.

Families with limited financial resources are likely to be more dependent on their local communities for their amenities, services and social networks, than more affluent families. They are also likely to be more exposed to the influences of the neighbourhoods in which they live (Jack and Gill, 2003). The reasons for this greater dependence and exposure include:

- Less ability to purchase access to leisure and educational resources outside the community.
- Less access to transport (which is linked to more restricted access to resources outside the community).
- Less access to social relationships which lie outside the community.
- Less control over the impact of the immediate environment (via, for instance, expensive home security).
- Increased vulnerability to the actions of others they live alongside because of smaller units of accommodation within more densely populated areas.

Underlying the dependence of low income families on their local communities is their restricted choice over where they live and who they live alongside, which is largely controlled by the allocation policies of local social housing agencies.

Children living in low income households in disadvantaged areas are liable to be particularly dependent on the resources of their local communities, for some (or all) of the following reasons:

- Families not being able to afford activities and entertainment provided by the private sector for children, and therefore being dependent on voluntary or community organisation provision, and some (cheaper) local authority services.
- Families having no access to transport to take children to activities and entertainment outside the local community.
- Children having no places to play other than the specifically designated play areas or 'adult spaces' within their communities.

All of this is at a time when resources for children and families are increasingly being located away from areas of residence because of economic pressures:

> *Decentralisation processes that particularly affect children include the trend towards closing local cinemas and swimming pools while opening large cinema and leisure complexes at motorway junctions or on peripheral retail sites which can only be reached by car.*
>
> (Freeman, Henderson and Kettle, 1999: 117)

Children are also likely to be uniquely exposed to the dangers and pressures that exist within their communities. An example of this is the way in which home and road accident statistics consistently show that children living in poorer areas have a much higher likelihood of being injured or killed than their counterparts living in more affluent areas (Spencer, 1996).

There is also increasing evidence of the importance of community for disadvantaged families as a whole. For instance Mumford and Power (2003: 31) in their study of family and community in a deprived area of East London, found that community mattered much more to the families in these neighbourhoods than those living in more favourable circumstances. Their study found that: 'Two thirds of the families in both neighbourhoods felt that community spirit exists in their area, but almost everyone – 90% – felt that community spirit mattered'. They also cite other research which indicates that this figure is far higher than the UK national average. They go on to stress the importance of community for families in a quickly changing and sometimes threatening environment:

> *Community therefore matters a great deal to families with children because it binds people together when they need support and it raises morale . . . In this way they manage to survive in a harsh urban environment where mothers often feel vulnerable to the unknown, the strangers and the changes they neither drive nor control.*
>
> (p. 268)

They sum up the findings of their study by concluding that:

> *People need both family and community, no matter how far they have travelled, how disrupted the community, how mixed fast changing or problematic the wider society-and possibly because of all these things. Low-income families tied by young children need a highly localised network of community organisations and activities in order to guarantee basic security, some control, and a sense of belonging and easy access to where they feel they can belong.*
>
> (p. 277)

Research evidence about the impact of living in disadvantaged communities on families and children

There is a wide range of evidence which highlights the impact of area and community influences on family functioning and the way that interactions between individual and area characteristics influence children's well-being and future life chances (Bronfenbrenner, 1979; Belsky, 1993; Jack, 1997, 2000; DoH, 2000).

Although it is clear from this body of evidence that the biggest influences on children's well-being tend to be exerted by their family's particular circumstances and characteristics, there is also consistent evidence highlighting the added difficulties faced by parents bringing up their children in disadvantaged neighbourhoods (Garbarino and Kostelny, 1992; Brooks-Gunn et al., 1993; Gill et al., 2000; Cebello and McLoyd, 2002; Kohen et al., 2002). Furthermore, much of this evidence also demonstrates that there are clear links between area of residence and various measures of well-being, independent of individual family characteristics and circumstances (Gatrell et al., 2000; Joshi et al., 2000; Pevalin and Rose, 2003; Cummins et al., 2005).

These links between area of residence and personal well-being are clearly highlighted in a large-scale, nationally representative study of parents living in the most disadvantaged areas in the UK, which found that they reported significantly poorer physical and mental health than the general population. The study also showed that the more deprived the area in which parents lived, the greater the proportion that experienced high levels of stress and the less satisfied they were with the area in which they lived (Ghate and Hazel, 2002). As noted already, many of the associations between the deprivation of the area and the difficulties experienced by parents living there are the result of economically, socially and politically structured selection processes, operating primarily through the education system and the labour and housing markets, which lead to concentrations of those with the greatest difficulties living in the most disadvantaged areas. However, the conclusions of this study of parenting in poor environments confirm the findings of other studies, that some of the difficulties faced by individuals are also determined by the area in which they live, regardless of their personal characteristics and circumstances (e.g. see Bottoms and Wiles, 1997; Ellen and Turner, 1997). The greater number of stress factors experienced by parents living in deprived areas meant that, whatever their personal circumstances and characteristics, they were less likely to be coping satisfactorily with parenting (Ghate and Hazel, 2002).

The most significant neighbourhood characteristic correlated with variations in the health and well-being of parents and children is the nature of the social environment in which they live (Furstenberg and Hughes, 1995; Garbarino and Kostelny, 1992; Sampson et al., 1997, 1999; Jack and Jordan, 1999; Jack, 2004). Variations in the levels of such things as health, crime and child abuse found between different areas matched for the individual characteristics of their residents are significantly linked to the way that individuals and groups interact socially with one another. For example, differences in rates of officially identified child abuse and neglect have frequently been found to be correlated not only with variations in the social networks of individuals, but also with what is referred to as the social capital of the wider communities in which they live (Garbarino and Sherman, 1980; Garbarino and Kostelny, 1992; Coulton et al., 1995; Vinson et al., 1996).

The definition of social capital that has been adopted by the UK Government focuses on the importance of 'networks together with shared norms, values and understandings that facilitate co-operation within or among groups' (Cote and Healy, 2001: 41). It can be seen, therefore, that this concept tries to capture some of the qualities of the social relationships that exist within particular communities. This includes the levels of trust and reciprocity that exist between people, the extent of their involvement in shared activities and organisations, and the degree of social cohesion between different groups. A government-commissioned review of the literature on this topic concluded that higher levels of social capital were associated with lower crime rates, better health and longer life-expectancy, better educational achievement, and improved child welfare, including lower rates of child abuse (Harper, 2001).

Unfortunately, the social networks of parents and children, and the social capital of the areas in which they live, tend to reflect individual and area levels of disadvantage, often leaving those most in need of additional help with the most restricted social support resources (Jack, 2000). This tendency was clearly demonstrated in one of the first national surveys of its kind in the UK, designed to measure five different components of social capital: civic engagement; neighbourliness; social networks; social support; and perceptions of the local area (Office for National Statistics, 2002). On all of these measures, the survey revealed that the most deprived areas of the country tended to display the lowest levels of social capital. For example, the proportion of people who were 'civically engaged' (i.e. who felt well informed about their local area and believed that they and other local residents could influence decisions relating to their neighbour-hood) was over three times higher in the least deprived areas compared with the most deprived. Similar differences were found in relation to the levels of trust between neighbours, perceptions of the facilities and problems in the locality, and a range of individual measures of social support, with a clear gradient from the least deprived areas, where social capital indicators were highest, to the most deprived areas, where they were lowest. These findings in the UK confirm similar associations between deprivation and lower social capital found in other parts of the developed world (e.g. see Putnam, 2000).

Despite the evidence that exists about the negative potential impact of living in disadvantaged areas on individuals and families, it is a mistake to view all such areas as having a similar impact on their residents. Not only do individuals and families vary greatly in the way that they react to their circumstances, but also, variations in the demographic characteristics of different communities will play a significant role, as we will now go on to consider.

Levels of child density and the age structure of disadvantaged communities

The levels of child density in a community can have a range of influences on children's lives. Typically, social housing areas have high rates of child density, with one study of housing association estates finding that the proportion of children to adults was five times the national average. Residents in these areas considered that this was acceptable, provided there were adequate local facilities including youth support services and provision for children's play (Cole et al., 1996).

One of the most obvious and immediate implications of the level of child density is its impact on the level of resources that are available within a community. If child densities are high, then it follows that there should be at least a degree of emphasis put on the resources needed to cope with this by local planning authorities and service providers. However, in practice this often does not happen, and the high proportion of children and young people living in a particular area may not be matched by correspondingly enhanced provision. This is a problem highlighted by Power (1997: 49) in her analysis of large housing estates throughout Europe, in which she found that there was often 'little regard for the dynamics of community and social problems until it was too late'. She paid particular attention to the age characteristics of the large, low income estates that she studied, highlighting both the large number of children on the estates, and the large number of young adults also living there. She concluded that:

> . . . the unpopularity and high turnover of estates meant that more households than average moved out and younger than average households moved in. Special lettings directed at young people were often introduced to fill vacancies . . . Such young households tended to have or be about to start young families, so high concentrations of young children went with high concentrations of young adults.
>
> (p. 294)

Illustrating some of the ecological processes at work in the lives of children, Power also drew attention the inter-relationships between social structural factors in disadvantaged communities and family life. In particular, she identified three factors that helped explain why estates deteriorated to the extent that they became increasingly problematic places to live:

1. Weakened adult control, linked with a high proportion of one parent families.
2. Conflict within families, linked to family breakdown and re-formation, with the appearance of new and unstable partners.
3. High concentrations of young adults within existing and often over-crowded families.

The decrease in normative controls that result from these processes, particularly in relation to children's and young people's behaviour, are central to Power's analysis:

> More stable areas have in-built resistance, controls and barriers to instability and crime deriving directly from people being anchors within the community. Community instability and weak controls in marginal estates sometimes led to the loss of normal boundaries of behaviour.
>
> (Power, 1997: 386)

Whilst research of this nature clearly identifies some of the problems associated with high child density, children and families living in areas of low child density can also experience significant difficulties. This may be a particular issue in the UK at the present time, with resources increasingly being allocated to communities on the basis of their level of deprivation. Areas with low child densities may not reach the required levels of deprivation to qualify for extra resources. Research for the Daycare Trust by Land (2002), for example, looking at initiatives designed to eradicate child poverty, has highlighted the fact that a significant proportion of disadvantaged children live in areas not targeted for help. One of the reasons is because they live in areas that do not score highly enough on indices of deprivation. This was also a problem identified in the evaluation of a largely rural Children's Fund programme, in which one of the author's was involved (Freeman et al., 2005).

The influence of geographical location

Much of this book focuses on the urban locations in which the majority of disadvantaged children and families live. However, there are also very significant numbers of children and young people living in disadvantaged circumstances in more rural and semi-rural settings. Having been largely overlooked for decades, the difficulties experienced by children and families living in rural communities have begun to receive increased attention over recent years. The National Youth Agency (1994) has identified five types of rural areas:

- remote rural areas, including isolated farms, single dwellings and scattered settlements
- villages
- market towns
- collapsed industrial areas
- coastal areas and hinterland

Although there will be differences of scale and impact for children living in low income households in different rural settings, a number of common factors can be identified. The first of these, which is linked to low rates of child density, is limited community resources and activities accessible by children living in low income households. Whilst children from more affluent families will often be able to afford to participate in a range of after-school and weekend activities and entertainment, for children living in poor families this will often not be an option. As we have already discussed, part of the reason for this disparity is the issue of transport. Facilities may be a considerable distance away from where a child lives, with only poor and expensive public transport services available in the locality. In these circumstances, the child coming from a household without a car will be seriously disadvantaged, as Davis and Ridge (1997: 68) have noted:

> . . . where there is sufficient affluence and mobility, localised lack of opportunity can be merely an inconvenience easily overcome. The burden of poor and inadequate provision falls most heavily on those with insufficient income and mobility to service their needs elsewhere. Of these children, those on a low income show clear indications of social and structural exclusion from the opportunities that exist.

As discussed in the introductory chapter, it is access to these constructive, organised activities that facilitate children's personal and social development, which has become an increasingly important determinant of relative life chances (Margo and Dixon, 2006).

Another key issue of rural life for children from low income households is that of the contest and conflict over space with more powerful, established, and older groups in the community. The issue of 'hanging around' and the negative imagery that this conveys is central, here, as Davis and Ridge (1997: 70) have noted:

> The issue of visibility is seen to be particularly acute for children and young people on a low income who already suffer from severely reduced opportunities to escape the confines of their villages and towns and are correspondingly contained and highly visible within their communities.

This is one aspect of the potential of rural life, compounded by the effects of poverty and lack of access to transport, to shape the social world of children and young people. Friendships may be more difficult to maintain, it will be more difficult to develop social contacts through paid-for activities, lifts may be difficult to accept because parents without access to a car will be unable to reciprocate, and there may also be barriers to inviting other children back to tea (Jack and Gill, 2003).

Living in a rural setting may also have implications for children's developing sense of identity. Compared with their urban counterparts, they may come into more direct contact with children and families who have far higher financial resources than themselves. For instance, in rural settings, children from low income families may be coming into daily contact with children from very different backgrounds at schools that serve the 'whole' community. This can have a powerful impact on children's experience of inequality, sense of identity, and where their family is socially located.

Many of the links between poverty, isolation and transport in rural setting, that have been highlighted above, are illustrated in the following practice example (Gill, 2001):

John and Helen Dunmore are a low-income family who have three children: Jade aged 10, Will aged 9, and Sapphire aged 3. They live in a small village about two and a half miles from a market town in Wiltshire. The village is an affluent one, where the majority of people commute out to work. The Dunmores live in a small group of local authority-owned housing in the village. They have little contact with their neighbours because they are wary of the people they live alongside, preferring to keep themselves to themselves.

There are few facilities in the village, particularly for the children. There is a weekly youth club, but as this is only for children and young people over the age of 11, so the Dunmore children cannot go there.

John receives incapacity benefit as a result of a back injury. The family are marginally above the income support level so they do not get the additional benefits associated with income support. Most significantly, they do not get free school meals.

One of the problems they face is that they live two and a half miles away from the shops, and other services and amenities. If they need to take one of the children to the doctor, for instance, they have to walk into town or else go to the expense of paying for a taxi. Where they live also has implications for their food budget. There is a village shop but the choice is small and the prices high. Once a week the couple walk to the supermarket in the market town to do their main shop. They then have to take a taxi back with all their purchases. Compared with their counterparts in the city, the family are living that much further below the poverty line because of the extra costs associated with buying their food and other household provisions.

The cost of transport and the Dunmore's lack of a car also have implications for the children's lives. Most of the children in the village are taken elsewhere to participate in activities and attend events, but the Dunmores cannot afford this. Nor can they enter into reciprocal arrangements whereby another family takes the children to activities one week and they do the same the following week. They are, in effect, restricted to the village, where there are no activities for children.

Besides the sort of isolated village locations illustrated by this example, there are other forms of geographical location that can contribute to the social exclusion that tends to affect children living in low income households. For instance, much of the social housing being built at the present time is being located in small brown field re-development sites. Consequently, there are small pockets of often 'income deprived' households living in generally more affluent areas. Particular historical circumstances can also have an impact at the local level. For instance, in one medium sized seaside town with which one of the authors is familiar, there are occasional houses in quite affluent owner occupied streets that accommodate families from the registers of social housing providers. The historical reason for this is that in the early 1990s, when there were a large number of housing repossessions, the local authority bought some of these properties and allowed the existing occupants to remain living in them, to avoid them being made homeless. As the original families have moved on, and these properties have become available for letting again, more disadvantaged families from the housing list have been housed in them.

Transience and community

So far in this chapter we have looked at demographic and geographical factors within communities that can either produce strengths or pressures for children and their families. A central point in this is that the most vulnerable children and families may be those who are only marginally linked in with the social networks and other resources of local communities. These processes of marginalisation and social exclusion are particularly evident in relation to children in families that are frequently on the move. The parents in these families, particularly the ones who display high rates of such transience, are more likely to be those with few informal networks, less knowledge of local resources, and less consistent contact with sources of help and advice. For their children, the impacts of transience will be especially strong, with friendships repeatedly disrupted and relation-ships with trusted adults more difficult to form and maintain. Concern and fear about a relatively unknown local environment is also likely to be higher, particularly if they lack support from their parents in mediating their interactions with children and adults in the new environment.

Transience may be the result of many factors, including family breakdown, domestic violence, housing problems, debt, or difficult relations with neighbours. For example, a study involving one of the authors identified a small group of parents living on a Bristol housing estate who had very limited social support networks. Often these families were transient and only stayed in the area for a short time. It was some of these families who also appeared to be experiencing significant difficulties in caring for their children (Gill et al., 2000).

Work with children in temporary accommodation has also highlighted how vulnerable they can be once they have been moved from their home area. It is often difficult to disentangle the interacting effects of family stress and substandard accommodation from those specifically related to the change of location and the breakdown of community networks. But there is no doubt that homelessness can place special pressures on children as a result of moving away from familiar friends, places and support. This is well illustrated by work undertaken in Bristol by Shelter (2002) in which children talked about being bullied as one of the added pressures of moving into temporary accommodation.

Another very vulnerable group of children, those who are separated from their families and looked after by local authorities, can also experience significant levels of transience and disruption of their family and wider social networks. This problem is particularly acute in areas such as London, where the accommodation provided is often a great distance away from the home areas of the children and young people concerned. For example, a report by Kent Child Protection Committee (Guardian, 2005) revealed that more than 1,250 children in care in the county – over half of the total number of children being looked after by Kent – had come from outside the authority, mainly from London boroughs. The report found that most of these children were placed in the east of the county in an area already facing severe economic and social deprivation, with potentially serious consequences for the children and young people who are placed there, as well as the local communities into which they have been moved.

Vulnerability and resilience in the lives of children

The above discussion has looked at some of the demographic and geographical factors and patterns of transience in communities that can have an impact on children's lives. But our focus in this book is on the lives of individual children, as well as specific groups of children. In any discussion of children and community, we therefore have to build into our understanding the way in which the well-being of individual children, or specific groups of children, is shaped by their environment.

Both the built and the social environment will have different effects on the lives of different children. For instance Freeman, Henderson and Kettle (1999) note that obstacles to movement on pavements (e.g. shop goods on streets) will have a far more significant impact on children who are visually impaired, and uneven surfaces will pose particular problems for children with impaired mobility. Levels of deprivation can also have an impact on the lives of individual children in ways which are not necessarily immediately obvious, as illustrated in the following quote from a mother, talking about the bullying her visually impaired daughter experienced, which led to her only feeling safe to play 'just outside the front door' (Allen, 2003: 30).

> She used to get called blind, deaf, she used to get her glasses took off her, where we lived before they were absolutely horrible, they'd pinch her roller blades off her, you know they really did, they were nasty people. It was, that's why I moved out. Because of five years of deterioration, I just didn't want the children, there was drugs there which there's drugs everywhere, there was car theft, there was children smoking the drugs and they were dealing it outside your door, there were house robberies. It just wasn't an environment to bring them up in.

In the UK and elsewhere, variations in the reactions of different individuals to stressful life events and situations have long been an important area of inquiry. For example, Rutter (1985) writing more than twenty years ago, noted that 'large individual differences in response to stress and adversity are a universal feature of empirical studies following all manner of research strategies' (p. 599). There has also been a more limited, but important, tradition of looking at the way in which families can help their children to successfully resist or overcome the pressures that are associated with living in disadvantaged circumstances. An early and important example of this strand of research came with Herbert and Wilson's (1978) study of parenting in the inner city. They were writing at a time when one of the dominant perspectives in understanding child and adolescent problems – particularly delinquency – was based on the idea of the subculture. This strand of theory and research identified that, in disadvantaged areas, where opportunities for success in culturally validated ways were blocked, delinquent subcultures developed with values and norms in opposition to the mainstream. Wilson and Herbert examined how parents supported and protected their children from adopting the values and norms of these oppositional subcultures.

Over recent years, on both sides of the Atlantic, there has been increasing interest in the concept of children's resilience (Fraser, 1997; Masten and Coatsworth, 1998; Bartley, 2006). Instead of focusing on difficulties and deficits in children's lives, this strand of research looks at how their well-being is promoted, and what makes some children able to cope with adversity better than others. This approach is particularly important when it comes to examining the relationship between the child, the family and the community of which they are a part, and it is therefore of direct relevance to the development of ecological practice.

Within this paradigm, resilience is conceptualised not as an inherent characteristic that some children possess and others do not, but rather as a process that involves the child's personality, development and interactions with the social systems of which they are a part. Yates and Masten (2004: 6) describe this in the following way:

> This dynamic view of resilience holds that the quality of adaptation results from interactive processes among factors operating at the levels of individuals, families and communities, as well as broader physical and social environments (for instance neighbourhoods, media, policy). Together these factors influence the operation of fundamental human adaptational systems that appear to underlie resilient patterns of adaptation.

Reviews of the empirical research which focuses on children's resilience clearly shows the combined importance of factors which are internal and external to the family. For example, Newman (2004: 6) identifies that resilience research, in diverse settings, has converged on a group of factors at individual, family and community levels associated with positive developmental outcomes, including:

- Competent parenting.
- Connections to supportive adults and other networks (e.g. religious affiliation).
- Good cognitive functioning.
- Social appeal (e.g. talents, attractiveness).
- Economic advantage.
- High quality schools and teachers.
- Community resources.
- A sense of self-worth, self efficacy and self-determination.

The relationship between children's resilience and community resources has been particularly emphasised by Gilligan (1998), who has highlighted the importance of positive school experiences and achievements for children living in otherwise disadvantaged circumstances. He points out that schools not only provide educational opportunities, but also rich sources of social relationships with both adults (teachers and other school staff) and fellow pupils, that may be important sources of support and advice. The role of schools has also been identified as an important issue in relation to the risk and protective factors associated with the development of offending behaviour by young people, which we look at in more depth in the next chapter. Schools may also have an important role to play in developing the capacity and social capital of disadvantaged communities, which is an issue that we consider in the concluding chapter, when we examine some of the challenges faced by organisations and professionals in developing ecological practice. The links between individual resilience and the social conditions that exist in local communities is also something highlighted by Newman (2004: 40) particularly in relation to the development of pre-school children:

> *Where levels of social capital . . . are higher, children show similarly higher levels of positive emotional and behavioural development. Mutual support and strong neigh-bour ties are health promoting factors even under unfavourable conditions. Where social capital is high children in even unfavourable environments are significantly more likely to develop resilient characteristics.*

Another important point for the development of ecological practice concerns the informal nature of the sources of support identified by parents and children as promoting their resilience (Jack, 1997; 2000). When asked about these issues, they rarely mention the help of paid professionals, instead focusing on support from their relatives and other members of their informal social networks:

> *. . . when children themselves are asked what helped them to 'succeed against the odds' the most frequently mentioned factors are help from members of their own extended families, peers, neighbours and informal mentors, rather than the activities of paid professionals.*

> (Newman, 2004: 26)

So, if we are to work effectively to build resilience in children and families, more often than not effective engagement with local informal networks will be more important than direct services to children provided by formal organisations.

Newman's conclusion, which confirms the importance of the links between the internal family world of the child and the external environment, may be of particular significance for work with refugee and asylum-seeking children:

> *In addition to supportive families, those who appear best placed to maintain positive mental health are able to identify with a community and the aims of that community, and have the opportunity to take part in meaningful social rituals which affirm their cultural values.*

> (p. 50)

Frank Furstenberg and his colleagues in the US have also made a major contribution to exploring the concept of resilience, and the relationships between children, families and communities which are at the heart of ecological practice. In particular, they have examined how disadvantaged communities can support parents in promoting the development and well-being of children and young people.

> *Investigating how individuals and families find pathways out of poverty is instructive for several reasons. First it may help eradicate the stigmatising idea . . . that disadvantaged parents are indifferent about their children's futures or inept when it comes to promoting their life chances . . . An added dividend of examining success is*

the information that they offer about what makes inner city families resilient to stressful conditions and what leads them to be creative in finding ways to help their children thrive. These attributes often take the form of individual qualities of parent or child, who may possess special beliefs, competencies, temperament or resources that contribute to success in the face of adversity.

(Furstenberg et al., 1999: 5–6)

Their detailed research work was carried out in a number of what they refer to as 'distressed communities' in inner-city Philadelphia. They looked at five hundred families and focused on the ways in which adolescent development and well-being are affected by growing up in a disadvantaged community. One of the key messages of the research is the importance of looking at differences, in terms of children's development and family functioning, *within* disadvantaged communities. They argue that sociologists have to take some of the responsibility for reinforcing negative stereotypes of families living in disadvantaged areas because they have tended to focus on 'crude aggregate differences between social categories . . . rather than pursuing sources of variation within groups' (p. 5).

Central to the thesis developed by Furstenberg and his colleagues is the importance of looking at how successful parents organise and manage the external environment for the benefit of their children. As we noted in the first chapter, they point out that studies of socialisation have typically focused on relations between parents and children rather than on how parents support their children and attempt to aid them in negotiating the outside world:

Generally speaking the identification of parenting processes has been limited to what happens inside households and specifically to dyadic encounters between parents and children . . . Yet parents also play an essential role in managing the external world by monitoring, locating and cultivating the social contacts in which their children engage outside the household.

(p. 12)

In this, they are arguing against what they refer to as the myth that disadvantaged neighbourhoods are inevitably linked to bad parenting. One of their key findings is that 'variation in social resources, family management practices and early adolescent outcomes is considerably greater within neighbourhoods than between them' (p. 167).

Using both quantitative and qualitative data, they identify the importance of parents' ability to manage the outside world for the benefit of their children. Three of the main, highly practical implications of this work are:

(a) Understanding the need to strengthen the family's capacity to manage the external world for the benefit of their children. This management involves accessing the strengths and positive influences of particular community and neighbourhood settings, while supporting children to avoid the dangers and pressures.

(b) The importance of building the social connections between families and the external world. This involves not only engaging directly with parents and children, but also linking them up with formal and informal organisations, agencies and groups in the community.

(c) The importance of developing the social capital of disadvantaged communities.

Although this work has been conducted in the United States, the general messages that it carries about the links between what happens within the family and what happens within the community is clearly relevant for the development of ecological practice in other countries, including the UK. Rather than seeing these aspects of a child's life as two distinct domains, their approach looks at the connections and the interplay between them, identifying not only the crucial role that parents can play in effectively managing their children's contact with the external world, but also the importance of agents of the external world reaching out to children and families living in disadvantaged areas:

> *Some existing institutions are committed to reaching out to parents, but too many others rely on active consumer mentality that simply is not widespread within the population of this study. Public schools in urban areas, in general, are conspicuously poor at engaging parents as active participants in the schooling of their children.*
>
> (p. 228)

This is an issue to which we return in the final chapter, when we examine some of the main challenges involved in developing ecological practice within the UK, including the sort of extended role for schools outlined above.

Conclusions

In this chapter we have mapped out some of the characteristics of communities which are likely to have the greatest impact on children's development and well-being. We have focused on disadvantaged communities and reviewed the research evidence on the links between community patterns and children's welfare. We have also looked at research which has made the connections between the community context in which the child is growing up, and the resilience of the child and the family.

This material has served to highlight the important impact of community structures, demographics and social interactions on children's lives, but it has also highlighted the role of the individual characteristics of children and their families in determining their resilience and vulnerability to the pressures that exist within communities.

In the second section of this volume, we use a number of detailed practice examples to illustrate ways of working that often cross existing professional and organisational boundaries in order to develop a wider perspective on individual children's lives, incorporating the interactions between the dynamics within families and the wider community setting in which they are located. However, before doing so, it is helpful to consider some of the main ecological processes that operate within disadvantaged communities. In the next chapter, as an example of these ecological processes, we examine the patterns and levels of crime and community safety to be found in different disadvantaged communities, which serve to highlight some of the connections that exist between population characteristics, group cultures, individual behaviour, and the responses of formal and informal organisations.

Chapter 4. **Ecological Processes in Disadvantaged Communities**

This chapter will consider:
- The way that social problems are geographically distributed in patterns related to interactions between individual, family and community level factors, best understood within an ecological framework.
- The risk and protective factors associated with criminal behaviour and child abuse identified by research.
- The role of neighbourhood cultures in mediating the influences of other area factors on individual behaviour.
- The way that apparently homogeneous communities are actually composed of a diverse range of groups with different perspectives, experiences and interests.
- Some of the ecological processes operating within particular community contexts, understanding of which is an important ingredient in the development of ecological practice.

Introduction: The spatial distribution of social problems

In Chapter 2 we looked at the spatial distribution of poverty and other forms of inequality in the UK. Research around the developed world, over many years, has highlighted the way that social problems, such as crime, child abuse, teenage pregnancy and drug misuse, also tend to conform to spatial patterns (Coulton et al., 1995). For example, areas characterised by economic deprivation, physical deterioration, and population instability are consistently associated with a range of social problems, including higher levels of criminal behaviour, and child abuse and neglect (Bottoms and Wiles, 1997; Cicchetti and Lynch, 1993). Whilst a significant proportion of the spatial variations in social problems can usually be explained by selection processes that result in concentrations of people with similar characteristics living in particular locations (Baldwin and Bottoms, 1976; Wikström, 1991; Murie, 1997), rates also tend to vary between neighbourhoods with similar populations, suggesting that area influences also play an important role (Hope and Foster, 1992). In relation to crime, for example, this point was illustrated by an analysis of the first two British Crime Surveys which showed that specific features of the social environment – sparse friendship networks, unsupervised teenage peer groups, and low organisational participation – underpinned the variations in rates of crime and delinquency identified between otherwise similar areas (Sampson and Groves, 1989).

Further research has demonstrated that it is actually *interactions* between selection processes and area influences, as well as wider conditions in society, that determine levels of social problems in local neighbourhoods. Using crime as a convenient example again, this has been demonstrated in a number of UK studies, including a detailed comparison between two areas of Sheffield, 'Gardenia' and 'Stonewall'. These two areas were separated only by a main road, and were similar in size and population characteristics such as age, sex, social class, ethnic origin, household size, proportion of single residents, male unemployment, education level, and length of residence (Bottoms et al., 1992).

However, recorded offences were three times higher in Gardenia than in Stonewall, which the research team attributed to small differences between the two areas, which started some 50 years earlier.

The process of differentiation began with differences in housing allocations, with tenants in greater need or with relatives and friends already living there being placed in the Gardenia area. Over time, these patterns of settlement were reinforced by other factors, including the stigma attached to residents because of Gardenia's growing negative reputation, as well as some minor differences between the main schools serving each area, and more significant differences in the parental and peer socialisation processes that developed in the two areas (Bottoms and Wiles, 1997). This study provides a good example of ecological processes operating, over many years, to shape the characteristics, attitudes and behaviour of two adjoining areas in one city. It demonstrates how aspects of the local public housing market can interact with other public services (e.g. education), the development of social relationships, and the responses of outside agencies and businesses to people on the basis of their home address. Mutually reinforcing patterns of influence were established in this example, resulting in two originally similar populations developing divergent social ecologies, with significantly different cultures and associated levels of criminal activity.

Other researchers have confirmed the important association between the social ecology of a neighbourhood and its level of crime. Most notably, Robert Sampson and his colleagues undertook a major study which examined the social ecologies and levels of crime in 343 neighbourhoods in Chicago, each consisting of about 8,000 residents, (Sampson et al., 1997). During the first half of the 1990s they interviewed a total of 8,782 residents, representing every neighbourhood, to identify their views about the levels of informal social control, social cohesion, trust, and violence in their area. For example, they asked respondents if their neighbours would intervene when they came across children involved in anti-social behaviour or truanting from school. Responses were cross-referenced with data about the socio-economic circumstances of residents in each neighbourhood and the levels of violence to be found there, based on the self reports of victims, the perceptions of residents, and police records.

They found that variations in the level of violence in different neighbourhoods were attributable to their levels of 'collective efficacy', a measure of mutual trust and informal social control. It is, in effect, a measure of *activated social capital*, specifically directed towards the supervision of children and the maintenance of public order. Neighbour-hoods with the highest collective efficacy scores had rates of violent crime 40 per cent lower than those with the worst scores. Although collective efficacy tended to be lower in the most deprived and unstable neighbourhoods it was, nevertheless, the best single predictor of the overall rate of violent crime, better than any other measure of disadvantage or the social environment such as poverty, race, or the density of friendship ties. Although this study is obviously only of direct relevance to understanding the dynamics between neighbourhood conditions and violent crime in one particular North American context, the ecological model of analysis that it adopts is now widely used, in many different parts of the world, to understand the factors that influence levels of a wide range of social problems, including child abuse and neglect (Belsky, 1993; Coulton et al., 1999; Garbarino, 1976; Garbarino and Crouter, 1978; Garbarino and Sherman, 1980; Vinson et al., 1996). For example, work by Coulton and colleagues (1995) in the

US identified three groups of factors that, *in combination*, explained 78 per cent of the variations in child abuse rates between different neighbourhoods. The first and most important group of factors related to 'impoverishment', which included measures of poverty, unemployment, vacant housing, population loss, and female-headed house-holds. The second set of factors related to 'child care burden', which included the ratios of children to adults and females to males, as well as the proportion of elderly people in the population. And the third set of factors related to 'instability', including the proportions of the population that had lived in their present home for less than ten years and less than one year, as well as the proportion that had moved within the last five years. In a multiple regression analysis, these three groups of factors (both separately and in combination) predicted the different rates of child maltreatment found within neighbourhoods.

The role of risk and protective factors

In recent years, the ecological model of analysis of human behaviour has increasingly been used as a framework for identifying the key risk and protective factors involved in the development of a wide range of different social problems. This can be illustrated by considering the findings of a number of studies, often following cohorts of children from birth to adulthood, which have helped to identify the roots of a wide range of social problems, including criminal and anti-social behaviour, and different forms of child abuse and neglect.

Offending behaviour

Comprehensive UK reviews of the evidence in relation to crime, for example, have concluded that its origins lie in the ways that a variety of 'risk' and 'protective' factors, operating at individual, peer, family, school, community and societal levels, interact with one another (e.g. Farrington, 1996; Rutter et al., 1998; Beinart et al., 2002). Whilst no single risk factor can be said to cause (or predict) future offending behaviour, the chances of such behaviour occurring rise significantly when several risk factors cluster together, and interact with one another, especially in the absence of protective factors (Rutter 1980; Anderson et al., 2001; France and Utting, 2005).

The longitudinal design of the studies upon which these reviews are based also makes it possible to identify the order of influence of different factors, thereby providing insights into the multiple causes (rather than the symptoms or consequences) of criminal behaviour, and the nature of the mechanisms of influence operating (Anderson et al., 2001). At the *individual level*, hyperactivity and impulsivity in childhood, which have strong genetic components, are consistently identified as risk factors for anti-social behaviour that tends to persist through adolescence into adulthood. Low intelligence and cognitive impairment are also identified as risk factors, even after controlling for variables such as low household income and large family size. Personal attitudes can also come into the equation, with factors such as lack of social commitment, alienation and acceptance of criminal behaviour (including drug misuse) all implicated as risk factors. Although protective factors can often be framed in terms of the opposites of risk factors (e.g. average/high intelligence, or social integration), there are a number of other protective factors, at the individual level, that are also worth noting. These include female gender (particularly in relation to offences of theft and violence), a resilient temperament, a sense of self-efficacy, and the social and learning skills that facilitate social acceptance and participation.

Peer level risk factors become particularly important during adolescence, and include friendships and alliances with anti-social children and young people, which may also develop into longer-term relationships with one another, sometimes producing children. Conversely, close friendships with pro-social peers have consistently been found to be a significant protective factor against criminal and anti-social behaviour, even for children and young people living in otherwise high-risk environments.

At the *family level*, children of low birth weight tend to be at increased risk of becoming offenders. Children of teenage mothers are also at increased risk of developing anti-social tendencies, including the early use of legal and illegal substances. Experience of poor parental supervision and harsh or inconsistent discipline are also regularly identified as important risk factors, as is experience of family conflict (whether in 'broken' or 'intact' homes) and a family history of criminal behaviour or the condoning of such behaviour by parents. Family poverty, when it is found in combination with poor housing and large family size, has also been identified as a risk factor, once again illustrating the importance of interactions between different variables highlighted by ecological theory (Jack, 1997; Jack and Gill, 2003). In relation to protective factors at the family level, secure attachment relationships with parents are important, as well as strong bonds with other adults including wider family members. However, as for peer level influences, the true value of these potentially protective relationships will, to an important extent, be dependent upon the pro-social attitudes and behaviour of the adults concerned.

Risk factors at the *school level* include low educational achievement (beginning in primary school), aggressive behaviour (such as bullying), and lack of commitment to schooling (perhaps involving truancy). Some of these factors may, themselves, be linked to aspects of a school's overall ethos and organisation. Schools also have the potential to exert important protective influences, including providing their pupils with opportunities to form supportive relationships with teachers and other school staff, as well as recognition and praise for achievement and other forms of positive behaviour, and the setting of pro-social standards for their pupils.

Finally, as was discussed earlier in this chapter, *community and societal level* influences also play an important role in the development of anti-social and criminal behaviour. At the national level, factors such as a country's economic conditions and levels of inequality, its education, employment, housing, criminal justice and leisure policies, as well as the overall political and media contexts, will all be significant (Bottoms and Wiles, 1997). At more local or community levels, inequalities between geographical areas which, as we have already seen, have grown in the UK over recent decades, have produced an increasing number of multiply deprived areas that are consistently associated with higher levels of crime. These neighbourhoods tend to be characterised by high levels of transience and social need, accompanied by a lack of social integration and informal social controls.

In such areas, social interactions tend to be more limited and trust between neighbours tends to be lower than that found in more affluent areas. Conversely, the presence of positive role models within the wider community, and a culture which transmits disapproval of offending and drug use, can be protective for children, whatever their individual or family circumstances. The protective potential of positive neighbourhood influences has been demonstrated in a housing mobility programme operating in five areas of the United States. This involved comparing the outcomes for children and young people belonging to randomly selected families who moved from disadvantaged housing projects to more advantaged urban or suburban areas, with the outcomes for those who did not move. The results revealed that moving to a better area, which brought with it potential improvements in peer influences, community and educational facilities, neighbourhood safety, and overall quality of life (for both adults and children), significantly improved outcomes for children across a range of measures, including health and behaviour, educational attainment, and employment prospects (Katz, et al., 2001).

Child abuse and parenting

Longitudinal and cohort studies examining the origins of child abuse and neglect have demonstrated that similar ecological processes, involving interactions between individual, family, area and society-level factors, are implicated (Belsky, 1993). For example, a study in Avon has followed over 14,000 children born in three health districts in that part of England (Sidebotham, 2000, 2002). It found strong associations between child maltreatment and poverty, at both family and area levels with, for example, children living in socially rented housing found to be seven times more likely to experience maltreatment than those living in owner-occupied homes. There were also significant associations found between child maltreatment and paternal unemployment, family mobility and lack of social integration.

The importance of an ecological framework for analysing human behaviour is also illustrated in a recent UK study of parenting in four neighbourhoods, three of which were disadvantaged and one affluent (Barnes, 2004). This study found that residents' feelings of attachment to their neighbourhood and ratings of the area as a good place to bring up children were associated with the extent of local social networks and levels of crime and anti-social behaviour. It also found that there were strong relationships between neighbourhood characteristics and neighbourhood-level parenting, which included local monitoring of children and the risk of retaliation in response to controls by neighbours on children's behaviour. However, family-level parenting was more closely related to individual child and adult characteristics, including children's behaviour and parents' personality, childhood experiences of discipline and mental health, rather than neighbourhood-level influences. Furthermore, some of these individual characteristics, such as maternal depression, were themselves found to be related to certain neighbourhood characteristics, such as social networks and attachment to the local area, illustrating the interactions between factors at different levels that could be said to be the defining feature of ecological theory.

Given the focus of this book, it is to a more detailed examination of neighbourhood level influences that we now turn, since these provide the context for the ecological practice examples which follow in the second section of the book.

Interactions between neighbourhood cultures and individual behaviour: Lessons from the Priority Estates Project

Some of the ways in which the cultures that develop in different neighbourhoods interact with criminal behaviour and child maltreatment have already been discussed, in relation to studies investigating the spatial distribution of these social problems in both the UK and the US. Other UK researchers, studying 'problem estates', have also noted the interdependency of a range of explanations for the social problems to be found in those neighbourhoods, including their high levels of crime (Rock, 1988; Power, 1989). However, in order to explain differences in behaviour between apparently similar people living in similar areas, there is a need to focus directly on the internal dynamics of disadvantaged communities.

We have already seen that a crucial component in determining levels of crime and anti-social behaviour in local areas is the degree of informal social control that exists, maintained through interactions between residents, participation in community organisations and activities, norms of conduct and trust, and the socialisation of children. These community and cultural aspects of social control were the subject of a UK study by Hope and Foster (1992) of an area regeneration programme, known as the Priority Estates Project (PEP), which is worth looking at in some detail for the light that it sheds on the complex interactions that can develop. The study compared two similar estates, only one of which was implementing the PEP model of intervention. The reputation of the PEP estate had been blighted since its origins in the early 1960s as a resettlement destination for families from slum clearance areas. However, the reputation of the 'control' estate was almost as bad, and they also had similar demographic profiles and crime rates at the start of the evaluation.

The aims of the PEP model were to improve the environment, management and social mix of the intervention estate. For example, to provide more 'defensible' public spaces in the housing areas of the estate, front gardens were added to some properties and walkways that were facilitating domestic burglaries were blocked off. Similarly, the land surrounding the tower blocks of flats on the estate was fenced off and landscaped, and CCTV and telephone entry systems installed. Housing management was improved with the introduction of an estate-based service, with dedicated caretaking, cleaning and repair services and close tenant involvement. However, attempts to improve the social mix of tenants on the intervention estate were thwarted by other changes occurring at the same time, resulting in relative increases in both the social needs and turnover of residents on the PEP estate, compared to the control estate.

Besides measuring changes in rates of crime during the period of the intervention, the research team were interested in examining the effects of the changes on the social interactions and informal 'cultures' of residents on the two estates and the way that these, in turn, influenced criminal and anti-social activities. Within the PEP estate they found that the areas with improved housing became occupied by relatively less deprived families, with more deprived families, including a growing number of single parent households, being allocated housing in the areas that had not been improved during the study period. At the same time, the tower blocks began to be used for a more transient population of younger, single adults, many with high levels of social need having previously been homeless or having recently left prison or institutional care, as previous elderly occupants were re-housed in low-rise accommodation.

Despite this increasing level of social need amongst new residents on the PEP estate, the evaluation team found that, by comparison with the control estate, there were significant reductions in both overall criminal activity, especially burglary and vandalism, on the intervention estate. However, these positive changes were offset by relative increases in theft from vehicles and offences against the person. A similarly mixed picture emerged in relation to non-criminal changes. On the plus side, residents' perceptions of having a say in what happened on the PEP estate, feelings of responsibility for the area outside their homes, and ease of identifying strangers all increased relative to the control estate, as did the number of households on the estate where respondents had friends. However, there were also relative increases in the perceptions of disorderliness on the PEP estate, including disturbances by youths, noisy neighbours and people hanging around drinking.

Cultural changes tended to mirror some of these behavioural changes. At the outset, the researchers identified three broad groups of families on the PEP estate – 'established', 'vulnerable', and 'problem'. The 'established' families tended to be long-term, stable and law-abiding residents who exercised close supervision over their children and managed financially, although often on very low budgets. By contrast, the 'vulnerable' and 'problem' families, distinguished from one another primarily by the extent of their difficulties, tended to lead more unstable lives. Both of these groups perceived themselves to be trapped in a cycle of deprivation that was largely beyond their control, characterised by financial and emotional problems, violence, and links with networks of criminal activity. However, the children from the small number of 'problem' families were, in addition, identified as causing particular problems for other residents, who perceived them to be beyond their parents' control and to constitute the core of troublesome youths on the estate, riding stolen motorbikes around the neighbourhood, defacing public areas, and being involved in theft, burglary and threatening behaviour.

During the study period burglary fell, overall, in both the improved and unimproved areas of the PEP estate. This was explained by the enhanced levels of overall informal social control associated with the PEP intervention, which had helped to provide residents with greater influence over the running of the estate and increased opportunities for participation in community activities, as well as an increase in the number of other households on the estate in which residents had friends. However, in the tower block area, changes in the resident population exerted a more powerful influence than the PEP improvements, resulting in a localised 'hot-spot' of burglaries. The influx of vulnerable, single people, allocated *unfurnished* flats, helped to create a market in stolen goods that formed a bridge between the previously separate adult and juvenile criminal sub-cultures. It also provided a new location for groups of young people to hang-out together, without adequate supervision by responsible adults, resulting in a rise in anti-social behaviour, including drug-taking. This study, therefore, provides a clear illustration of the way that physical, organisational, and population changes can interact with one another in ways that affect both neighbourhood cultures and levels of criminal and anti-social behaviour in different locations (Hope and Foster, 1992: 501–2).

Lessons from more recent studies

The PEP study refers to work which took place some 20 years ago now. More recently, a study of twelve disadvantaged areas around the UK, designed to trace the dynamics of neighbourhood decline and renewal, helps to shed further light on the ways that the local cultures of different areas can influence the behaviour and attitudes of the people who live there (Lupton, 2003).

Interviews with residents in these disadvantaged neighbourhoods revealed the perceived strengths of the community spirit to be found in each area, based primarily on local kinship networks but also including informal relationships with friends and neighbours. For some, these ties also included links with networks of illegal activity such as trading in stolen goods. As other community studies of disadvantaged neighbourhoods have identified, the illegal economy was well established in these areas and was considered a normal and rational response to a combination of personal and structural disadvantages (see, for example, Jordan et al., 1994). For instance, in 'Sunnybank' (Newcastle-upon-Tyne), a number of respondents talked about door-to-door sales of stolen goods, and in 'Kirkside East' (Leeds), a local community worker identified that the illegal economy provided a widely accepted survival technique for living on benefits (Lupton, 2003: 112). As in the PEP study discussed above, every area contained a small number of households that created a disproportionate number of problems, involving a mixture of criminal and anti-social behaviour, including excessive noise and movements late into the night, aggressive attitudes towards neighbours, dumping rubbish, and damage to public and private property. Although the impact of these households was usually restricted to a small number of streets, or even sections of streets, it could be very damaging, driving other residents away and leading to rapid and long-term decline.

Whilst most areas had active tenants' or residents' associations, and semi-formal community networks based on participation in organised voluntary activities, the mainstay of most residents' social support networks in the twelve deprived neighbourhoods in Lupton's study were close relatives. One woman in 'East Docks' (Inner London) identified a dozen households containing members of her immediate family within a few hundred yards of her home. It was not uncommon for extended families living in another area in the study, an estate in Knowsley in the West Midlands, to involve as many as five generations. Even in areas where extensive inter-generational networks did not exist, such as the predominantly Asian area of 'Middle Row' in Birmingham, kinship (and faith) networks were still the foundation for shared values and support, providing 'a stable core, even though some residents were transient, unsettled and isolated' (Lupton, 2003: 113).

Similar findings have emerged from a range of studies of the social networks of families living in disadvantaged areas in the UK and elsewhere (e.g. Gill et al., 2000). Disadvantage creates a dependence on local networks, primarily consisting of kinship relationships, for day-to-day support with things like child care, transport to appointments, and borrowing money, tools and food. These family relationships tend to be supplemented by usually weaker, less numerous and more transient ties with friends and acquaintances in the immediate vicinity. By way of contrast, the social networks of families living in more affluent circumstances tend to include a larger proportion of close friendships, usually being sustained over long periods of time and over a wide geographical area, as well as a more diverse circle of acquaintances (Jack, 1997, 2000).

A dependence on local kin-based networks can facilitate the emergence of insular cultures, which sometimes serve to support or at least tolerate criminal and anti-social behaviour and attitudes, including child abuse and neglect (Korbin, 1989). In their turn, such cultures can help to reinforce an area's negative reputation and serve to limit residents' social relationships and access to services and opportunities outside the area, including housing, employment, and personal credit. Through these processes, it can be seen that particular neighbourhoods may collect together those who are already socially excluded, as well as contributing further to their social exclusion (Lupton, 2003: 121).

Variations in perceptions of trust and safety in local areas

The cultures that develop in different neighbourhoods are also intimately connected to the perceptions of trust and safety held by local residents. This is illustrated in a study of two economically matched, predominantly white, high crime neighbourhoods in Greater Manchester (Walklate, 1998). In this in-depth study, adults and children who lived, worked, or went to school in the two neighbourhoods were asked where they thought it was safe or risky to go in their area, and how they managed any fears that they had. In 'Oldtown' perceptions of safety tended to be shaped by a culture based on shared understandings amongst almost all residents, no matter what their age, gender or background. Essentially this consisted of assumptions that people were alright as long as they were local, and that local people 'wouldn't rob off their own'. A form of self-policing was also widely accepted by people living in this area, partly enforced by members of the local criminal gang, who 'sorted out' trouble within the area. By way of contrast, there were some significant differences between the perceptions of different groups of respondents within 'Bankhill', the other neighbourhood in this study. Adult residents described it as an area in rapid decline, characterised by mistrust in other people – 'even in their own sons' as one local police officer put it. Perceptions about safety were often expressed in terms of fear of young people by older people, and there was no sense among adult respondents that being 'local' carried with it any meaningful level of protection. Young people (13–15 year olds) however, expressed views that were quite different to those of older respondents. They thought that the area 'wasn't so bad' and considered that coming from the area and 'being known' did provide a measure of personal protection.

This piece of ethnographic research indicates the dangers inherent in making assumptions about the community-level social ecology of any geographical area or neighbourhood, including the level of social cohesion or disorganisation to be found there. Any location, whatever the apparent homogeneity of its residents, will actually consist of a number of different social groupings, whose attitudes and interests are likely to both overlap and diverge, in often complex ways. Factors such as age, gender, social class, religion, ethnic background, family structure and length of residence may all play a role in shaping the social ecology and local culture of different neighbourhoods for different groups of people (Coulthard et al., 2002). As we discuss elsewhere in this volume, concepts of what constitutes the 'neighbourhood' or the 'local area', as well as participation in community organisations and networks, and use of local facilities and social spaces, are all influenced by interactions between personal, household and neighbourhood characteristics. Inclusion for some almost inevitably means exclusion for others (Lupton, 2003: 115). For example, length of residence can become a significant source of divisions within disadvantaged communities, with longer-term residents often avoiding newer residents, primarily because of fears about crime and anti-social behaviour. Over a period of time this, somewhat paradoxically, is likely to lead to *increased* levels of crime and anti-social behaviour, due to a weakening of informal social controls over local behaviour and conditions.

The heterogeneity of experiences and perspectives to be found within different communities is clearly demonstrated by the results of a number of UK surveys of people's perceptions of their local areas which, for example, reveal clear notions of what are considered to be safe and unsafe locations and activities for different groups in particular areas. One study, which explored the perceptions of 12–15 year olds attending two schools in relatively deprived wards in a town in south-east England, revealed the way that young people perceive certain sites in their local areas as unsafe (Morrow, 2002). Fear of crime associated with drunks, gangs and racist residents were all highlighted by the young people in this study, with particular locations, including a local park and the adjoining shops, an area surrounding a local pub, and the houses of known racists all identified as scary and dangerous places. Other young people in this study talked about the general sense of distrust shown towards them by adults, summed up in the comments of 'Mike', who said that adults 'expect you to be no good . . . they don't give you the benefit of the doubt, they just write you off before they've even met you' (Morrow, 2002: 177).

The young people interviewed also highlighted the role that they thought lax parental supervision played in the anti-social and criminal behaviour of some young people in the town, with one boy commenting that some parents didn't care what time their children came home in the evening, and a girl ('Kerry') alleging that mothers in one area of the town 'just let their kids go everywhere' (Morrow, 2002: 178). Parks, which were identified as an unsafe place by children and young people in this study, were also widely reported as unsafe in a study of 13 and 14 year-olds living in the English Midlands (Jones et al., 2000).

The differences in the perceptions about safety between different groups, according to factors such as age, gender, ethnic background, individual and area levels of deprivation, and rurality, are also clearly demonstrated in two recent national surveys. One of these, carried out on behalf of the Home Office, explored the views of over 2,500 children and young people about their community safety and participation (Farmer, 2005). Whilst 93 per cent of the respondents said that they enjoyed living in their particular neighbourhood, some significant variations were apparent in the responses given by different groups of children and young people on more specific issues. For example, in relation to differences along ethnic lines, Black and Asian young people (aged 11–15 years) were about four times as likely to report having experienced racial prejudice as white respondents. Possibly linked to this finding, a higher proportion of white young people said that they trusted 'many people' in their neighbourhood, compared to Asian and Black young people. Trust was also higher in the least deprived areas, where young people were twice as likely to say that 'many people' could be trusted as those living in the most deprived areas, and in rural compared to urban areas. The main reasons cited by young people for feeling unsafe were strangers, feared especially by girls, bullying, feared more by boys, and traffic. The same reasons were cited by the children (aged 8–10 years) surveyed, but in different proportions, with an even higher number of them citing fear of strangers, followed by fear of traffic and then bullying. Similar fears were also expressed by 10–11 year-olds living in four areas of England – Huddersfield, London, South Gloucestershire and Bath – in another recent study (Thomas and Thompson, 2004).

The other national survey that reveals the contrasting perspectives of different groups of people about community safety involved nearly 8,000 adults (aged 16 and over), interviewed as part of the General Household Survey 2000 (Coulthard et al., 2002). As in the children's and young people's survey discussed above, the proportion of respondents who said that they enjoyed living where they did was high, with people of Pakistani and Bangladeshi origin the group most likely to say that they enjoyed living in their local area, whilst Black respondents were the least likely to say so. Overall, the majority of those surveyed expressed positive views about their local facilities, including health and transport services and rubbish collection. However, only a small minority rated facilities for teenagers as 'good' or 'very good', with a low proportion also giving the same ratings to facilities for young children. Traffic speed and volume were identified as problems by the greatest proportion of residents, followed by parking, teenagers hanging around on the streets, and alcohol and drug misuse.

Whilst the great majority of respondents said they felt either 'safe' or 'very safe' walking alone in their neighbourhood during the daytime, this fell after dark with over a quarter feeling either 'a bit unsafe' or 'very unsafe', and one in five respondents admitting that they never went out alone after dark. Women felt less safe than men walking alone in their neighbourhood, especially after dark, and older people were the least likely to feel safe walking alone, both during the day and after dark. Younger people were the group who felt safest walking alone in the neighbourhood, despite the fact that they were also the group most likely to have been the victims of inter-personal crime in the past twelve months. There were clear associations between a wide range of measures of area deprivation and higher levels of dissatisfaction with the local area among residents.

A more local study, of young people aged 13 and 14 in three locations in the English Midlands, to which reference has already been made, further illustrates some of the differences between perceptions of safety and appropriate behaviour according to the type of environment in which people are living (Jones et al., 2000). For example, young people living in a high-density urban environment were less likely to use bicycles or to travel unaccompanied, even within their local area, whereas, in suburban and rural locations, lone travel (even after dark) and cycling were more common. Also, although all young people viewed 'hanging-out' together, away from their homes and parents, as being important, there were significant differences in how such 'gangs' or groups were perceived, according to location. In the urban area, for instance, they were considered to be essential for ensuring physical safety outside of the home whereas, in the suburban and rural locations, they were viewed more casually as serving a purely social function.

This study also provides some interesting insights into the ways that young people deal with parental concerns about their safety. Their strategies, especially those of the girls in the study who, as a group, tended to have more restrictions placed on their independence than boys, involved a mixture of careful information management and outright lies. They often kept to themselves information about situations or incidents that they thought would alarm their parents, and frequently failed to reveal the full extent of their plans for an evening out, perhaps stating that they were spending time at a friend's house when this was only where they intended to meet up together at the start of the evening. The general approach taken by the young people in this study was summed up by a girl living in the suburban area who said that 'what parents don't know won't harm them' (Jones et al., 2000: 322).

Many of the same issues emerged from a more recent study of the perspectives of parents and children living in four disadvantaged areas with high levels of anti-social behaviour in and around Glasgow (Seaman et al., 2006). For example, despite the problems that they acknowledged existed in the neighbourhoods where they lived, both parents and young people also identified many positive aspects of their local areas, often associated with the presence of familiar and trusted family, friends and neighbours. The main concerns expressed by adults and children living in these neighbourhoods were the threats posed by youth gangs and the misuse of drugs and alcohol by both adults and young people. Young people, however, viewed groups or gangs as a necessary form of self-protection, although some of them recognised that others found the presence of such groups threatening. Children in this study generally interpreted parental interest in their activities and the imposition of rules as evidence of appropriate concern for their welfare. However, as they got older they were increasingly likely to either ignore or subvert such rules in order to increase their own freedom and independence. They took responsibility for keeping themselves and their friends safe by sharing their very detailed local knowledge about hazardous people, places or situations, looking out for one another, and moving around in groups.

Conclusions

What all of these surveys and research studies highlight are the often varying perceptions and social ecological niches of different groups of people living within the same communities. For example, young people, who are statistically the group most likely to be the victims of street crimes, view collecting together in groups or 'gangs' when out of the house as both an enjoyable social arrangement and a necessary protective measure against bullying and assault. Conversely, older people and younger children tend to perceive groups of teenagers as threatening to their personal safety and troublesome for their quality of life. There is a complex web of inter-connections and associations between an individual's personal and family characteristics, the location in which they are living, different perceptions about trust and safety in the area, and the ways in which all of these factors interact with the local cultures, including parenting behaviour and levels of crime and other forms of anti-social behaviour. This is the sort of information with which practitioners wishing to develop ecological practice need to be familiar in order to help children and families living in disadvantaged communities to improve the quality of their lives.

Chapter 5. **The Development of Practice Approaches to the Connections Between Child, Family and Community**

This chapter will consider:
- Ecological practice and the five *Every Child Matters* child well-being indicators.
- The importance of listening to children and parents: A precondition for ecological practice.
- Different levels of ecological practice.
- Questions about the meaning of 'community' for children and families.

Introduction

So far we have looked at some of the main principles underpinning ecological practice and reviewed the research evidence behind the present policy context, as well as considering the impact on children and families of living in disadvantaged communities. We have also examined some of the complexity to be found in the community-level ecological processes that operate in disadvantaged neighbourhoods, using variations in crime and anti-social behaviour as an example.

Our aim, now, is to explore the relevance of all of this information for practice, and to consider various ways in which ecological theory and research can be incorporated into welfare work with children and families. To set the tone and provide an insight into some of the issues involved in such practice, we begin by considering a first hand account of the importance of social networks and community-level factors in the life of one parent and her disabled son. Support within communities, and the links that children and parents have with their communities, are often complex, as the following example illustrates. It is taken from an interview with Maureen, a lone parent with a 13 year old son, Jack, who has severe learning difficulties. The case study illustrates a number of themes about support in communities, including:

- Support from local people or people in the same situation – a community of interest – may be more significant than the support and help of professionals.
- Support from the social networks available to families may change over time.
- At a local level, there may be a wide variety of groups that either offer support, or increase the pressures on parents.

Maureen describes living as a lone parent with Jack as being cut off from the rest of the community: 'once I shut this door it's like living in a "secret little world"'. She particularly emphasises how support from both professionals and family has changed over the years, as Jack has got older:

I can remember in the beginning when Jack was diagnosed with learning difficulties and we started having all the people doing home visits and introducing themselves. I thought at least we've got all these people coming and they're going to help. And they're going to do this and they're going to do that. But after a little while it's wavered away and you just get left to get on with it and find things out from the other mums and find things out for yourselves . . . its actually been the other mums in the same boat who've been the ones supporting me.

As the interview proceeds it is apparent that Maureen is unenthusiastic about the support she has received from professionals:

The professionals I feel at a loss with really. It's like all the pouring out I've done to them over the years, it's been like a waste of time. I might as well have been talking to that wall. The difference is like someone understanding, listening to me for a few minutes. It would be more beneficial than talking to a professional for five hours. I really mean it. That's the way it is . . . They do just come and go. They just don't quite get it.

Maureen emphasises that the main support she gets is from other mothers who are in the same situation as she is in herself:

I know I could get up at 2 o'clock in the morning and ring other mums and they wouldn't go, 'Oh what . . . are you ringing me now for'? If I was at the end of my tether I wouldn't go to the professionals. Not in the slightest. Other mums of special needs children are my biggest support. It's more likely to be a phone call because we're so busy with appointments and things like that. Sometimes you've barely got time to get on the phone, but you just manage to slot it in. I'm getting up willy nilly and seeing to Jack, and I'm saying 'Hang on, he's put something in his mouth', or 'He's climbed up on the table'. So a phone call is even difficult.

Maureen also says that the help she has received from her family and friends has changed and diminished over the years:

Talking to other mums, they have said that families and friends drop away when a special needs child comes along. I thought this was just me, but talking to other mums its 'My family don't bother, my sister used to come around but now she doesn't bother'. As for people visiting me, it doesn't really happen a lot. I don't know why they don't come and see me. I always try and make them welcome . . . I try hard, but they can't deal with it.

Other factors, specific to Jack's daily routine, tend to cut Maureen off from contact and support. For instance, because Jack has transport away from the local community to a special school, Maureen doesn't get the chance for a chat with the other parents, and hear what's going on. Her description of her situation also shows how different people in the community may be supportive, whilst others increase the pressure that she is under:

I've taken him down the cricket club . . . the supporters do not say 'Hello', or anything. Just looking around and staring when they hear the noise that Jack is making, and then carrying on with their game . . . All the mum's down there, they spread their blankets out and have a day long picnic. They call their children away when they go too near Jack. But I find the football players and the people who support the team have a different attitude. They say 'Oh, here comes Jack. We're going to have a good game today (Jack)'. Like they have a little chat . . . It's like a warm glow inside. It makes me feel lovely. And now the local team's asked Jack to be their mascot when they do their cup final. And that's just made me feel like I've flown to the moon and back.

Another important point that talking to Maureen illustrates is that social support, at a community level, doesn't exist in a vacuum. It is in part dependent on the skills of the parent to access it:

On meeting people that live locally, I have to make more effort than they do. I do the groundwork and the hard work. I make a big effort on approaching people and having a chat with them. So I don't think I'm segregating myself. I'm making an effort. I overcompensate for their lack of understanding.

Maureen also talks about the impact of community networks when they don't meet her needs:

I'll give you an example. In the holidays Jack got up at 4 o'clock in the morning and he's very vocal and loud. And he repeated shouting all day. By about tea time I went and stood out the back by the field. I was trembling because he was shouting so much. I stood out there and a woman came down the field with her dog and said, 'Is Jack in the house on his own? Is he alright?' I was stood there and I almost burst into tears. She was more or less saying, 'Oh, you've left your son in there on his own.' She wasn't saying, 'Oh, are you alright?' I went back in but I felt bullied by the situation rather than helped.

Ecological practice and the five *Every Child Matters* well-being indicators

As we identified in the first chapter, the UK government's strategy for children's services, set out in the Green Paper *Every Child Matters* (HM Treasury, 2003) and the Children Act 2004, places new responsibilities on local authorities in England to safeguard and promote the well-being of all children, through the development of integrated local services, commissioned and co-ordinated by children's trusts. Central to these aspirations is the requirement to safeguard and promote children's well-being through the achievement of five inter-related outcomes: being healthy; staying safe; enjoying and achieving; making a positive contribution; and achieving economic well-being. Formulated in consultation with children and young people, and expressed in simple language that captures all of the important aspects of their development, these outcomes have been favourably received, and have come to be seen as understandable by policy makers, practitioners, parents, and children alike. They also provide an effective framework for the development of ecological practice.

We argued, however, that one of the main obstacles to the development of effective approaches to the safeguarding of children and the promotion of their well-being is the absence of holistic, ecological practice frameworks that can be used within mainstream children's services. In an attempt to address this deficit, we have developed the following diagram, which illustrates the way that the five *ECM* outcomes can be integrated within an ecological framework of child development.

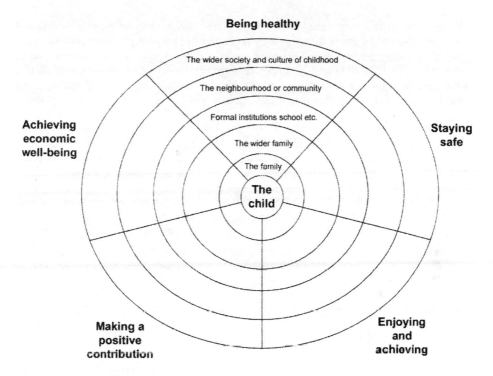

Figure 1. The *Every Child Matters* outcomes within an ecological framework

The spider's web diagram enables the social ecology of individual children to be mapped out, identifying the key strengths and pressures to be found at different levels within the different systems that have an impact on the child's life, in relation to the five *ECM* outcomes. It also allows practitioners and family members to see some of the main connections and interactions between different aspects of a child's life. For example, we can think about the situation of a particular child in relation to factors that either promote or threaten their safety: in the household; in the wider family; within formal institutions, such as school; within the communities of which they are a part; and in the wider society and its cultures, in which everything else is embedded. We can also map out the dangers or risks for the child within all of these spheres of their life.

Crucially, the diagram helps us to examine the connections between the different domains of the child's life. In relation to 'staying safe', for example, what is happening within the family, such as a child receiving inadequate support and guidance about keeping safe, may be linked to the child being at increased risk in the community, or at school. Equally, the wider society and culture may be impacting on what is happening within the family, such as the danger of internet contacts impacting on the child's safety. The diagram also allows the connections between strengths and pressures in one area of a child's life to be tracked through to impacts in another area of the child's life. For instance, safety issues may have an impact on the child staying healthy. If the child does not feel safe in the community in which they live, this is likely to have a detrimental impact on the child's ability to stay safe by accessing the benefits of community facilities.

What the diagram helps to illustrate, therefore, is the way that the achievement of each of the five *ECM* child well-being outcomes is influenced by a combination of factors which are both internal and external to the family. Another way of representing these interactions is to set the different variables out in a table, as we have done in the example below.

Table 3 Internal and external factors and the *Every Child Matters* outcomes

Outcome	Factors internal to the family	Factors external to the family
Staying healthy	Provision by parents of adequate health care, emotional security, and a balanced diet	Healthy activities accessible at school and in the neighbourhood, and access to good quality health care
Staying safe	A home environment that provides protection from harm through accidents, neglect or abuse	Safety from harassment, abuse, and dangers in the built environment (e.g. roads)
Enjoying and achieving	Entertainment and stimulating activities provided within the family, and parental support for education and learning	Availability of pleasurable and age-appropriate activities, homework clubs, and positive local role models
Making a positive contribution	Child's viewpoint taken seriously within the family, child contributes to secure and affectionate relationships within the family	Children consulted on school policies and neighbourhood plans, and involved in initiatives that contribute to strong communities
Economic well-being	Family has adequate resources for needs of the child, and equitable distribution of resources between family members	Adequate provision of community resources, including public transport, and good quality training and educational opportunities

Whilst we think that diagrams and tables, such as the examples above, provide helpful ways of gathering a considerable amount of information together in one place, presented in a clear and comprehensible manner, some of their limitations also need to be recognised. For example, there is a danger that, in representing what are actually often complex, fluid and even contradictory pieces of information in these rather simplified and abbreviated forms, under separate headings, that the true nature of the interactions between different influences on children's well-being will be lost. In the above table, therefore, it must be understood that the demarcation between family and community factors is not real, and is made for illustrative purposes only. In reality, the quality of children's home environments will influence their behaviour, attitudes and interactions in the local community, and *vice-versa*. These interactive processes are fundamental to ecological theory and the form of practice that we are outlining in this book, which is concerned with the whole child, and their functioning in lots of different settings. It is, therefore, always important to bear in mind, when using tools such as these, that they can only provide somewhat simplified representations of more complicated realities.

Listening to children and parents: A precondition for ecological practice

As indicated above, and throughout the rest of this volume, one of the key challenges in ecological practice is the development of practice approaches capable of addressing the interplay between different levels of influence on children's lives. It is our contention that practitioners are in a central position when it comes to recognising and understanding the complexities of these connections. Coming into daily contact with children and families, the practitioner is repeatedly presented with information about the interplay between the individual and the social and physical world they inhabit, and the ways in which children and families are either supported or undermined by the characteristics of the environments which they inhabit.

If practitioners listen carefully to the children and parents they work with talking about their lives, they will become aware that, on many occasions, children and their parents adopt what is essentially an ecological perspective. Their descriptions often move between different levels of explanation or interpretation of their difficulties and, crucially, they often identify some of the connections between factors in different areas of their lives. For instance, parents may identify that tensions in the family are linked to housing problems, or explain that children's behaviour within the family is linked to what is happening at school. Similarly, children may explain that their lack of self confidence is linked to issues at school, or that the lack of access to appropriate leisure opportunities in their local area is affecting their sense of safety in the community. Often children will be experiencing and possibly talk about quite extreme pressures, both within and outside their families, as the following brief case description from a piece of Barnardo's neighbourhood work illustrates.

> *The worker visited a lone parent with a seven year old child. The lone parent suffered from depression and there were occasions when her son had to provide caring functions such as bringing his mother drinks in bed.*
>
> *The child also talked about life with other children in the immediate neighbourhood. He said 'It's frightening. They kick and punch.' and 'People fall over and there's lots of pushing outside'.*

Although listening is fundamental to all child welfare practice, practitioners all too often exercise a form of selective hearing, albeit often unconsciously, based upon the requirements, procedures and service arrangements of their employing organisations and the definitions and understandings of their different professions. However, parents and children are under no such obligations. Talking, and especially listening to children and parents, in order to understand *their* subjective experience and interpretation of the circumstances in which they are living their lives is, therefore, a fundamental starting point for developing ecological practice. In this respect, ecological practice is directly linked to the whole participation agenda in which children's and parents' own words about their lives, and what they think would make a difference, are of central concern. Whilst this aspect of ecological practice does not negate the need to consider other, perhaps more objective, views and data, alongside these subjective accounts and analyses, it is the latter which are the key to understanding the weight which children and parents attach to different factors, and the connections that they make between them.

Different levels of ecological practice

Although we now have national frameworks for the assessment of children in the UK which incorporate elements of ecological theory (e.g. DoH, 2000) we currently lack equivalent frameworks for *practice*, which incorporate an ecological approach. Without such practice frameworks, much of the information that is currently collected during assessments of the needs of children and families, about the wider family and environmental factors affecting their lives, is rendered largely irrelevant when it comes to making decisions about the interventions and services that might be required.

However, it is unrealistic to expect that every practitioner will be involved at all levels of all of the systems which might influence the development and well-being of children and the functioning of their families. Instead, what we are arguing for is a widening of the perspective and targets of intervention considered by any organisation which has an interest in the well-being of children and their families. Underlying this widening of perspective will be an understanding of the impact of structural and cultural processes in the lives of children and families, in general, as well as the impact of these forces on specific groups and individuals.

Below, we outline some of the different elements of ecological practice relevant for working with children and families in disadvantaged communities, based on the relationship between ecological practice, the five *ECM* outcomes, and the links between the different sectors in the spider's web diagram provided earlier:

- *Sharing information across the different domains of the child's life*
  This involves bringing together information from different professional perspectives to identify important interactions between different factors within the various domains of a child's life, and to use this knowledge in service planning and resource provision. For instance, sharing information about the impact of housing provision on the mental health of family members, such as the depression experienced by a young single parent, which is linked to the social isolation created or reinforced by the area where she lives and the people that she has for neighbours.
- *Developing pieces of work which incorporate aspects of the different systems of which the child is a part*
  The key point, here, is that practice should usually consist of different pieces of work that simultaneously address important aspects of the child's life, both within the family and in the community. For instance, in the case of dual heritage children living in white families, which we return to in a future chapter, there may be important issues of identity that need to be addressed at a family level (the child's conception of who they are and their links to important family members representing different elements of their heritage), and at the community level (links with positive role models, and addressing issues of harassment in the community).

- *Using contacts in one domain of the child's life to develop initiatives in another domain*
  This involves the possibility of using the contacts and networks established in one system, to operate more effectively in another. Often children or families will feel at ease developing relationships with practitioners in one setting, which can then be used as the basis for effective work in other settings. For example, positive relationships may be developed between workers and individual children in the context of social activities and other initiatives in the community, such as a children's participation project, which at another time might be used to address problems that the child is experiencing within the family.
- *Working with the community around family and child welfare issues*
  Often there is potential for bringing members of a community together to tackle issues that are of collective concern to local families and children. Some of the clearest examples of this aspect of ecological practice involve issues of community safety, when people can be brought together to address their concerns at a community level (see Chapter 7 for more details).
- *Working at the immediate community or neighbourhood level for the benefit of individual children in achieving the five* ECM *outcomes*
  The aim, here, is to develop local networks which are supportive of children and families, harnessing the strengths of the community to support children in achieving the five *ECM* outcomes. Examples of this can include the development of supportive local networks for parents who are under pressure or socially isolated, thereby indirectly contributing to a number of different *ECM* outcomes, or members of the community working together to develop more opportunities for children in 'enjoying' their leisure time.
- *Working with the individual child and family to access the benefits of the community (and thereby be in a stronger position to achieve the five outcomes)*
  Here, the aim is to work with the child and family to understand and access the resources of the community, extending the support they get at a neighbourhood-level, whilst at the same time developing resources in the community and the involvement of individual children and families in those resources.
- *Gathering information and influencing across the different settings of children's lives*
  In this final aspect of ecological practice, the aim is to ensure that, where appropriate, knowledge gained in one area of work is used to influence provision in another. This often involves ensuring that knowledge gained in work with individual children and families is used to influence allocation and resource decisions affecting wider groups of children and families in the local area. An example of this approach could include recognising, at an individual family level, the damaging impact of transience on the families concerned, and using this knowledge to inform an understanding of the impact of high levels of transience on overall community stability. Intervention strategies might involve trying to cut down both the extent and impact of transience, by influencing housing allocation policies at the same time as developing support mechanisms for the families directly concerned.

Practice questions about the meaning of 'community'

In addition to developing practice that consistently strives to integrate issues across the different domains of a child's life, we suggest that ecologically-minded practitioners also need to adopt an enquiring approach to the communities in which they work. Individually-oriented child welfare professionals, who already adopt an enquiring approach to understand the uniqueness of each of the families with whom they come into contact, may need to develop a similar approach to the communities in which they are operating. Likewise, those who already adopt more of a community focus in their work may need to extend their practice to encompass a fuller understanding of the impact of community characteristics and interventions on individual children and families.

Based on a combination of our own practice experience and the messages that can be gleaned from research, we suggest that, underlying this enquiring approach to ecological practice, there are a number of questions that practitioners in different settings might need to address about the children and families with whom they are working, and the communities in which they live.

What constitutes the 'community' for different groups of children and families?

One of the first tasks in developing ecological practice is to be clear about the membership of different communities, and where they begin and end. In doing this, it is important to move beyond official definitions of communities and the boundaries that contain them, since they are often the product of administrative convenience, efficient service delivery requirements, and attempts to produce consistency of size.

Instead, it is important to understand, almost in an ethnographic sense, where local children and families think that their communities begin and end, and who is included and excluded. The key to this approach, yet again, is talking to children and parents. Three important points need to be made about this:

1. Anybody who is experienced in working with community groups will be familiar with the often impassioned and confusing debates that can develop about these issues. However, it is important to be aware of the different views that exist, because they convey important signals in relation to people's perceptions about who they are, and what they understand to be some of the key characteristics of the place in which they live, or the communities of interest to which they do (or do not) belong. For example, asylum-seeking or refugee families are likely to frame their understanding of community in terms of their identity and mutually supportive networks with other similar families, wherever they live, rather than in terms of the immediate geographical area, which they might experience as much less supportive and meaningful. However, this will not always be the case, since such 'communities' may also encompass tensions and divisions that have been carried over from their countries of origin. People who appear to share a common identity may originate from different geographical areas, or belong to different religious or social groupings, and the refugee experience, itself, may also have created conflicts that serve to push people apart, so that there is only a limited sense of shared identity remaining.

2. Definitions of areas of residence and community membership are often complex and somewhat contradictory. As we discussed in the previous chapter, children and parents will often have detailed and, in some cases, very precise and minutely delineated conceptions of where areas and neighbourhoods begin and end, and what are problematic and supportive settings. Whereas administrators, and even re-

searchers, will often take fairly large areas for the focus of their activities and concerns, child and adult residents of communities will often use much more subjective and local frameworks.

3. Children's conceptions of community are likely to differ markedly from those of adults. Younger children, in particular, may have a much more limited notion of community than adults, and different children's views about where the community begins and ends may also differ markedly. For instance, in Children's Fund work over recent years, one of the authors has managed projects where the starting point has been to talk to children about their communities and neighbourhoods. In talking about where they feel safe and unsafe, and where they have the opportunities to 'enjoy and achieve', children have very often talked in tightly and almost microscopically defined small areas – for instance a very small play area next to the block of flats where they live.

What are the key aspects of community which are likely to impact on children and families?

Any practitioner experienced in working with families living in disadvantaged communities will be familiar with the accounts that parents give of the pressures that their circumstances put on them, and the way that this stress impacts on their family. The pressures created by inadequate housing and a lack of safe play areas for children, the pressures created by living alongside people who parents and children find threatening, and the pressures created by fear of crime and anti-social behaviour in the neighbourhood, can all have a profound effect on the tensions that develop *within* families.

These community pressures can be wide ranging and operate at different levels, simultaneously, through a combination of inadequate community resources and supportive networks, and the social, economic and demographic characteristics of the local area, with the difficult mix of needs and lifestyles that is often created. Before practice that links the internal world of the family and the external world of the community can be developed, the often complex nature of the mixture of pressures and supports experienced by children and families have to be fully understood.

What are the different experiences of community?

To understand the impact of community on individuals in the family, practitioners also need to recognise that community patterns and processes can impact not only at the level of the family, but also at the level of individuals and different groups within the community.

For example, as noted in the previous chapter, gender will often be of key significance in this. Women who are parents are likely to be more linked into the social networks of the community. Mumford and Power (2003) have shown how, in disadvantaged areas, social interaction and participation in local activities are linked to women's distinct roles, and Wilkins (2004) has shown how women's experiences of the local built environment is also likely to be very different from those of men. Gender is also a key issue in the different experiences of boys and girls and their use of the community and its resources, as the following example, taken from a local piece of work, which we describe more fully in a following chapter, illustrates:

The workers were approached by a group of girls who said that there were very few leisure facilities for them in the town. They said that all of the resources were either geared more to the needs of boys, or else they were dominated by them. The girls wanted somewhere they could pursue their own interests, where they weren't constantly on view to boys.

As we discussed in the previous chapter, other factors such as age, disability, social class, ethnic origin and religion, are likely to significantly affect the experience of community as well. Taking age as one example, it is easy to understand that older people, parents, young people, and children are all likely to perceive and experience the community in different ways, depending on the mix of facilities and the characteristics of the social networks available in local areas.

How do children and young people use public spaces within their communities?

It is also important to understand the way in which children use their community and its resources. Matthews (2001) has discussed the way that children are often:

. . . seemingly invisible on the landscape. At best they are provided with some sort of token space – commonly a playground – but otherwise they are required to fit into the alien environment of the adult world.

(p. 50)

He goes on to emphasise the importance of the 'street' in children's lives, using the term as a metaphor for a range of public outdoor spaces, including alleyways, cul-de-sacs, shopping parades, car parks, vacant plots and derelict sites (p. 52). Echoing a point made above in relation to gender differences, Matthews also emphasises the different ways in which boys and girls use public spaces:

Girls and boys often use the street in different ways. The main activity reported by the girls was talking and chatting with friends; boys were more likely to see the street as a venue for informal sports such as football, skateboarding and rollerblading. For both boys and girls, there is a strong sense of theatre and being on display when out and about.

(p. 60)

The importance of understanding the scale of community for children's lives is also apparent in much practice work, and is illustrated in the following example:

In a piece of local development work, contact was made with children and their families living in a very small housing association estate, which had an equally small play area adjacent to the housing. It had no play equipment except for two very small wooden horses on which the children could sit and pretend to ride. The play area was not in good condition and there was evidence that older children had tried to set the play horses alight. Nonetheless, the play area was identified as a very important resource by the children. Not only did it provide the only (albeit very limited) play equipment in the immediate area, but it was also an important meeting point for younger children. Being only yards away from their front doors, parents felt it was safe for the children to go there. Unfortunately, soon after the start of the project, following a community consultation with parents (but not children), the play area was covered with tarmac in preparation for its use as a car parking area.

What are the links that the family has with the community?

Questions need to be asked about the connections and links that the individual child and family have with the communities of which they are a part. For instance, do parents positively identify with them and do they have supportive links within their communities? Are these supportive links easily accessible to them? Do the difficulties of being a member of a particular community outweigh its advantages? As we highlighted in the previous chapter, factors such as a transient lifestyle can seriously weaken the community social networks of all family members.

It is also important to recognise that networks and sources of support are likely to be different for children and adults. In addition to the influence of parents' social networks on children's development, children and young people develop their own networks which take on increasing importance in their lives as they move towards adolescence and beyond, and which have a direct impact on their well-being throughout their childhoods. Often the qualities of parents' networks in the community will be mirrored by those of their children, but this is not inevitable. Sometimes there will be major differences with, for example, a child experiencing problems within their own social networks, such as bullying and ostracism, whilst also being a member of a family which otherwise has strong links of support in the community.

Assessments of children's use of community resources and the nature of their social networks can usefully be linked with the framework of the five *ECM* outcomes. For example, how do the community resources (both physical and social) that are available to a particular child in a particular family affect their chances of staying healthy, staying safe, achieving and enjoying, making a positive contribution, and achieving economic well-being?

What factors help to make children and families resilient to the pressures of community?

At one level, the ecological model can appear to be somewhat deterministic. Focusing, as it does, on the relationships between the internal and external worlds of the child, it can be assumed that the external pressures of the society and community will impact equally on different individuals. However, in real life this is very far from the truth. It is therefore important for practitioners to have an understanding of the ways in which different families manage to resist some of the main pressures and disadvantages of their situation, facilitating good developmental outcomes for their children. An understanding of the difficulties and pressures that some families are experiencing in particular neighbourhoods needs to be matched by an understanding of how particular families manage to resist these pressures.

Although different families will experience the same environmental and community disadvantages, different levels of parental resilience will have a dramatic effect on how children experience their lives. A prerequisite of developing ecological practice is, therefore, for the practitioner to explore the particular sources of strength that exist within particular families.

The following practice example, based on interviews with families living in a disadvantaged, semi-rural community producing what were considered by local social workers and other professionals to be disproportionate numbers of child welfare referrals, helps to illustrate what we are talking about here:

> One of the concerns of local parents was the lack of activities and events for children. The interviews were conducted at the beginning of the autumn term, when the memories of the summer holidays were still fresh in people's minds. In one street, we interviewed a lone father, living on state benefits, who had health difficulties and few supportive networks. He talked about his son and the fact that, at the beginning of the summer holidays, he had got into fights with other children in the street, leading the father to 'ground' him. As a result, the child had spent much of the summer holidays alone inside the flat where he lived.
>
> By way of contrast, just a few doors away in the same street, we talked to a group of lone parents who were also living on benefits but who, between them, had scraped together enough money to arrange a holiday for their children. One of them had a car, which the three parents and their children had piled into and taken off for the countryside. They were full of stories about arriving at an isolated farm, begging the farmer to allow them to camp, the farmer taking pity on them, and the whole group having a wonderful holiday.

However, as we noted in the previous chapter, resilience in mitigating the impact of living in difficult and disadvantaged circumstances is not only a question of personal attributes. It also involves the wider family and community resources to which families have access, as the following notes, again based on work in the community described above, illustrate:

> Another lone parent, living in the same street, and again on benefits said that, although she didn't have the money to do anything herself with her son over the summer holiday period, her own parents had been actively involved with him over the summer, and had taken him on trips to local adventure parks and other places of interest.

Practitioners are regularly presented with examples, like these, of the ways in which disadvantaged families, often with the aid of their wider family and community support networks and other resources, play a very active role in resisting and surmounting their difficulties. The challenge for practitioners, working within the ecological model, is to be alive to the strengths of individual children and families, to think closely about what those strengths are, and to work to foster them. We return to the practice implications of these issues later in the book.

Conclusions

In this chapter we have sought to move from research and theory towards putting the ecological approach into practice. We have outlined a model that links ecological practice with the five *ECM* child well-being outcomes, and we have illustrated this by providing examples of work which take this ecological perspective. We have also highlighted a number of questions that practitioners might need to ask themselves when they are working with individual families, or particular groups of parents and children, who are living in disadvantaged communities.

In the chapters that follow, we develop the themes of this chapter, once again using practice examples to illustrate the issues that we are discussing. We start, in the next chapter, by describing four specific practice locations, from Barnardo's work in the South West of England, which help to draw out the links between the child, the family and community, and ways of working that attempt to link these different domains of the child's life.

Chapter 6. **Ecological Processes and Practice in Four Community Settings**

This chapter illustrates the context for ecological practice by describing four different community settings. The connections between the internal world of the family and the external world of the community are drawn out in each description. The four community settings are:
- A large estate on the city periphery.
- Children and families in Bristol's Somali community.
- A small estate in a relatively affluent market town.
- The centre of a large seaside town.

Introduction

In this chapter we explore ecological process and practice in four different community settings in which one of the authors (O.G.) has been involved, either as a practitioner or a manager. Between them, these settings cover some of the main categories of disadvantaged communities in the UK at the present time: a peripheral housing estate; a refugee community in an inner city neighbourhood; a small estate in a rural market town; and the central area of a large coastal town. All have involved local action research work, undertaken by Barnardo's, which attempts both to understand the connections between the internal and external worlds of children and families living in these disadvantaged communities, and to address some of the problems that these connections have produced.

In each of the descriptions that follow, we look at the community context of pieces of practice and at the connections between community patterns and resources, and the lives of children and families. We then look at some of the practice initiatives and learning points for ecological practice that have emerged. This material is not intended to capture all of the work of the projects involved. Rather, we have selected out particular aspects of the projects which illustrate some of the main connections between the child and the community, and some of the main elements of the ecological practice which has been developed in response to those connections.

As these examples are all taken from on-going pieces of work, the practice is in a constant state of review and change, and is at different stages in its development, in each of the four locations at the time of writing. For example, the second piece of work described – working with Bristol's Somali community – is of relatively recent origin and, although the links between community and children's lives are fairly clear, the practice initiatives to address these are still in their early stages.

The aim of these descriptions is to assist practitioners, together with the children and families with whom they are working, to construct analyses of their own local communities, and to develop integrated approaches to practice, both of which are underpinned by ecological theory and research.

Whilst the four localities described in this chapter are different from each other, in a number of significant ways, underlying many of the problems faced by the children and families living in these communities are similar levels of poverty and disadvantage, often exacerbated by demographic factors. Given the current levels of inequality that exist in the UK, between different groups within the population as well as between different geographical areas, we consider that a fundamental requirement of ecological practice is to recognise and attempt to address the impact of these inequalities on the daily lives of the children and families who experience the greatest levels of disadvantage.

It will be seen that the work undertaken in the four locations also varies considerably. However, it shares at least one common feature, which is the emphasis placed by ecological practice on listening to children and parents talking about their own lives. This is a fundamental starting point for developing ecological practice, linking it to the wider participation agenda in which children's and parents' views about their lives, and what would make a difference, are given a central role.

One important consequence of this approach is that, when children and parents are talking about their lives and the issues they face, they do not typically keep to the often more narrowly defined perspectives of professionals. In describing their situations, they will often move backwards and forwards between a wide range of different aspects of their lives, including information about different members of their immediate and wider family, as well as issues connected with things like community resources, aspects of the local culture, and the roles of formal organisations. This contrasts with the usual approach of professionals, who tend to operate within more clearly demarcated arenas, either focusing on the internal, or the external elements of family lives.

Crucially, in such discussions, children and parents will often identify the connections between the different areas of their lives, either explicitly, or implicitly. For instance, tensions in the family may be linked to housing situations, children's behaviour within the family may be linked to what is happening at school, a young person's sense of confidence may be linked to peer-group issues in the community, and children's safety may be linked to the lack of appropriate and accessible resources within a community. Each of the descriptions that follow looks at elements which, in our attempts to develop ecological practice, appear to be important in terms of the links between the characteristics of communities and the lives of the children and families concerned. Five of the most important of these are:

- **Levels of community disadvantage.** These can involve both the characteristics of individual families that come together in a community, as well as the cumulative impact of the grouping together of families with certain levels of disadvantage.
- **Community resources.** In particular, the resources of informal support that a community has at its disposal for the benefit of children and their families.
- **Community demographics.** Including issues about who lives in a community, what is the economic and age profile of the area, what is the ethnic composition, and what is the level of child density?
- **The characteristics of networks.** Includes the characteristics of the social networks of families and children, and the ease with which they are able to access various sources of informal help, as well as the exclusion of some families from networks of support in the community.

- **Levels of transience in the area.** Some areas are relatively stable, in terms of their populations, whilst others show high rates of turnover, which may impact negatively on the lives of children and families. Also, there may be mixed and complicated patterns of movement, with some families being highly transient, whilst others in the same geographical location are far more settled.

A large estate on the city periphery

The first practice setting is a large, primarily white estate on the outskirts of a city with the practice input being provided by a family centre that has been in existence since the 1980s (see Stones, 1994).

Various pieces of local research, over a number of years, have highlighted the characteristics of this particular area and illustrate the context in which this integrated family centre has operated. For example, one study looked at the strengths and pressures in a part of this area which was producing disproportionately high rates of child protection referrals (Gill et al., 2000).

It is often assumed that even quite large residential areas are relatively homogeneous in their family and community characteristics. The picture to emerge from this piece of work was of a community in which many of the families had high levels of wider family support, with strong links across the generations. These links provided help across all the main areas of informal family support, including advice, guidance and practical support. The majority of parents talked about the frequency and importance of these family contacts. And this was apparent, in spite of high levels of family disruption and consequent changing family structures in this area, which affected not only the current generation of parents but also their own parents. This pattern of three generational contacts also held true for the majority of the lone parents in the sample.

So, whilst it is often suggested that there is an association between the breakdown of 'traditional' family structures and a weakening of wider family ties, there was little evidence of such an association in this area. The study illustrated that, although there had been dramatic changes in family structure over a number of years in this area, patterns of family and kin support had developed to accommodate these changes. For instance, one parent talking about the family of her former partner described the contact between his family and her children in the following way: 'They come over once a week . . . They get things for them if I need them, like, clothes and toys. They will also baby-sit if I need it, but my mum does that anyway.'

However alongside this general pattern of residential stability in the area, and strong links between the generations within families, there was also a relatively high degree of transience which affected a smaller but significant group of families. These families had a history of frequent moves and had very limited wider family and social networks in the area, and those that they did have were often problematic. For instance, a lone parent with four children, who had been living in the area for less than a year, described the difficulties she encountered in being accepted: 'I don't get to know them that well. They're really funny. So I don't really know what they're really like. You walk out in the street and they'll give you a funny look. It's like I got two heads or something. I don't know.'

Other pieces of local research in the area have pointed to the difficulties faced by particular families that are again linked to community characteristics. For instance, the residents in the area, although primarily white, also included a small but significant number of multi-racial families. Typically, these were families where there was a white lone parent mother with dual heritage children. There had been high rates of racial harassment in the area and it had been recognised that the dual heritage children potentially faced particular problems, including social exclusion and issues surrounding their identity, because they were rarely coming into contact with other Black people.

The family centre based in the area operated in the context of these community characteristics, and attempted to make links between what was happening for individual children and families, and what was happening, more generally, in the communities that it served. This involved combining different levels of practice, with a number of interlinked components to the work, including:

- *Individual family work* – including couple work to address issues in the family, intensive work with individual children experiencing difficulties within their families, and financial advice or debt counselling to individual parents.
- *Semi formal group work* – including parenting groups, and women's groups.
- *Informal groups* – providing support for people who lacked adequate social networks, or were isolated in the community.
- *Community development and community action* – local community groups were supported to take action around issues such as play facilities, and children being housed in high rise blocks.

In the terms of ecological practice, as we are defining it in this book, it can be seen that the family centre in this area had developed a range of work, much of which ran concurrently, which attempted to address a number of inter-connected issues which were both internal and external to the family. One important aspect of this was the development of a joint language, which both staff and parents could use to understand what was happening at the centre. For instance the term 'confidential family work' was used to identify work about internal family issues from wider, more public, community development work.

The work with children and parents in multi-racial families illustrates the way in which these different elements of work – the internal and the external – are often interrelated and can complement each other. Through its multi-racial staff team, the family centre in this primarily white area was able to offer individual counselling to parents in multi-racial families, focusing on issues of identity and connection within the families. Also, in the confidential internal domain of work, it was able to offer sessions with individual children specifically around identity and heritage. At a wider and more external level, it was also able to bring families of the same ethnic composition together. For instance, a long running and valued group for multi-racial families has operated in the family centre for many years, playing a significant part in developing informal support networks for the families and countering their social isolation. A community development and community action approach also evolved around Black and multi-racial issues on the estate, which complemented the other areas of work. For example, as a founder member of the local Black Support Group, the family centre was involved in research which looked at police response times in cases of reported racial harassment. This revealed that these incidents, often directed at children, typically involved a long response time. As a result of this study, police response times were reviewed and improved, demonstrating an increase in the importance that they attached to cases of racial harassment, particularly when they involved children. The family centre also took the lead in developing creative responses to issues of social inclusion and the experience of Black and multi-racial families on the estates that it served. One of these initiatives, for instance, involved the linking of schools in this predominantly white area, with schools in the multi-racial centre of the city.

The following case description (developed from Jones et al., 2002) illustrates the way that this approach has worked with one family.

Mary, a white lone parent, came to the family centre wanting to talk about the difficulties she was experiencing with her oldest son Dean, aged seven. Her three children had the same father, an African-Caribbean man who had not lived with the family for three years.

Mary told the worker, who was herself Black, that she was finding it difficult to cope with Dean's behaviour and was thinking about asking for him to be fostered. She said he was naughty all the time and did not listen to her. She said that any punishment she tried did not work and he often shouted and swore at her when she told him off.

During the initial meetings with Dean it emerged that he was very angry with his mother and blamed her for his father's lack of contact. It also emerged that Dean was struggling with the image he had of his father. On the one hand, he was a man whom he idolised, but on the other, he was a Black man whom his mother and her friends described in negative terms. It also emerged that Dean was the victim of racial harassment. He said he had to look over his shoulder the whole time because he never knew when he was going to be attacked.

The worker felt that Mary's general standard of parenting was good. However during early discussions it became clear that Mary was unaware of the impact of her own negative views about Black people on Dean. It also emerged that, because of being in a multi-racial family, Mary had little support in this primarily white neighbourhood.

In order to address the different but interconnected levels of difficulty that Dean was experiencing the following programme of work was undertaken:

Racial harassment in the neighbourhood. The worker supported Mary in a move away from her immediate neighbourhood. Although the move was only four streets away Mary felt that the reaction to Black and multi-racial families there was much more positive and supportive – an example of the very local differences in communities that, from the outside, may appear homogeneous. Action was taken against the perpetrators of the harassment, but both the worker and Mary felt that an immediate change of accommodation was in Dean's best interests.

Racial harassment at school. A meeting was arranged with the head teacher which focused on improving the handling of racist incidents at the school.

Support group. Mary joined a group for white parents of dual heritage children. This group not only provided an opportunity for the parents to explore their complex reactions to their current or former partners; it also provided support for Mary in her own community.

Individual work with Dean. The aim was to help Dean to develop a positive view of himself as a child of dual heritage.

Identity group. Dean eventually joined a group of other dual heritage children from the local community in regular sessions at the family centre. One aim of this group was to reduce the isolation of these children in the community.

The combination of these different approaches to Dean's apparent 'behaviour difficulties', addressing the different systems of Dean's 'ecology' was eventually successful. Not only did Dean develop a more positive perception of himself but, equally important, community supports were developed for both Dean and his mother.

For children and parents, the advantages of operating in this integrated and holistic way have included:

- Parents can find their own level of involvement with the family centre, which may include becoming part of a community group, or engaging more detailed and intensive family work.
- The different levels of involvement can be complementary, allowing families to receive support for confidential issues, internal to the family, at the same time as they receive (and can reciprocate) support in the community, through involvement in groups, thereby developing their social networks through informal contacts made via the family centre.
- Because a wide range of activities are happening in the family centre, any stigma that might otherwise be associated with a service is minimised. Parents seen going into the family centre are just as likely to be going there to book tickets for a community event, or to take part in an open-door community group, as to be going there for personal counselling or an assessment of their parenting skills.
- Community action can involve families who are experiencing high degrees of pressure, but whose capacity to participate in activities that are intended to benefit others living in the area can be encouraged and supported at the same time.

Finally, there are a number of messages for ecological practice that can be derived from this family centre's work that have not been mentioned so far. It demonstrates that, to firmly embed ecological practice in a particular setting takes time. Time is needed for workers to build up the necessary contacts and detailed knowledge about what is happening in the local community, and time is needed for families to develop sufficient trust in a local agency. Ecological practice, that focuses on the links between community patterns and what is happening within families, is not just something that can be hurriedly bolted on to the initiatives occurring in a particular area. It has to be embedded over a longer period.

The work of this family centre has also demonstrated that ecological practice involves not just focusing on the difficulties and pressures that people are experiencing. It is equally important to focus on the strengths of families, and the community and neighbourhood settings in which they are living, and to try to bring those into play for the benefit of all concerned. We have also learned that the full impact of ecological practice can be difficult to capture. Because of its strong preventative orientation, specific and measurable impacts can be hard to quantify (we return to this last point in Chapter 10).

Children and families in Bristol's Somali community

Capacity building work with children and families in Bristol's Somali community has been on-going since late 2004. This community is often referred to as being 'hard to reach', so the approach to this work has involved working directly with a local Somali-led community organisation, to develop services relevant for the children and families who belong to their community.

Bristol's Somali families have almost all come to the city since the beginning of the 1990s following the increase in civil war in their country. Although there are no completely accurate figures, it would appear that more than half have arrived in Bristol since 2000. It is, therefore, a very quickly changing community in which the experience of transience, for children and parents, is a major issue. The way in which members of this community are coping with the major disruptions in their lives is testament to their resilience, but it also presents challenges, particularly for the children involved. At the time of writing, there were estimated to be between 12,000 and 15,000 Somali families in Bristol, with Somali children comprising the largest Black and minority ethnic group in Bristol's schools.

The journeys of the families to Bristol show considerable diversity, with some of them arriving directly from Somalia, whilst others have come via different African countries, often involving extended stays in refugee camps. Many of Bristol's Somali families have also arrived in the UK after extended periods of time spent in other Northern European countries, including France, Sweden and Holland. In some cases, members of individual families have arrived at different times, with children often joining their parents only when the latter have become established in the UK. These re-settlement experiences have had a significant impact on internal family relationships, with children often having been separated from their parents for significant periods of time.

In 2005 extensive community interviewing was carried out, which involved talking to 55 children in 33 families (Awad et al., 2006). The interviews were viewed as an important aspect of an overall capacity building strategy, with members of the Somali community therefore being asked to play a key role in deciding, not only on the questions to be asked, but also how they should be asked. As a result, members of the steering group were trained as interviewers, and subsequently carried out all of the interviewing with the children and their parents, and the steering group reflected on the findings and their significance.

This piece of community research was the most detailed yet done with Bristol's Somali community and, given that we are confident it is a representative sample, the findings illustrate some key characteristics of the community and the issues the members of that community face. Demographic factors have a key impact on the nature of the challenges faced by this community and, therefore, on the children's ability to achieve the five *Every Child Matters* child well-being outcomes. Some of the most important demographic factors to emerge from the interviewing were as follows:

- More than half of the families in the sample had arrived in the UK since 2000, illustrating the fast changing nature of the community.
- Only a relatively small proportion of the younger children in the families had been born in the UK.
- Some of the children had been living continually with their families, but others had experienced major family disruption and had lived separately from their parents.

- A majority of the families were headed by lone parents, in the sense that an interviewed mother did not identify a father as living in the household. The reasons for the high proportion of lone parents appeared to be the complex combination of factors relating to family disruption basic to the refugee experience, issues related to the benefit system, and the pressures on Somali men who found themselves marginalised in the UK.
- The families are typically far larger than is the average for the UK. Approximately half of the families in our sample had five or more children, and some families had as many as eight or nine children.

The interviews with children showed the extreme pressures they faced as a result of community change and migration. Here, for instance, a 13 year old girl (through an interpreter) talks about arriving in the UK. The interview took place more than two months after her arrival, but she had yet to be allocated an accessible school place:

When I started to come it was paradise. A place I can be educated . . . Then when I arrived I couldn't see my dream. When I arrived at Heathrow it was a beautiful place. When I am stuck at home things become upside down.

Another girl new to the UK, who had started attending school, talked about struggling to become accepted by other pupils:

The first time I came I thought Britain would be a good place to live. Then when I joined the school I have met with a lot of problems with other children. It was a very bad experience to go through that situation to the extent I hate going to school. When I report things to the teacher things don't get changed. I report through the other children. My strategy is not to report now.

Since they arrived in the UK, the Somali families in Bristol have experienced high rates of relative poverty, directly related to some of the demographic factors identified above. For example, we know from other research that Black and Minority Ethnic families are amongst the most economically disadvantaged groups in the UK (Craig, 2005) and that large families are likely to be more disadvantaged than smaller families, even when both are dependent on welfare benefits (Bradshaw, 2005).

One of the key findings to emerge from the interviewing and subsequent practice initiatives with these families was the way in which community factors had a direct impact on children's ability to achieve the five *ECM* outcomes. In particular, interviewing the children and parents showed how, at a community level, factors affecting the achievement of the outcomes interact, with the ability to achieve one of the outcomes directly impacting on the ability to achieve others. In the case of Somali children in Bristol, the clearest example of this was the way in which issues around children staying safe impacted on the achievement of other outcomes. For example, nearly half of the children interviewed answered 'yes' when they were asked whether they had ever been picked on because they were Somali. Some of the experiences the children talked about were extreme, by any measure. They included children being subjected to racist verbal abuse, including a girl who was afraid a racist neighbour would run her over, and knives being brandished against families. In response to these experiences of racism, some parents adopted a policy of not allowing their children to go outside their house to play. For instance, one lone parent told us:

> *When the children go to the park there is a lot of fighting and intimidation. My children don't go out. I keep them inside. They don't have any friends. I take this action as a precaution.*

In other cases, there was evidence of a clear reluctance, on the part of some of the children interviewed, to go out of the house. The following example of this reluctance was taken from a transcription of an interview with Ahmed, an 11 year old boy:

> *Ahmed: 'I don't take much exercise.'*
> *Interviewer: 'Why do you say that?'*
> *Ahmed: 'Because I don't go out much.'*
> *Interviewer: 'When you say you don't go out much, why do you say that?'*
> *Ahmed: 'Because I'm scared if I get trouble . . . sometimes people throw things at you and say you're not welcome because you're Black.'*

These responses to racism in the communities in which Bristol's Somali families have been re-settled also have a direct impact on the children achieving at least two of the other *ECM* outcomes – *enjoying* and *staying healthy*. Safety issues, therefore, have to be addressed for children to achieve some of the other *ECM* outcomes.

As already stated, this piece of work is still in its early stages. Future plans for work with Somali children and parents in this community, designed to further the achievement of the *ECM* outcomes include:

- A forum for Somali children in Bristol, so that their views can be conveyed to policy makers (children making a *positive contribution*).
- A series of educational trips, in and around Bristol, including to the universities, that involve parents and children so that knowledge about job and educational opportunities becomes more embedded in families new to the UK (children *achieving*).
- Developing a longer-term family play scheme, building on the success of the initiative given as an example of community capacity building in Chapter 8 (children *enjoying*, *staying safe*, and *being healthy*).

Perhaps the key point to emerge, so far, from this developing work with Bristol's Somali community is the benefit of fully engaging with the community, building its capacity to provide resources for its own children. Whilst traditional agency responses to the needs of children and families in refugee communities are, of course, important, the ecological approach that underpins the practice initiatives outlined above has served to emphasise the particular importance of supporting the development of informal networks. This appears to be the most appropriate way of engaging with children and families who would otherwise be regarded as 'hard to reach'.

A small estate in a relatively affluent market town

The market towns and apparently affluent commuter villages in the South West region of England often include small areas or estates in which there are high concentrations of children living in poverty (Gill, 2001). One father in a small area of housing association property in North Somerset described these areas to us as the hidden estates of the region. He said that all of the resources and attention goes to the large estates in the region, and areas like his were overlooked. Another parent described the area where she lived as 'a tiny little estate cut off from everywhere else'.

The 'hidden estates' have a number of important characteristics for families and children and, in particular, the way in which poverty and social exclusion are experienced. For example:

- Most adults commute out of these areas for work, and children (in families who can afford to) are transported out for their activities. This leaves children who are in families that have very little money, and no means of transport, particularly vulnerable to social exclusion.
- Because of the smaller areas of concentrated child poverty, there is often very limited provision for children's activities and family support services in these areas.
- The cost of living for poor families in these areas can be higher than for their urban counterparts. For instance, if the family live in a commuter village, where the local shop only sells a small range of items at a relatively high price, they will spend more on the goods or, alternatively, spend more time and money travelling to places where goods are cheaper.
- Children in families with low financial resources in these areas may be more aware of exclusion and difference than their urban counterparts, as they will constantly be coming into contact with children whose families have very different access to material resources.

The particular market town in which this third piece of work is based illustrates some of the main characteristics of these 'hidden estates'. The town has, like many others, developed into a commuter zone for large centres of employment – Bristol, Bath and Swindon. It has seen extensive new private housing in recent years. However, in the centre of the town is an estate which has high rates of family income deprivation. When we started working in the town in 2000, 44 per cent of the children under 16 in the central ward of this apparently affluent market town were living in poverty (defined as being in households dependent on means-tested benefits).

Our work in this town clearly demonstrated one of the central characteristics of these hidden estates – the way in which children on very low incomes come into regular contact with children whose family resources are far higher, particularly at school. This experience of relative deprivation came over particularly poignantly when one lone parent on income support described her tactics for the beginning of the September term:

> *This parent knew that, in the first days of the term, the children would be asked to write something about 'what I did in the summer holidays'. She also knew that, compared with many other children her son had done very little in the holidays – there was simply not enough money. So that her son would have something to talk about, she said that, before the beginning of term, she sat with him and helped him to make up things he could say.*

The ecological practice interventions in this town, which have developed over a four year period, include:

- The provision of activities for children, with a particular emphasis on the 5–13 year age range. These activities, such as trips, workshops, community events, and holidays, directly address the national anti-poverty agenda, in the sense that they are directed at the level of the personal experience of children and families affected by poverty. They also offer an important means of making contact with the most disadvantaged families in this community.

- Building the capacity of parents and grandparents in the local community, so that they can take a direct lead in organising events and activities, making their communities more responsive to the needs of their children. Training and support have also been provided to parents (e.g. in applying for funding) so that the work can move towards sustainability.

- Using community networks to make direct contact with the most disadvantaged children and families. Local parents and grandparents, who have been centrally involved in organising activities, have also identified children and families who can benefit from these resources. Local people are most likely to know the families in difficulty. They will know which parents and children do not have strong family support systems and who has just arrived on the estate with no sources of support. They will also know the children who are being excluded from friendships with other children, and who are experiencing bullying and other forms of social exclusion.

- Encouraging the development of safeguarding strategies, and strengthening social networks in the community. Supporting local families to support other local families and to access services or make links with other sources of support.

- Encouraging those children and parents who are regarded, locally, as vulnerable or as outsiders to participate in community decision-making that directly affects them, and supporting them to speak out about the difficulties they face.

The work in this setting clearly illustrates the way that ecological practice attempts to target the interactions between different levels of the children's experience and the different social systems of which they are a part. One of the main aspects of this piece of work has been around children *enjoying*. Rather than seeing child poverty only in relation to its effects on the *futures* of children (e.g. their educational attainment and future employability, or the likelihood of transferring deprivation to another generation), the work has also focused on the *here and now* aspects of children's well-being. We need to be just as concerned about how children experience their lives at the present, as we are about the way that these experiences help to shape their future life chances.

In terms of the lessons that the work in this setting has for ecological practice, perhaps the first thing to note is the way in which children in families with similar levels of income deprivation may have very different experiences. This may be due to: family factors, such as the health and resilience of parents; network factors, such as the proximity and involvement of grandparents, adult siblings and other wider family members; or community factors, such as the level of resources available and neighbourhood networks of support. It also illustrates how the organisation of activities and interventions at a community level enables connections to be made with what is happening within families. Families develop confidence in a service which is obviously providing activities and events of tangible value to their children. This can lead to their developing enough confidence to talk to the workers and volunteers involved in these activities about some of their more private and personal issues. There have been examples of this happening in relation to a range of parental issues, including difficulties with children, financial problems, and worries about the threat of eviction.

Children in the centre of a large seaside town

The fourth practice context is the central area of a large seaside town. Family poverty and disadvantage have typically been understood to be concentrated in the relatively large estates on the periphery of this town. Little attention had previously been paid to the situation and circumstances of the smaller number of disadvantaged children and families living in the centre of the town.

In addition to economic disadvantage, with a high proportion of families dependent on benefits, three factors have particular relevance for understanding the child's experience of community in this area, and the impact of community patterns on children's lives:

- *Housing patterns*: The area is characterised by particular types of housing. Research for the local regeneration partnership, in 2001, highlighted the nature of housing in the area. It found that many of the older properties had been converted into flats for rent in the private sector. Many of the older family hotels had become residential homes and single room lettings. The report stated that this had led to dramatic increases in the proportion of single person households, consisting mainly of young adults and retired people. The characteristics of the housing in this area have an important impact on the children who live there. In particular, the housing is not designed for families, and play facilities and gardens are in short supply.
- *Child density*: The area contains a significantly lower proportion of children than other areas in the region. In the local area as a whole, children under 16 comprised 19 per cent of the total population whereas, in this central seaside area, they made up only 13 per cent of the population. Relatively low child density of this nature means that services and other provision for children and families have remained underdeveloped, with resources going to the areas where there are higher rates of child density and concentrations of children experiencing disadvantage. This had the effect of placing children in this area (and other similar areas around the country) in a position of double jeopardy, being exposed to the effects of economic disadvantage, compounded by a particular deficit in appropriate community resources. Informal social networks in this area of low child density were also restricted, leaving families with a lack of social support and sources of local contact.
- *Rates of transience*: Partly because of the pattern of housing, the centre of the town has also traditionally been associated with high rates of transience, reflected in the 30 per cent annual turnover of pupils in the main school serving this part of town at the start of the project. Lack of continuity of schooling can have important developmental implications for children. Also, in a community setting, networks of support for both children and families are likely to be disrupted by such high rates of transience.

It was in the context of these community patterns that the project was set up, with the aim of providing play and learning resources for children and families in their local area. Linked to this was an equal emphasis on supporting individual children and families within their community.

The project has worked at different levels of the child's and family's experience. To start with, given the importance of informal support and the particular implications of transience and low child density for social networks, it has addressed the basic issue of bringing parents together. It also targeted the interactions between two *ECM* outcomes, *enjoying* and *economic well-being*, by developing the play facilities and activities in the area, where there was originally very little provision and parents couldn't afford to provide access to these opportunities away from the area. In addition it addressed what was happening within families, with workers able to use contacts made through the provision of activities in the community to follow up difficulties with individual parents.

Early work in this area illustrated how children are likely to be particularly exposed to some of the dangers that exist within this community (*staying safe*). We talked to young children living there about their safety concerns. The accommodation the children lived in was typically small, with front doors leading directly on to busy narrow town centre streets. The following are examples of what some children said about what made them feel unsafe:

> *Cars, you can get run over.* (girl aged 5)

> *Feel unsafe when the cars come around.* (boy aged 6)

> *On the roads; the cars crash into me. They go straight across like that. It scares me . . . (I would like it if) the roads get a bit wider and the cars don't go so fast to the edges.* (girl aged 6)

As already indicated, the area also had high rates of transience. Often this meant that families and children were coming into the community with few social contacts. One of the roles of the project was, therefore, to focus on these children and families, facilitating the development of their local social networks. Two specific pieces of work illustrate this aspect of the project:

> *A project worker made contact with a family new to the area. They had moved without any accommodation and, for a period, were living in a caravan. The project worker supported the children to become involved in community play activities and to develop friendships in the area. She also worked with the mother to support her in finding accommodation. Because of the particular characteristics of the housing in the area, the family experienced a number of moves until they eventually settled in more permanent housing outside the area. The project worker supported the family through these moves and acted as a point of continuity for the children within the area, supporting friendships and a sense of belonging in the community through their involvement in activities.*

> *The same project worker also provided support to a child who had recently moved to the area to live with her mother, who had recently arrived in the area herself. The child became involved with the activities of the project, and it soon became evident, through contact with the child, that the mother was struggling to provide satisfactory routines for the child, including getting her ready to go to school on time. Not only was the project worker able to work with the mother and the child to develop better routines, but the project was also offering something positive for the child, in terms of play activities. These two aspects of the work with this family proved to be mutually reinforcing, with the result that the mother came to trust this particular worker, although she found it difficult to trust other workers who were coming into contact with the family at the same time. One aspect of this was that, through activities (enjoying),*

confidence and support for routines developed, and the child attended school more regularly (achieving).

In subsequent evaluations of the ecological practice in this community, we have become aware of further connections between the provision of activities in the community and achieving the five *ECM* outcomes. Sometimes this has happened in a way that would not be immediately obvious. These connections are best illustrated by extracts from interviews with parents, undertaken as part of the evaluation exercise, which was conducted after the project had been operating for over two years:

Being healthy

We go swimming. Nice to be sociable. Important for mental health. Friendships have been made.

Otherwise they're cooped up at home.

We look forward to activities and doing them together. Energy is released. My son has ADHD and has a lot of energy to use.

It has made them happier in themselves . . . (she) is more confident, can express her opinions more and has become more confident in herself.

Staying safe

You know where they are. Properly looked after and with the right people.

Safer in groups, otherwise (she) would have been out the back and that wouldn't be safe.

Because when we take part in the activities she is not running around and me not knowing where she is.

They love it. Children don't mix with the other children in the street as it ends up in arguments with parents and the police get called.

Enjoying

Opportunity to do new things. They talk about it for ages.

I know from the huge smile on his face when I pick him up. And six months later he is still talking about it as if it is yesterday.

In the same evaluation, when we talked to some of the children who had been involved, they also made some connections between the *ECM* outcomes and activities in the community provided by the project, which otherwise might not have been apparent. For instance, one 13 year old boy, who previously had a poor record of school attendance, said that being involved in the project had helped with his confidence which, in turn, had helped his school attendance:

Because of the confidence I've gained, I attend school all the time now because I'm not bullied. I used to stay away sometimes because of bullying.

Conclusions

We have presented these descriptions of ecological processes and practice, developed in four different community settings, because they illustrate some of the ways in which practitioners can helpfully intervene at the point at which the different domains of children's lives interact with the characteristics of the communities in which they live.

Although the settings described cover a range of the different types of disadvantaged communities to be found in the UK, they are, of course, far from exhaustive. However, the key point which they do illustrate is that ecological practice needs to be developed in ways which are compatible with the community contexts in which it is undertaken.

In this respect, ecological practice requires something of an ethnographic approach to assessing the dynamics of particular communities, which has to be combined with the assessment of the internal dynamics of individual families, and an understanding of how these two aspects of children's lives influence one another. In illustrating how this ethnographic approach might operate in particular communities, we have concentrated on the way in which various factors shape communities and the experiences of the children and families living within them. These factors have included levels of disadvantage, community resources, child density and transience.

Another lesson that emerges from looking at these different practice settings is that, instead of looking for deficiencies in the community and its families, it may be more important to ask 'given the high pressures on families, what is it that protects the children in the neighbourhood from the immediate impact of these pressures?' In other words, what are the strengths to be found within the communities that enable individual families to withstand the pressures created by lack of financial resources, lack of choice in the housing market, and poor or non-existent community resources?

Chapter 7. **Community Approaches to Safeguarding Children**

This chapter will consider:
- The historical focus on individual approaches to child protection in the UK.
- The limited success of attempts to establish community approaches to safeguarding children.
- The main elements of ecological practice in the safeguarding of children.
- Some of the limitations and risks involved in community approaches to safeguarding children.

Introduction

The previous chapter considered some of the main ways in which ecological practice can be applied, in four different disadvantaged community settings, both to support families under pressure and to help children achieve the developmental and well-being outcomes identified in *Every Child Matters*. We now move on to examine the way that certain aspects of ecological practice can be used to address one particular ECM outcome – that of children *staying safe*. In doing this, we will also consider some of the organisational and professional barriers that exist to the development of ecological practice in this area of children's services, concluding the chapter with an examination of some of the limitations and risks that might also be involved.

Many of the key components of ecological practice that have been discussed in previous chapters, such as connecting the internal and external worlds of the child, developing the community resources and social networks accessible to parents and children, building the capacity of disadvantaged communities, and strengthening the links between community groups and more formal child and family welfare organisations, are directly relevant to the safeguarding of children. We use the term 'safeguarding children' to encompass the whole range of issues that can have an impact on children *staying safe*, including:

- Factors within the family (e.g. physical, emotional or sexual abuse, and neglect).
- Factors within the community (e.g. physical, emotional or sexual abuse and neglect, including those that might occur in formal or semi-formal settings such as clubs).
- Harm that other children might cause (e.g. bullying, racial harassment, and inappropriate sexual contact).
- Environmental dangers (e.g. buildings, public spaces, and road traffic).

Individual and community approaches to the safeguarding of children

Historically, the UK has developed rather limited links between services directed at the safeguarding of individual children and community approaches to enhancing children's overall safety and well-being. The two approaches have tended to develop separately, with few connections being made between them at either practice or policy levels (Jack,

2004). This is in spite of there being considerable research evidence about the mutual influences and interactions between community characteristics and patterns, and the safety of children (Jack and Gill, 2003). Where initiatives have been developed that explicitly recognise these connections, they have tended to be either rather short-lived, or have emerged in response to specific local difficulties. For instance, in the early 1980s, The Barclay Report (NISW, 1982) which examined the role and tasks of social workers, and recommended the introduction of a 'community social work' approach that focused on the development of informal networks based on community groups and associations, led to the establishment of some community projects that included the explicit aim of reducing child abuse (see, for example, Eastham, 1990).

More recently, Baldwin and Carruthers (1998) provided information about the Henley Safe Children Project in Coventry. This was developed at a time when, due to heightened public concern about child abuse, crisis work focused on 'high-risk' families tended to dominate statutory child care services. However, the Henley project took a broader view of the factors affecting children's health and safety, as the following comments make clear:

> *The facts and figures on health in the Henley area alongside low income, pockets of very high unemployment and high levels of crime and danger on the streets give some indication of the difficulties parents face in bringing up their children in health and safety ... This is the context in which high child protection referrals and childhood accidents have to be understood.*

(Baldwin and Carruthers, 1998: 38–9)

As a result of this analysis, the approach developed towards child protection within the Henley project incorporated neighbourhood-based family support, action with young people for a safer environment, partnerships between agencies and communities, and positive action to build on the strengths of families and communities. Subsequent elaboration of this perspective resulted in a process called 'Comprehensive Neighborhood Mapping' (CNM), which involves children, young people and families identifying 'risky places, people, situations and activities' within their local communities. This information is collated and fed into statutory, voluntary and community organisations to facilitate the development of protective initiatives (Nelson and Baldwin, 2002: 215).

Nelson and Baldwin argue that CNM helps to build communities which are 'informed and thoughtful' about child protection, and they state that 'CNM is grounded in an ecological perspective which sees partnership approaches as essential and believes an overarching view of neighbourhood needs, based on detailed local information and understanding of how different forms of harm interconnect, is crucial in developing child protection strategies' (p. 214). More recently, the same authors have described the way in which CNM has been piloted on the Craigmillar estate in Edinburgh. Although the approach started with a focus on mapping the risk of sexual crimes against children, it broadened out to include the identification of dangerous physical environments, physical violence, neglect, and the risk of school truancy (Nelson and Baldwin, 2004).

Another example of a community approach to safeguarding children, called the 'Safe Kids' project, has been developed by the NSPCC in Tilbury, to the east of London. The starting point for this project, in 2000, was a recognition '. . . that a small pool of professionals could only have an impact on the safety of a relatively limited number of children through traditional casework-based approaches and that a cultural distrust of child protection professionals prevented many children and families accessing child protection services' (Wright, 2004: 385). The project has a number of key aims:

- To promote community responsibility for the protection of children.
- To ensure that communities are well informed about risks to children and are armed with strategies to protect them.
- To increase the safety and confidence of children in their communities.
- To work towards breaking down barriers between professionals and communities.

Part of the programme involved the development of a 'protective behaviours' programme for schools, which aimed to support children in identifying situations in which they felt unsafe, and actions that children and young people could take to achieve a greater level of safety.

There have also been initiatives to develop community-oriented children's safeguarding strategies with families in Northern Ireland, in the context of heightened awareness of the impact of community tensions on local people (Heenan and Birrell, 2002), and with Black and minority ethnic groups (for example, Atkar et al., 2002) about which we say more later in this chapter. Underlying these approaches is the recognition that, to work effectively to safeguard children, it is necessary to understand how children's safety is understood within particular communities.

However, examples of this kind in the UK are small in number and often prove difficult to sustain in the long-term. Even within organisations that have, at some stage, adopted a clear commitment to this way of working, subsequent changes in priorities, brought about by central government policy directives, changes in key personnel, or the resistance of staff wedded to more formal and individualised child protection practice, have usually meant that community development initiatives have been relatively short lived (see, for example, Jordan, 1997, and Davies, 2004).

The subsidiary role played by community approaches to safeguarding children in the UK is highlighted whenever tragic incidents of child abuse shake the child welfare world. Invariably, at these times, recommendations are made that view the problem almost entirely from an individual family perspective. For instance, although the official inquiry report into the death of Victoria Climbié noted that: 'the 'eyes and ears' of the community are not used enough in the identification of children potentially in need' (Laming, 2003, para. 17.30), only one of its 107 recommendations touched on community issues in any way, highlighting the need for local authorities to 'establish strong links with community-based organisations that make a significant contribution to local services for children and families' (Rec. 7). Almost all of the other recommendations are made from the perspective of the dominant systems for the individualised protection of children. In our view, given the circumstances of Victoria's death and the range of people she had come into contact with in the months immediately prior to her death, the report fails to adequately recognise the community dimensions of this case and the important potential that the community could have played in protecting her. Bob Holman, in commenting on the Green Paper which followed the Laming Report, made a similar point when he suggested that the services that are of most relevance to vulnerable children are those nearest to them, provided by churches, local voluntary bodies or by other families in the street, which *Every Child Matters* largely ignores (Holman, 2003).

Practice guidelines for ecological practice in safeguarding children

The community aspects of approaches to safeguarding children are, as we have seen, relatively underdeveloped in the UK. However, combining what we know from the research evidence with the limited number of practice-based projects described above, and our own practice and evaluation experience, we can identify some of the main ways in which partnership and engagement with local communities, and community development approaches, can be utilised to safeguard children.

First of all, it is important to recognise that, every day, in every neighbourhood, there are almost constant child safeguarding measures being taken by members of local communities. Totally informal activities and actions to protect children abound. Parents look out for the children of neighbours, residents campaign for safer streets, and community groups organise events in which the safeguarding of children may not be highly articulated but nevertheless underpin what happens. What we are going on to consider, therefore, are the ways that those who have responsibilities for planning and delivering a wide range of more formally organised services and programmes that have an impact on the lives of children and families in some way, can support or extend these informal community activities.

Listening to children and adults

Underpinning the safeguarding of children in the community is the necessity for a range of interested and supportive adults to be engaged with children on a regular basis, contributing towards a local culture in which the views of children are listened to and valued. This approach has to start from the perspective that the real experts in children's lives are children themselves. Genuine attempts to communicate with children about their lives and their experiences of living in their community can provide important insights into the conditions required to promote their healthy development and to safeguard their well-being.

Talking to children in their communities not only allows local adult residents and practitioners to hear directly what children and young people are saying about where they live, but also has the related effects of contributing to their self-esteem and empowerment, sending out the clear message that their views are being taken seriously. This approach gives young people increased confidence in expressing any concerns that they might have, at an individual level, to known and trusted adults. Without these active listening networks, children are left in a more isolated and vulnerable position.

Alongside this active orientation to listening to children, one of the key ways in which community approaches can help to safeguard children is through working with local adult residents, to bring into the local community arena issues relevant to the safeguarding of children. Through this, concerns about safeguarding children can be validated, and local community members can be provided with channels for their concerns to be conveyed to the statutory agencies responsible for safeguarding children. The welfare of children and the threats they might experience are typically amongst the most powerful concerns of local communities. However, such concerns are often restricted to the private sphere of the family, with no channels for communicating these concerns to other community members or, ultimately, to those involved with children's services. At a more general level, there can often be insufficient clarity, for community members, about how they should act if they have concerns about the welfare of children. The work developed by the NSPCC in Tilbury, already discussed, provides an example of an approach that explicitly promotes the benefits of developing these channels of communication with adults, for children's welfare (Wright, 2004).

The role of community initiatives in safeguarding children is to work with individuals and groups to develop consensus and share ideas about practical ways forward when there are concerns about the welfare of children. This involves identifying and working with the natural sources of protection for children that already exist in any community – the most powerful of which are the concerns of other parents living there. The following example, described previously by one of the authors (Gill, 1996) illustrates one way in which an agency, in this case a neighbourhood family centre, and the concerns of local parents, can productively be linked with each other:

A worker from the family centre received a telephone call from a local woman who had been involved in various activities with the centre. Her own children were on the child protection register at the time.

She was reporting her concerns about the welfare of a ten year-old girl, who was visiting the block of flats where the woman lived, on a daily basis, to see her father on her way home from school. However, the father's supervision of the girl was very lax, and the girl had been seen hanging around a neighbouring flat where two men in their early twenties lived.

Through another local woman, who knew the mother of the girl, she had arranged what she referred to as a 'case conference' with the mother, at which she suggested that the child's mother should contact the family centre to discuss what was happening and obtain advice about what to do (which is what subsequently happened).

Perhaps one of the reasons that it has proved difficult to maintain community approaches to safeguarding children is the time that is often required to ensure their success, which may not be compatible with the short-term, time-limited orientation that prevails within children's services these days. Another practice example illustrates the need to allow community approaches time to take root:

A family centre was involved in a piece of neighbourhood development work in an area in which there were high rates of child protection registrations and in which there was evidence of a high number of risk factors.

One of the initiatives developed involved setting up a safeguarding children group. The plan was to encourage local parents to come together to identify their concerns and to decide what action should be taken to keep children safe in the neighbourhood. Unfortunately, it proved very difficult to establish a group with this remit and this particular initiative was not successful.

However, subsequently, several groups were set up with the more general aim of developing the social networks of vulnerable and isolated parents. Over time, these groups became established and appeared to meet a real need in the lives of parents. But they also allowed parents to develop trust in each other, and the groups began to include discussions and initiatives around keeping children safe in the neighbourhood.

Supporting local people to protect children

Nowadays, professionals are typically somewhat remote from the communities in which they operate, with few choosing to live in the areas in which they work. This means that they will often not be available when there are crises in children's lives, or when issues of safeguarding children arise. By contrast, local residents are much more likely to be available when difficulties arise and they are also likely to have a good understanding of the immediate context of local children's lives. The following practice example, from action research with the Somali community in Bristol, illustrates this point:

> Adults in the Somali community were very concerned about the racism and intimidation being experienced by children from their community in one of the local parks. Because of their concerns, they devised a rota to cover the after-school period, to ensure that when children from their community were using the playground there would always be a Somali adult present as well, to deter or deal with any intimidatory behaviour.

What this example illustrates is the important role that local people can play in ensuring children's well-being in their own community. The following example provides an illustration of the way that community work to safeguard children can support the efforts of local residents or members of communities of interest:

> A local volunteer, who was active in her community (and was paid for a small number of hours as a neighbourhood networker), made contact with a single parent with a ten year old son who was new to the estate. This family had moved from approximately 20 miles away because, in the previous community, the child had experienced bullying.
>
> One evening, at approximately seven o'clock, the mother got on the phone to the community networker and said that her child was getting bullied again in his new area. She said that, at that moment, children were surrounding the house and not allowing him to go out.
>
> Because it was 'just around the corner', and the local networker knew the children involved, she was able to go out and talk to the children who were surrounding the house. They listened to her, and allowed the boy out into the street to play with them.

There are, of course, difficult issues tied up in work of this nature. Local residents may not be able to deal with situations in an impartial way. Events and incidents, happening in their immediate neighbourhoods, will often impact on the lives of their own children and families. Equally, local people may be reluctant to get involved because they fear that to do so may lead to threats against themselves or their children. In these circumstances 'staying out of it' or 'keeping ones self to ones self' may be natural reactions. Other problems with this approach can include over-reporting, vigilantism, and a false sense of security within mainstream organisations, which can develop a belief that the community is protecting its children more effectively than is really the case.

Bringing parents and workers together to address specific issues

In developing community perspectives to safeguarding children, it is also important to create settings in which practitioners can discuss and share ideas with community members. It is through joint discussions, and the sharing of ideas between professional workers and community members that effective and coherent community practice is developed. One of the best ways of bringing workers and local residents together, especially in the early stages of a project, is through the organisation of joint 'training' events, as in the following example:

In the work on the estate in the market town, training days were put on for local people and a wide range of practitioners active in the community. The training days were designed to facilitate the involvement of local parents, taking place on a shortened-day basis, from 9.15 a.m. to 2.45 p.m., so that parents with children at school could attend. The content of the training days included:

- *What do we mean by good parenting?*
- *What might you notice that would make you concerned about a child in your community?*
- *What kinds of things might a child say which would make you concerned?*
- *If you were concerned, what would you do about it and how would you contact the authorities?*
- *How do you think the community ought to support children and families where there are concerns about parenting?*

One aspect of this approach is that it needs to be based on the particular issues facing the individual community. For instance, the same worker who led the training in the market town in the above example, where the community was mainly white, is adapting the contents of the programme for work with the Somali community in inner-city Bristol.

Organised activities and specific initiatives to develop protective networks

One of the key ways in which communities can safeguard and promote the welfare of children is through the development of a range of opportunities in which children can come into contact with (safe) community members. The following practice example illustrates this point in relation to disabled teenagers living in a seaside town, many of whom had become socially isolated from their non-disabled peers because they had attended special schools out of the local area for a number of years:

After about a year in post, a social worker with experience of community work, specialising in work with disabled children within a mainstream local authority children and families team in a rural/seaside district, found that she had about six male teenagers with learning disabilities on her caseload. They all attended special schools outside of the district and were experiencing the effects of social exclusion in their local area as a result. Their primary need was to be able to access local facilities and develop social networks with their peers. The worker initially tried to meet their needs individually by supporting their attendance at local youth clubs and cubs/scouts, but she met with a lot of fear, misunderstanding and opposition. It was also very difficult for the young people concerned, for instance being the only one attending a youth club who didn't go to the school where it was based, looking different, or having limited communication and social skills.

This led the worker to try a more ecological approach. Instead of trying to make local clubs and activities more inclusive, she decided to set up a new inclusive club, based around the young people with learning disabilities but open to all young people in the area. Getting the group off the ground involved networking with a wide range of other professionals in the locality, including teachers and occupational therapists, an education welfare officer, a community education worker, a youth support worker, and the manager of the local volunteer bureau. The group needed a meeting place with a positive image for young people. The teacher running the Duke of Edinburgh scheme at the local secondary school was enthusiastic. He saw that the club would also provide an excellent opportunity for pupils on the Duke of Edinburgh scheme to undertake volunteering activities, and arranged for the group to meet in the same premises used for all out of school hours youth activities.

Over the next three years the club ran very successfully with more young people from the school having 'drifted' into the club, not as volunteers but just as ordinary members wanting to spend time with their peers in the evenings in a place where they said they felt welcomed. In order to promote the wider social inclusion of those attending, regular trips out into the local community were also arranged, using mainstream facilities and services to help the young people to develop greater confidence and independence in the local area.

The club was organised by a committee consisting of parents, professionals, and young people, some of whom were on the Duke of Edinburgh scheme and some of whom were disabled. The disabled young people on the committee were supported to take part, by training and a buddy system. For example, one learning disabled young person was able to act as chairperson of the committee, with the support of a professional buddy.

Probably the main benefit for the young people who attended the club was the development of friendships with disabled and non-disabled peers in their local community, in many cases leading to inclusion in social activities outside of the club. The disabled young people, in particular, also developed their social skills in a natural social setting with their peers, leading to greater confidence in themselves as well as a degree of independence from their parents and other family members, on whom they had previously relied for the majority of their leisure time activities.

Six years after it started, the club was still going strong, with approximately 60 young people attending every week, and with many of the original disabled young people having subsequently registered as official volunteers at the club.

Amongst other things, this practice example illustrates the way in which all of the different aspects of community life are interwoven. By helping to build the capacity of communities to meet their own needs and develop resources for their own children and families, powerful forces are harnessed that can help to safeguard children by promoting their social inclusion and contributing to their overall well-being.

It is important to acknowledge, however, that organised activities, and the social networks and contacts that they generate, can be a danger to children as well as a potential source of support and protection. In our experience, though, children are likely to be protected by strengthening the networks and organised activities of the communities in which they live, provided that the risks inherent in these activities are recognised and that they sit alongside the other initiatives discussed in this chapter, that serve to validate community concerns about children's well-being, and that facilitate effective channels of communication, enabling any concerns to be articulated and acted upon.

The advantages for children of being involved in organised activities in their neighbourhood are perhaps obvious, but it is worth restating them in the specific context of efforts to safeguard children. Organised activities not only provide disadvantaged and vulnerable children with enhanced opportunities for contact with other children and adults living in their local areas, thereby extending their social networks, but they also help to provide helpful structure to children's time. The local adults who are in contact with them will, as Holman (1981, 2000) has persuasively argued, also have the advantage of knowing what is going on in their lives and local community settings, and be aware of any significant changes or difficulties.

Parents themselves are often very aware of the difficulties that lack of organised activities can present for children. It will often be one of their biggest concerns for their children that the area in which they live provides very few opportunities for engaging with other local people in social events and activities. Often parents will link this directly to safeguarding issues, as the following example illustrates:

A 13 year old girl lives in a lone parent household in an area which has poor provision in terms of after-school and holiday activities for children. She spends a great deal of time with the father of a friend of hers. There is concern, both amongst professionals and community members, about the appropriateness of the contact between the girl and this man.

The mother is also concerned about the situation. Although she struggles to provide adequate boundaries around her daughter's behaviour, she thinks that the best way to divert her daughter away from her involvement with this man is for her to be involved in other activities. She says she needs help to find her daughter 'something to do in the evenings'. The mother is concerned that very little happens for children on the estate, thereby making a direct link between organised activities for children and her daughter's safety.

Sometimes, specific initiatives to address particular problems challenge us to look at exactly what we are trying to protect children from. Are we only concerned about the traditional evils of neglect and abuse, or are we involved in a wider exercise of safeguarding children and promoting their well-being? For instance, as the case study in the previous chapter shows, initiatives to address a problem such as racial harassment, using community development methods, can be used to promote children's well-being, in general, as well as having an impact on the protection of individual children.

Involving vulnerable children and adults in community development

At a practice level, it is also important to work hard to involve vulnerable children and families in community development initiatives – not only as the recipients of activities but also as active participants in their planning and organisation. One of the dangers inherent in community approaches is that powerful local groups emerge to take the lead, excluding more vulnerable families in the process. If this tendency is allowed to develop unchecked, vulnerable or marginalised families can feel that things are being done *for* them, rather than feeling that they are involved in determining the course of their own lives. At its worst, the danger is that yet another layer of power, influence and intrusion has been created in the lives of vulnerable families.

Involving vulnerable families in planning and organising community initiatives can have a positive impact on their sense of power and capability in their local community. It is difficult to quantify this, in research terms, but practice experience reveals the importance of this aspect of community development. The family that begins to feel a sense of involvement and empowerment in their local community can also experience a sense of empowerment and competence in terms of dealing with their own difficulties.

There are obviously some complex and sensitive issues to be balanced in work of this nature. For example, involving vulnerable children and families in planning and organising community activities demands significant groupwork skills of practitioners, who must attempt to produce balanced groups where those with power and confidence in their community are successfully integrated with those who are experiencing greater problems and who, as a result, are in danger of being socially excluded from their communities.

Conflicting cultures

The above, then, are some practical ways of combining child safeguarding and community development approaches to children's well-being. It is, however, important to recognise that there are significant practical barriers to the integration of these approaches that are, perhaps, most apparent in the different organisational and professional cultures that exist within these branches of children's services.

One general difference in the cultures of those who are involved in community development and regeneration activity, as opposed to individualised approaches to safeguarding children, concerns their perceptions of community. For the former, community networks tend to be viewed as potential sources of strength whilst, for the latter, they may more often be perceived as sources of risk.

These different perspectives on the strengths and risks posed by community networks are accompanied by a number of other contrasting perceptions and assumptions, as set out in Table 4.

These cultural differences are most apparent when specific difficulties arise in attempting to combine a community development approach with one based on the individualised safeguarding of children. The key issues, here, are accountability and confidentiality.

Accountability

Workers operating on the basis of an individualised approach to the safeguarding of children are obviously accountable for their actions. But this accountability is to groups and representatives who are often far removed from the communities concerned.

Community groups are typically not involved in discussions about what constitutes child abuse or child safety. One result of this is that there is rarely a clearly articulated

Table 4 Different perceptions of community

Culture of individualised approaches to safeguarding children	Culture of community development approaches to safeguarding children
Knowledge about safeguarding children and what constitutes danger mainly resides with agencies and professionals.	Experts about what constitutes danger in local communities are local children and adults. Community development works to validate this knowledge.
Decision-making is largely in the hands of formal agencies and professionals.	Members of local communities are empowered to take decisions in relation to their own lives.
Primary partnerships are between formal agencies and professionals.	Primary partnerships are between community development workers and community organisations or representatives.
Accountability is to the employing organisation and the elected representatives of the local authority.	Accountability is to the members of local communities.

consensus within communities about what constitutes danger to children. There is no baseline for understanding in what circumstances action will be necessary on the part of the authorities. 'Knowledge' about protecting children is generated almost entirely from a professional perspective and value base. If communities are aware of this, it is at the level of handed down or received wisdom, rather than definitions and expectations which they have played a part in shaping themselves.

In the absence of this consensus, there is often misunderstanding and mistrust about the action of social workers and other child welfare professionals. At best, community members will not know what action agencies are taking, and, at worst, there will be suspicion and antagonism when action is taken. This may be a particular shortcoming in the case of communities of interest. For instance, one of the major dilemmas of practice in recent years has been how to ensure the safeguarding of children in Black and other minority ethnic communities. In relation to this issue, Atkar and colleagues describe work with a local Asian community to understand child safeguarding issues (Atkar et al., 2002). Their starting point was discussion about whose standards were used to define 'child abuse' and what constituted child safety. Their project explored a range of understandings, meanings and expectations in relation to children's needs, discipline, harm to children, teaching about sexuality, and sexual abuse. It also looked at differing cultural expectations around issues such as confidentiality, consultation and partnership. They found that '. . . differing cultural definitions of physical punishment and where the line between it and physical abuse should be drawn were sometimes seen as creating considerable strain between Asian families and the services they encountered' (Atkar et al., 2002: 329).

Confidentiality

Another key challenge, in relation to community initiatives to safeguard children, is developing shared understanding around issues of confidentiality. The obvious reasons for this are that issues concerning individual children and families cannot be put into the public domain, thereby creating barriers to the two way sharing of information.

Being identified as a recipient of child protection services can be one of the most stigmatising markers for families in a community, often creating powerful tensions between neighbours. At its most extreme, this tension is illustrated by the anxious and often very vocal concern of residents about sex offenders living in their communities. But it can also be an important issue in the everyday business of working in communities with children and families. The challenge is to find ways of respecting the confidentiality of what is happening within individual families, whilst at the same time using professional and local knowledge to get appropriate and timely services to the children and families who most need them. This challenge is illustrated by a community project in which one of the authors has been involved, where it has proved difficult to work effectively with the community whilst, at the same time, dealing with issues that are rightly regarded as confidential:

> *The project was concerned that its activities and events should be made available to the most vulnerable children in the community. This raised the question of how those children should be identified. Both methods of identification – professional and community – presented difficulties. There were obviously difficulties in sharing information held by the agencies with the community group but, equally, there were issues about local people coming to the group and expressing views about the vulnerability of children and families they knew in the community.*

The role of the worker who liaises with community groups is, therefore, a difficult one, simultaneously trying to act as a channel for this information and the identification of children and families, without confidential information coming into the public arena of the community group.

Some limitations and risks

Whilst most of what has been discussed so far has concentrated on the potential contribution of community development approaches to the safeguarding of children, some of the limitations and risks of such approaches also need to be recognised.

One limitation is that the families in the communities that are the focus of safeguarding initiatives may be hard-pressed and lack the resources of time and energy to become involved in these community-level activities. It may be unrealistic to expect families already trying to cope with a lack of household resources, poor community facilities, and the tensions that often go with living in a disadvantaged neighbourhood, to become directly involved in offering support to others, or to actively contribute to a protective environment for the wider benefit of all children.

Also, child protection may particularly be an issue with the children in those families who are cut off from the rest of the community and its potential strengths. This separation from community may be due to a wide range of factors, such as frequent moves, the stigmatisation of the family, or their lack of skills in accessing social support. Often it will be a combination of all of these factors. This was a challenge in a piece of work referred to earlier (Gill et al., 2000):

> *In this community there were very different family groupings. On the one hand, there were the well established families, who often had wider family members in the community who could act as sources of support and assistance. On the other hand, there were a small number of (often transient) families who did not have these supports and who, as a consequence, suffered much higher levels of stress in this disadvantaged area.*
>
> *In a situation such as this, there are clearly limitations on an approach which looks, in broad terms, at the capacity of the community to protect its most vulnerable children. More differentiated strategies are called for to address the particular needs of different groups of families. In this location, transience was a particularly important issue, and transient families faced particular problems, as far as the development of protective networks was concerned. The children at most risk appeared to be those in families which were moving frequently, either because of scapegoating, housing difficulties, or family breakdown.*

Another important limitation may be that there is not necessarily a direct correlation between the strength of community networks and the extent to which children are protected. This point is illustrated by the piloting of the Comprehensive Neighbourhood Mapping approach in the Craigmillar area of Edinburgh, which has already been discussed. Here, the close family networks that existed within the area, which were undoubtedly an important source of support to many residents, also served to limit the freedom that people felt to report any concerns that they might have had about the welfare of children in the area. The researchers who monitored the impact of this programme noted that 'Many local people were related, resulting in fears of splitting extended families and inviting recriminations if someone reported violence or abuse: "you daren't say anything because everyone is somebody's cousin"' (Nelson and Baldwin, 2004: 419).

We should also recognise that community approaches towards issues of safeguarding children may carry certain risks, as well as potential advantages. No intervention into the lives of children and families is neutral. All have the potential for negative as well as positive impacts, and it is important that these are recognised so that any risks can be properly managed. One of the inherent risks of this approach to safeguarding children goes right to the core of community development, which is fundamentally based on bringing people together to try to resolve the problems that they face and improve the quality of their lives. There is a wealth of evidence that social networks have the potential to be both helpful *and* dangerous for children (Korbin, 1989; Thompson, 1995; Jack, 2000). There are many cases of networks and organisations being used to facilitate the sexual exploitation, or the more general abuse of children (Monk, 2004) and these networks may not only be the more organised ones. We should never ignore the possibility that individuals within communities, who present a potential danger to children, may get involved in community activities primarily to gain access to them. In order to minimise the risks that such individuals pose to the well-being of children, it is probably safer if all community development activities are established with the explicit understanding that unsupervised contact is not allowed between adults and other people's children.

However this is only half the story. Adults who are a potential risk to children may also use their involvement in these activities to establish or heighten their general credibility in the community. As their credibility is increased, so also is their danger of accessing children *outside* of the context of these community activities. This potential risk will come up fairly regularly in community groups which set out to work directly with families and children in the community. In organising activities for children and families, there will be questions raised about particular adults who are involved. Sometimes there will be information coming directly from official channels about the potential dangers posed by particular adults. In such cases, the appropriate course of action will be clear – that the persons identified are prevented from becoming involved. More problematically, situations also arise in which there is some degree of uneasiness in a community about a particular adult, but without any concrete information which confirms the threat that they might pose to children. The following case example illustrates some of the dilemmas that these situations present to community development programmes:

> *A community worker was organising a series of summer activities for children and their parents who were at risk of social exclusion. A health visitor referred a family consisting of a mother and father and two children aged twelve and ten. When the community worker received this referral she was told by a local person there was information in the community that the father in the family was a risk to children.*
>
> *The community worker had to decide whether to exclude the family altogether, and therefore deny the children the chance to become involved (and the father and his children the chance to be in a situation in which there could be beneficial contact), or to encourage only the children and their mother to come, or include all members of the family. In the event, a request for guidance was made to social services who advised that the man himself should not be allowed to be part of the activities.*

One important element, in managing these kinds of risks, is to ensure that they are acknowledged and discussed from the outset and on a regular basis thereafter, both within professional supervision and as a routine part of any community planning around events and activities. The potential for danger to children has to be recognised in all kinds of community activities, demanding that workers successfully integrate an awareness of individual child protection issues with their commitment to the contribution that community initiatives can make towards the safeguarding of children.

Conclusion

In this chapter we have not been arguing for a model in which the statutory authorities simply access the 'the eyes and ears' of the community to be better informed about the welfare of individual children. Ecological practice, in relation to safeguarding children, goes a lot further in its ambitions. It aims to embrace the totality of children's lives, which do not have clear cut boundaries between individual, family and community level influences on their development and well-being. What is happening, at a community level, will have a major impact on all aspects of children's lives. The challenge is to bring together all the resources that professional and non-professional people have available to them to safeguard children.

On the basis of the preceding discussion, it is evident that community approaches to safeguarding children should aim to incorporate a number of key strategies. First of all, we want to stress the importance of creating and maintaining a culture of listening to children and adults, with workers tuning in to what children and adults can tell them is happening in their local communities, paying particular attention to hearing what children think is most dangerous for them, from their own perspective. Secondly, it is important that child welfare agencies identify the particular situations and contexts which place children at risk in different communities. Once again, this will involve talking to local children and adults, as well as working closely with colleagues in other agencies who might have information about community-level risks. Next, ecological practice should seek to validate local concerns about child protection, utilising the value placed on safeguarding children (by the vast majority of adults), and creating opportunities for residents to express their uncertainty about issues such as what constitutes good enough parenting and child well-being.

Capacity building is another central component of ecological practice, and workers should always aim to increase children's local social networks and enhance the community's social capital by developing activities and events which provide additional opportunities for personal development and the overall safeguarding of children. They should also encourage the development of a culture in which the safeguarding of children and the promotion of their well-being is seen as a key element in all community activities. And, finally, it is important that child welfare organisations and practitioners acknowledge the limitations and risk factors inherent in community development approaches to safeguarding children, working to minimise the limitations and manage the risks.

Chapter 8. **Community Capacity Building for Ecological Practice**

This chapter will consider:
- The importance of community capacity building in policy for children and families.
- The complexity of communities in relation to capacity building.
- The principles of capacity building for ecological practice.
- Different aspects of capacity building for ecological practice.
- Practice examples.
- Practice issues.
- Sharing between communities

The importance of community capacity building in policy for children and families

Over the last decade, the idea of capacity building has been central to government approaches to the regeneration of disadvantaged communities, with a succession of statements and initiatives underlining the importance attached to this aspect of their overall strategies. For instance, *Building Civil Renewal*, the government's strategy document on this subject, stresses '. . . the key part that local people, community organisations, groups and networks can play in providing a wide range of local services' (Home Office 2003: 17) and states the government's intention to:

> . . . make sure that the support for community capacity building, which includes the development of social capital, necessary for the start and ongoing development of the community sector, is effectively planned and efficiently used. Government's aim is to build strong, empowered and active communities, in which people increasingly do things for themselves and the state acts to facilitate, support and enable citizens to lead self-determined, fulfilled lives for the common good.
>
> (p. 6)

The notion of community capacity building is also central to some of the government's child welfare initiatives. For instance, the Children's Fund had, as one of its main objectives:

> To involve families in building the community's capacity to sustain the programme and thereby create pathways out of poverty.
>
> (DfEE, 2001: 15)

However, much of this government material is strong on exhortations that promote community capacity building, but much weaker when it comes to providing concrete guidelines and practise-based information on how capacity can be built. This is an important gap in present guidance because often, the nearer the practitioner gets to communities (and away from strategy documents), the more varied the opportunities and barriers to capacity building appear to become. Much of the material from policy sources about capacity building has something of a feeling of unreality for the practitioner immersed in the tensions and complexities of working in local communities.

In this chapter we attempt to address this imbalance. The focus of the chapter is not on the large scale 'capacity building' initiatives in communities, such as working to provide population-level education and work opportunities, but on the smaller scale everyday contexts which also impact on the lives of the children and parents, and on which the individual practitioner can have an impact. Such capacity building for ecological practice involves working with community groups to make community settings and networks more supportive for children and families and working with specific children and their families so that they benefit from the potential strengths of involvement in their local community.

A major potential advantage of this approach is that local community groups are likely to have considerable knowledge about a wide range of people living in their communities. They will often know not only about many of the people who are experiencing (or causing) the most difficulties in the area, but also about community members who are able to make positive contributions to the life of the community. This is often the sort of information which is lacking within more official child and family welfare agencies. Local community groups are also likely to have extensive natural networks which can be used to facilitate contact with families and others living in the community. These networks can often be used to powerful effect to bring people together and to develop support. Another potential advantage is that, in building the capacity of community groups, relationships of support can potentially 'spill over' into other areas of community life, leading to the development of often intricate and supportive community relationships at a more general and long-term level.

The complexity of community capacity building for ecological practice with children and families

We have emphasised that communities are complicated entities, consisting of multi-layered groupings of people often perceiving themselves to have different, even conflicting, interests. As Hoggett (1997: 15) states:

> . . . each neighbourhood is a site for a multitude of networks, interest and identities which help determine how people see the place where they live. What comes across, even from the strongly working class neighbourhoods, is the heterogeneity and complexity of communities. And yet it is this that policy makers and practitioners still seem to be largely unaware of.

The heterogeneity and conflicts of interest that tend to characterise all communities mean that capacity building within communities, for the benefit of children and their families, is itself a complex undertaking. This complexity can be especially marked when working with several different communities of interest within a geographical community, as is the case, for example, in multi-faith or multi-ethnic neighbourhoods.

Also, addressing the needs of children and families, at least in part, through local community groups can have some potential disadvantages. The membership of community groups, and the networks linked to them, can be unbalanced and idiosyncratic. Some children and families in need of additional support may actually be excluded from membership or assistance by particular groups because of the divisions and conflicts of interest which exist within all communities. For instance, families exhibiting criminal or anti-social behaviour problems, such as illegal drug dealing or use, may be excluded because they are seen as dangerous or undeserving, bringing extra difficulties to the community. For other families, the way that community groups operate may actually serve to reinforce the disadvantages that they are already experiencing as a result of where they live. For example, the difficulties faced by a family with a disabled child, who have poor access to formal and semi-formal support services in their local area, will be exacerbated if the more informal groups active in their community do not promote the inclusion of disabled children and other family members in the activities that they organise.

Given the complexity of community life, part of the skill of the practitioner must include the ability to weigh up, in a particular locality and for a particular child or family, the extent to which working with specific community groups will be a help or a hindrance. And, more generally, to what extent is support for specific community groups likely to contribute to improvements in the well-being of children and families living in a particular area? Making these judgements requires that practitioners and their employing agencies not only have good knowledge about the needs of individual children and families, as well as of different groups of people within their area, but also that they develop and maintain up-to-date information about the community groups and networks in existence.

Principles of community capacity building for ecological practice with children and families

It is important not to be overly prescriptive about community capacity building for ecological practice. There is a great deal of variety both within and between different communities, including the extent to which their capacity is already 'developed', and the potential for further development. This means that practitioners need to have the scope to proceed on the basis of their assessments of the particular community context in which they are working, and what are likely to be the most effective ways of operating in that context.

However, despite community diversity, it is possible to identify four principles that can be used to guide practitioners and managers in the development of effective small scale local capacity building within a wide range of disadvantaged communities.

Capacity building in the community is about empowerment

Capacity building is essentially about the empowerment of communities, or groups within communities, to make positive changes for the benefit of children and families.

Simon (1994) identifies five elements of practice in the empowerment tradition, which are particularly appropriate for ecological practice:

1. Collaborative partnerships with clients, client groups and constituents.
2. A central practice emphasis on the expansion of clients' capacities, strengths and resources.
3. A dual working focus on individuals and their social and physical environments.
4. The operating assumption that clients are active subjects and claimants.
5. The selective channelling of professional energies towards historically disempowered groups and individuals.

Capacity building can incorporate the aims of external agencies but it is primarily about the self-determined needs and potential of the community

Since community capacity building has taken centre stage in government regeneration strategies, there have been a significant number of examples in which external agencies have, either wittingly or unwittingly, attempted to mould the views and activities of communities to fit with their own agendas. There have, therefore, been a correspondingly large number of communities and individuals who have become disillusioned with the notion of 'capacity building'.

The starting point for all community capacity building should be where the community is, at a particular moment in time, in terms of its own self defined needs and potential. The ambitions and aims of external agencies can be incorporated into capacity building programmes, but these should never be allowed to take precedence over the self identified needs of communities. As noted by Chanan and West (1999) capacity building also needs to build on the existing strengths of communities.

Practitioners involved in capacity building need to recognise the many different groupings in communities and any tensions or divisions that exist between them

Perhaps the first question that needs to be addressed in any attempt to develop 'community capacity' is: Whose capacity are we building? As we have noted, tensions and divisions exist within all communities, and these barriers often go to the heart of children's lives. For instance, tensions might have developed between different age groups, divisions arisen between groups from different racial or ethnic backgrounds, or hostilities exist between people from adjoining neighbourhoods. Linking this with poverty and disadvantage Wilkinson (2005: 23) has argued that members of disadvantaged communities are likely to be disproportionately affected by these social dislocations:

> *Inequality promotes strategies that are more self-interested, less affiliative, often highly anti social, more stressful and likely to give rise to higher levels of violence, poorer community relations and worse health.*

Recognising the existence of the tensions that exist between different individuals and groups may be particularly important for understanding how social networks operate within particular disadvantaged communities.

Capacity building and local agencies

Capacity building is not just about achieving change for people in local communities, it also has to involve change within mainstream child and family welfare agencies. The capacity of communities cannot be enhanced if agencies themselves are not prepared to change and adopt more flexible ways of working. To be effective, capacity building with local people has to be undertaken within the context of a partnership between local agencies and the communities that they serve. If local people are encouraged to change and develop, for the benefit of their children and families, then agencies must also be willing to change and develop their own working practices

We look in more detail at some of the challenges that the development of ecological practice (including capacity building) present to organisations and their practitioners in Chapter 11. At this stage, we identify some of the main ways in which agencies are likely to have to change their practise if effective capacity building is to develop:

- Being prepared to go at the pace of the people whose capacity they are attempting to develop.
- Actively listening to what community members are saying about the issues in their community that are having the most impact on children and parents, rather than trying to fit what children and parents are saying into already decided organisational categories of 'problem' and 'response'.
- Being prepared to commit sufficient staff time and other resources to working on community capacity building.
- Actively working on ways of evaluating the impact of capacity building initiatives, particularly in relation to achieving the five outcomes from *Every Child Matters*.

Working to build community capacity also presents some specific challenges for practitioners, in their day-to-day work, particularly in relation to issues about confidentiality. Ecological practice, which encompasses community capacity building, involves combining work on issues that are internal to the family with work in the community on issues which are external to the family. This combination of approaches can present problems, because it involves working with two different levels of confidentiality, with information relating to internal family matters bound by tight organisational and professional controls, whereas most information relating to community initiatives will be in the public domain. This situation requires that clear guidelines and protocols about confidentiality and information sharing are developed in local areas. For instance, in the pieces of project work described in this book, clear ground rules had to be developed with local people about the circumstances in which they could share information about children and families with others.

Capacity building and ecological practice

There are many forms of small scale community capacity building which form an important part of ecological practice. Whilst the list below is far from exhaustive, it illustrates the broad range of approaches which are relevant for building the capacity of communities within a framework of ecological practice. Under each element, we give everyday practice examples of what might be involved.

- *Developing the capacity of the community so it can voice the concerns of children and parents to external agencies that are responsible for provision and services in the area*
  - Providing opportunities for parents and other adults, as well as children and young people, to voice their concerns about children's safety in the community.
  - Promoting community discussions about issues such as lack of play provision in local areas, and the impact this has on children.
  - Opening channels of communication with official agencies so that parents and other adults can express their concerns about such things as housing allocation policies and the use of housing stock, which are perceived to be having a detrimental impact on family life.

- *Working so that the voices of as wide a range of families as possible can be heard*
  - Supporting the development of local groups that represent the views of specific groups of children or families (e.g. disabled children, BME families).
  - Working to facilitate and support the full participation of parents, children and young people in groups and decision-making bodies within the community (e.g. community partnerships).
- *Assisting community members to develop skills in organising events for children and families*
  - Supporting community members to organise events for children and families, such as trips, holidays, outings, and workshops.
  - Supporting community members to develop skills in seeking funding for these activities.
- *Working with the community to develop networks that support adults in their parenting role*
  - Developing more formal resources, such as parent support groups.
  - Providing community centre facilities, such as accessible parent-child drop-ins.
  - Developing more informal networks in the community, such as reciprocal 'helping' relationships between parents.
- *Developing the social network resources of the community for the direct benefit of children*
  - Developing mentoring schemes, providing access to personal advice and positive role models.
  - Facilitating opportunities for positive contacts between the generations within the community.
- *Working to enhance the protective aspects of community that help to safeguard children and young people*
  - Organising community discussion sessions about safeguarding issues.
  - Developing family safety groups.
  - Helping community groups to develop child safety protocols.
- *Working to support the community in establishing norms around children and childcare*
  - Setting up discussion groups about parenting and child development issues.
  - Linking older/more experienced parents with younger/less experienced parents, through neighbourhood groups.

The wide range of practitioners now involved, to a greater or lesser extent, in the provision of children's services, will need to consider how the sort of activities outlined above might influence children's progress towards the achievement of each of the five outcomes from *Every Child Matters*. Similarly, the Children's Trusts or other bodies responsible for the planning, commissioning and delivery of children's services in each local area, will need to consider how the sort of community-level changes intended to be brought about by successful capacity building are likely to impact on their existing organisational arrangements.

Three Case Examples of capacity building in relation to ecological practice

The following three case examples, all taken from current or recent Barnardo's work, illustrate some of the aspects of capacity building for ecological practice. In each example projects have attempted to do something more than simply be 'community based' or 'provide a service for the community'. They have attempted to work alongside the local community or community of interest so that its capacity to meet the needs of children and parents has been developed and strengthened.

The Carrickfergus Child and Parent Project

The first example is of a project that has a well articulated theory of the relationship between community and family. It is perhaps no accident that this example of ecological practice is based in Northern Ireland where over many years the sectarian nature of local communities has been acknowledged to have a very significant impact on family life:

> The Carrickfergus Child and Parent Project in Northern Ireland is part of a larger initiative, Parenting Matters, a Barnardo's service based in Belfast but covering the province and working with a range of parenting issues in local communities. One of its principles is to incorporate community development and capacity building principles into parent support services.
>
> The project delivers a range of local programmes including parenting pre school children, parenting children with behaviour difficulties, parenting in ethnic minority communities and supporting families affected by imprisonment. The programmes involve parents (and grandparents) for 8–10 weeks after which they have the opportunity of joining locally based support groups.
>
> Evaluations show the project to be highly effective in terms of parents' perceptions of positive change within their families and the impact of the programmes on children (Barnardo's 2005).
>
> The project's community development and capacity building approach has the following elements:
>
> - Engaging with the different networks around the life of the child – for instance grandparents and immediate local networks.
> - Systematically trying to find out what is happening in the community. The project employs a research and information officer whose role is not only to evaluate programmes but also to gather information from the community and to adapt parenting material to the specific needs of the community. For instance responding to the changing demography of the area the research and information officer has worked with the local Chinese and Japanese community groups in Carrickfergus to develop appropriate parenting programmes.
> - Using local networks to ensure widespread access to the programmes. The project employs and trains facilitators from the local community and these people are able to use their local networks to encourage involvement in the programmes and be immediately responsive to supporting local parents. As the manager of the project notes 'we've sent out 500 letters and only one parent has come forward. But personal contact always brings in families'.
> - Developing parent support skills and expertise in the local community. There is a philosophy that what happens in the project should also flow out into the community.

One particular aspect of this is that some local parents who have come to the groups because they themselves were experiencing serious difficulties with their children have eventually been trained up to go back into their communities as facilitators. For instance in the case of one family, a parent under a great deal of pressure with a child with behaviour problems, came to the parenting group but also brought her own parents. After finishing the course and being involved in local support networks the parent and her own parents are now actively involved in facilitating other local groups.

Another case description illustrates how the benefits of the approach may 'ripple out' into the community:

Margaret is a mother of four boys aged 15, 11, 8 and 7. Her second youngest child has severe learning difficulties. Margaret came to a 'parenting a child with behaviour difficulties' programme to help her manage the behaviour of her son.

The programme ran for 10 weeks and Margaret found it a great help. She did however realise that some difficulties would be ongoing so she joined the community based parent's support group. With developing confidence and the experience of the impact of the programme on her own family's life, Margaret decided to take the 'parent facilitator' training programme run by the project. She also volunteers for the project as well and is currently co-facilitating a 'parenting pre-school children' programme.

Margaret also has encouraged local parents with severe learning difficulties to come to the project. Again some of them went on to join a support group after the programmes finished. She is currently working with the project to try and organise a programme in her children's primary school. Margaret says 'it's all sort of networking now. We're broadening out and finding more things out.'

Reviewing the above project, the relationship with the local community and the capacity building inherent in that relationship appears to be based on the process shown in Figure 2 (overleaf).

Play in the Park

The above example relates to capacity building around parents. But capacity building in local communities can also focus directly on children's lives and the interface between the child and the community.

In the second practice description we look at approaches to capacity building and developing ecological practice with disabled children. The work described and case example are from an innovative Barnardo's inclusion project in Somerset which focuses on participatory approaches to work with disabled children and their parents.

Ecological practice involves working at a community level to make provision accessible both in the physical but also in the social sense. The project illustrates two central elements of ecological practice – working to make community settings and networks more supportive for children, in this case disabled children, and working with specific children and their families so that they benefit from the potential strengths of involvement in their local community.

Issue identified at local level and fed back to project.

Research and information officer is able to clarify needs from the community through local research and focus groups. The content of the provision (parenting group etc.) is developed.

Local networks are involved identifying and supporting appropriate local people to come forward to the service.

Local people are involved in the provision of the identified service.

The benefits of the service 'ripple' back out into the community through support groups, networks being extended and fresh community information.

Figure 2   The ripple effect of capacity building

The setting for Play in the Park was the local park in a large county town.

The starting point for the work was the knowledge gained from individual families that many disabled children weren't getting the chance to be involved in local play opportunities. In part, this was because the parents lacked confidence that the community was a safe place for their chilfren. But it was also the result of a consultation exercise with disabled children themselves, which emphasised that they wanted to play and 'hang-out' in their own neighbourhoods, without their parents or other carers present, like any other children of their age.

The aim of the project was, therefore, to make the park a safe and accessible place for disabled and non-disabled children, alike. Workers were initially based in the park to ensure that the play experience was safe for all concerned, and to facilitate friendships between disabled children and other children.

The above case study illustrates the importance of involving children in planning processes affecting their local environment. It serves to demonstrate some of the main components of ecological practice, working at individual, group and community levels, simultaneously, and emphasising the importance of understanding the ecologies of individual children which can be understood by asking four questions:

- How does a particular child relate to and integrate into their community?
- How do the parents and workers support the child in question to access the strengths of their local community?

- How do the parents and workers support the child to avoid the dangers and difficulties of their community?
- What barriers do the parents and the child experience in terms of involvement in their community?

Summer Playscheme involving Somali children in Bristol

The following example, also taken from a play setting but directly addressing family support and isolation, illustrates a recent piece of local work which adopted a joint community and family capacity building approach. This piece of work developed from the community research with Bristol's Somali community referred to earlier in the book.

In reading this case example it is important to remember that this community is typically regarded as a 'hard to reach' community.

In summer 2006 following a community consultation exercise with parents and children, which identified a need for safe play provision, a playscheme was developed with Bristol's Somali families.

The scheme however also addressed wider outcomes such as supporting parents to learn about community resources and increasing community cohesion by actively involving isolated and highly pressurised children and parents.

The scheme, which involved trips out of the area as well as increased use of local parks and other play facilities in the area, had the following elements consistent with a capacity building approach for the benefit of children and families.

It worked alongside members of the Somali community to build their capacity to provide play opportunities in the city for children from their community (for instance through jointly working on planning, risk assessments etc).

It directly used the networks of the community group to achieve family access. Working through the normal channels of service provision, this playscheme might have been hard to organise. But working alongside the Somali community group, we were able to link in with their networks so that, far from being 'hard to reach'; we often had over-demand for the activities of the scheme. In total more than 320 children were involved.

Members of the Somali community group were also able to identify families who were experiencing difficulties (for instance racial harassment and fear of going outside), children who were under great pressure (for instance children coming to rejoin their parents in a strange country after being in refugee camps) and children who were disabled but not accessing play facilities.

It focused on children and their parents playing together and getting jointly involved in the activities. One aim of this was that the parents' capacity to provide play for their children should be enhanced by them finding out about play opportunities.

Evaluation of this scheme by children and parents was very positive. It highlighted that they 'enjoyed' and learned together in a stress free setting.

Practice issues

Broadening our perspective from these specific practice examples, it is also possible to provide more general information about some of the key practice issues involved in community capacity building work. These include identifying individuals in the community with the potential to play a significant part in these activities, as well as issues about timescales, the involvement of vulnerable families, and the importance of promoting shared learning between different communities.

Identifying people with strong local networks

The most effective community activists working on behalf of children and families tend to display a number of common characteristics. Chief amongst these is their access to extensive natural networks in the community that usually consist of well developed family and friendship networks, and a wide circle of acquaintances and other contacts. They are also people who tend to have the trust and respect of others in the community, combined with the ability to empathise with disadvantaged children and parents, often based on their own experiences as parents or grandparents bringing up children in similar environments. Importantly, they have the time and personal capacity, without too many other pressures in their lives, to be involved in this type of work, which can include membership of groups, individual networking, advice and support, advocacy with local agencies, and organisation or participation in a range of communal activities, all with the ultimate aim of improving the lives of children and families in their community. In contrast to many others living in their community, they will also tend to see themselves remaining in the area for the foreseeable future, and they will usually feel some pride in the area in which they live (or the community of interest to which they belong), which is an element in their motivation to help others.

These are, therefore, the sort of personal experiences, attitudes, attributes and circumstances that we are looking for in people who may be suited to take on a helping role on behalf of children and families within communities. However, they are also the characteristics that capacity building will be working to develop in others who are not yet at the stage where they feel able to take on community roles. This process will often have begun with their involvement in local activities to support children and families, but as a recipient of support rather than as an organiser or leader of those activities. This involvement should help to extend their own networks and will normally provide opportunities to reciprocate some of the support that they are receiving from others. During the course of their own involvement, the leaders of community activities, be they paid workers or volunteers, are likely to become aware of participants who demonstrate some of the personal attributes identified above. They may either directly express their wish, or show the potential and motivation, to become more involved. This is how the process of capacity building for the benefit of children and families proceeds, with the provision of support to families being the starting point of what is likely to be a long and slow journey, that involves helping to increase their confidence and coping skills, and providing opportunities that enable them to reciprocate some of the help they are receiving and extend their personal networks and local knowledge.

The following example illustrates the way in which extensive networks and the personal capacity to be involved in community activity can link to make a person effective in community capacity building:

Margaret is a grandmother in her late 50s. She has lived on her estate for nearly 30 years and her daughter and grandchildren live nearby. Margaret has been involved in residents' associations for many years and is now very active in a Family Action Group which works to put on activities, outings and holidays for children and families, and provides groups for parents. Her great advantage in this role is that she has very extensive social networks in the community, not only through people she knows herself, but also people her daughter knows. In one way or another, she knows the parents and grandparents of many of the children with whom the project is engaged. Because her direct childcare responsibilities are now in the past, Margaret has the time to be involved in community activity. She is committed to the estate and wants to maintain her work in a voluntary capacity, rather than move to paid child care employment. Although she says she finds it over-demanding at times, Margaret also admits that she gains a great deal from the experience, particularly the new friends that she makes and the fun and enthusiasm that are involved.

In what has been discussed already, the issue of personal motivation to provide help to others has been identified. Altruism, in the shape of giving something back to members of the community of which you are a part, perhaps based on having been a recipient of similar help in the past, is one possible motivating factor. However, it is naïve to think that people get involved in their communities only out of a sense of altruism. Whilst it may be one factor, there are likely to be other factors motivating those who take on either an informally acknowledged or more formal helping role, within their community, including:

- Getting something out of it for their children or grandchildren.
- Addressing issues in their community which are having a negative impact on their personal lives (e.g. crime or antisocial behaviour).
- A sense of personal status, fulfilment, or value.
- Taking the first steps towards a career.
- The development of personal networks.

Often these aspects will be linked. For example, in becoming involved with a piece of community activism, a local person may feel strongly that they are giving to their community but at the same time they will enjoy it. This enjoyment might take the form of getting to know more people, or seeing resources come to their community for their own and their family's benefit. They might also 'have a laugh' – the importance of humour and enjoyment in community capacity building should never be underestimated.

Timescales
One of the key issues in capacity building for children and parents in disadvantaged communities is that of the time needed for these processes to work effectively. Unfortunately, the timescales necessary for effective capacity building are often inconsistent with the requirements of the outcome driven short-term funding of many programmes and initiatives. This mismatch has repeatedly been one of the most serious issues confronting practitioners and community groups, ever since capacity building became a central component of the UK government's regeneration strategies in the mid-1990s.

Some communities, particularly communities of interest, may have the potential for the relatively quick development of capacity, although lack of access to decision-making processes (and power to influence decisions) may still limit their effectiveness. The Bristol Somali community, for instance, includes many people with well developed skills but, at this stage in its history, it lacks access to channels of power and influence. In other communities it will be a matter of starting from a lower skills base which, combined with other factors in the lives of their members, may mean that capacity building is likely to be a long process. In the case of working with parents, one of the key factors likely to slow the process of capacity building will be the pressures that they are under in the early stages of their family's life cycle. For instance, in family centre work concentrating on families with under fives on the south Bristol estates, considerable staff time was spent on working with families so they could play a more effective part in having their voice heard on what really affected them on the estate. It should be noted these families were at the most demanding stage of their family's development, and it was unrealistic to expect many of them to be able to put a great deal of their time into community activities. However these early seeds of community involvement did eventually come to fruition for some of the parents as their children grew up and became more independent.

Capacity building takes place in a situation of flux

In an ideal world, ecological practice with communities would proceed in an orderly fashion from the initial stages of research and consultation, through a partnership development and capacity building phase, and on to well planned and co-ordinated forms of individual, group and community action. However, such neat, linear development is generally a long way from what happens in practice, where the pressure to meet funding deadlines and the intrusion of events, often causing delays, dead-ends and retreats are usually the order of the day. Just when things appear to be going well, something is likely to happen which completely disrupts the whole process and appears to put everything in jeopardy. Community initiatives can go backwards as well as forwards. Equally, the demography or pressures of a neighbourhood may change, making what was once seen as urgent less important, and producing new priorities. As noted by Gilchrist (2000) amongst others, these are not factors over which agencies or workers generally have much control:

> Many community workers will recognise that what happens in practice is usually a combination of serendipity and strategy in which professional interventions play a catalytic but not controlling function.

> (p. 269)

Involving vulnerable families

One of the aims of community capacity building for the benefit of children and families in disadvantaged communities should be to involve more vulnerable family members in community action. This can have powerful benefits in a number of ways:

- It can put the real experiences of vulnerable families into the public (community) arena, so that agencies and local families hear what they have to say about issues that affect their lives.

- It can help to break down barriers between families who are perceived to be coping and those who are not.
- It can activate processes of immediate and local support.
- Sharing in community empowerment processes can lead to enhanced personal confidence and effectiveness within the family.

This last point is an important one, and links in with a central theme of talking about the whole person in the variety of settings in which they find themselves. The following case example (taken from Jones et al., 2002) and based on the family centre work already referred to illustrates the way in community and personal development may have important links:

John and Cathy have two children, eight year old Charlie and four year old Laura. Charlie has cerebral palsy.

Cathy talked about her depression and her difficulties in accepting Charlie's disability. She began to see a counsellor but her depression worsened. Eventually she was admitted voluntarily to hospital.

John felt increasingly unable to cope with looking after the children. By the time of Cathy's hospitalisation both the children were distressed. Neither John nor Cathy had supportive family living nearby.

A community development worker suggested that John might join a group of residents campaigning for better play provision. John became involved in the group and began to see it as an important respite from the stresses and turmoil of family life

John's new sense of purpose carried over into his family life. He realised that he could be effective within his family as well as within the group, and John's new involvement gave his family access to a wider and richer set of local networks. Pressures on the family are still high, but the informal supports that have developed and a new sense of the potential for change have been maintained.

Earlier in the book we pointed to the particular difficulties experienced by children and families who are highly transient. We suggested that these families may be particularly disadvantaged because they are either missed by agencies that attempt to support families, or the level of support that is developed does not have any significant impact before they move again. Family transience is also a significant issue in terms of community support and capacity building for children and families. Just as agencies are less likely to be able to offer effective support to these families, so also are community groups.

Community groups may be particularly resistant to the incorporation of some families because of powerful perceptions about the sort of people local parents think are suitable to be involved with their children, as the following practice notes illustrate:

One of the workers has been involved with Sharon, who has expressed an interest in getting involved with the group and 'doing something for the children around here'. Sharon is herself a parent who is struggling with a number of issues in her family.

At the meeting this morning Sharon's wish to become involved in the group was raised. Strong feelings were expressed about Sharon not being the 'kind of person' that ought to be encouraged to be in contact with other people's children.

Sharing between communities

Another important element of community capacity building for work with children and families involves creating links with other communities. Although it is commonplace for professional workers to spend a considerable amount of their time linking with other professionals, it is just as important that community members are given similar opportunities to link with people from other communities, to offer one another mutual support, share ideas about practical issues and to learn what has been effective elsewhere.

It is particularly important for children and families to be given these opportunities since, maybe more than other community members, they are typically confined within the boundaries of their own communities because of time and resource constraints. Within communities, particularly disadvantaged communities, it is the parents and children who are typically less likely to have the chance of leaving those communities, thereby missing out on opportunities to develop new links and gain ideas and information from people who live outside their own communities. The following description of community meetings bringing parents together from different communities, illustrates some of the potential benefits of facilitating these kinds of opportunities:

> *Conferences and other gatherings were set up under the title 'In Our Own Communities', with the aim of bringing people from different communities in the region together to share information around common problems and what had worked in overcoming them in particular areas. The events included representatives from communities which were at different stages of 'development' and individuals who were at different stages along the journey to being involved in their communities.*
>
> *Besides sharing practical ideas and information, these events were also intended to develop capacity by enhancing people's skills and confidence in their ability to present their ideas and experiences to others, including both community representatives and professionals. The meetings were also intended to 'inspire' community members about what could be achieved, something which has been overlooked in the 'official' literature on capacity building. The inspiration that participants gained from the meetings seemed to be particularly important to them. It was referred to in feedback from the event, and people talked about going back to their own communities enthused to carry on their involvement.*
>
> *The events included a wide range of presentations, all focused on activity undertaken by people in their own communities for the benefit of local children and their families, including:*
> - *A group on an estate badly affected by drug taking which was providing local support and counselling for young men involved with drugs (and their families).*
> - *A local support group in a market town for families with an autistic child.*
> - *A group of local people that had achieved funding for holidays and outings.*
> - *A local group of Black parents who had been instrumental in developing a supplementary school for their children.*
> - *A local group providing support for parents with children with learning difficulties.*

At these events there were also descriptions of more personal journeys. For instance one parent gave a presentation entitled 'From Service User to Service Provider' in which she described her own experiences of being a parent with a disabled child and how she and other parents had developed a 'Special Needs Network'. This eventually ceased operating but the parents kept on getting requests for assistance from other local parents with a disabled child and eventually, with the support of a local community centre, a successful funding application was made and the work has continued to grow.

Feedback after one of these events included the following comments:

'Good to see so many people and to know that you're not alone. There are other people fighting the same battles as yourself only in a different area.'

'Raised my awareness of what is going on and inspired me personally that I do make a difference.'

Some practice difficulties

For all the potential benefits of capacity building within communities, it can also bring practitioners face-to-face with major child care and community issues and dilemmas. For instance, community capacity building inevitably involves making what are, essentially, political decisions. There will never be sufficient resources to support every community group that has a potentially positive contribution to make to the lives of families and children.

Furthermore, whilst providing support to a range of different community groups is entirely consistent with current government approaches towards the strengthening of communities, it must be appreciated that this approach also has the potential to *weaken* communities, by reinforcing some of their existing divisions. This is a major current issue with opinion divided about whether the power and identity of faith groups in the community should be supported or whether public policy should be attempting to move towards more 'integration'. By supporting and working with individual community groups agencies could, in effect, be supporting the development of what have been referred to as 'parallel' communities. In other words, instead of supporting the integration of communities and working towards 'community cohesion', capacity building efforts might be contributing to increased separation.

In our view, the key to these apparent dilemmas is for policy makers, mainstream agencies and individual practitioners to adopt a dual approach, working to enhance the capacity of individual groups, whilst at the same time promoting and supporting their links with different organisations and faith groups, both within and between different geographical areas.

A second difficulty of this approach is that being a volunteer or paid worker in the local community for the benefit of children and parents can put particular pressures on the persons concerned. The expectations placed on them may be high, and it may prove difficult for them ever to feel properly 'off duty' in their own community. Despite only volunteering or being contracted to work for a limited number of hours each week, they are likely to be perceived by others as being constantly available. If they do not make themselves available in this way, they may be perceived as not wholly committed to their role by local people. There are also powerful emotions attached to most issues concerning children, and it is often difficult for local volunteers or workers to avoid accusations of behaving in a preferential way towards particular local children and families at the expense of others, whether this is really the case or not. In other cases, work and private family issues may intermingle in a problematic way, as the following case notes illustrate.

> *Jean is a local person volunteering to develop activities for families in a large inner city area. One of her children is in conflict with a child from another family that lives nearby. This conflict spills over to affect the adults involved. The mother of the other child accuses Jean of not including her children in events and activities she is organising. She makes a formal complaint to the organisation for which Jean volunteers.*

Sustainability in the employment of local people is another important issue. The local person who is employed within an initiative which aims to benefit local children and their families can be particularly disadvantaged if that work ends because of, for instance, short-term funding. Their work skills will have been defined, at least to an extent, by their contacts with the local community and, even after their contract ends, expectations of their contribution to the community may remain high.

Conclusions

In this chapter we have attempted to address some of the gaps which currently exist in relation to community capacity building practice.

We have also pointed to the dangers of making simplistic assumptions about capacity building. It is important not to be naïve about communities and their potential for change. In many of the most disadvantaged communities, there will be powerful processes at work which serve to counter initiatives, and which create tensions and transience, which may mean that the benefits of community capacity building are mitigated.

But, get it right and powerful processes can often be set in motion for the benefit of individual children and families. Although we have deliberately not attempted to produce a blueprint for community capacity building, applicable to all community situations, we have, nevertheless, tried to look at some of the practical ways in which the social capital of disadvantaged communities might be enhanced, and to present some of the challenges that practitioners are likely to face in achieving this.

We finish the chapter on an optimistic note, with a statement from a parent who was in at the beginning of a capacity building initiative in one of our projects:

> *. . . (the workers) came knocking on my door doing like a survey and I let them in . . . They asked me about things and I told them it's like there's nothing to do in the centre of . . . (the town) nothing for kids to do – no facilities. They asked us about things we wanted and what we like to do and I can't believe that like three or is it four years later all this is here. Like they did something about it and made something happen-not just ticked some boxes and went away. I think that's amazing. Like all this has happened and it's brilliant.*

Chapter 9. **Regenerating Disadvantaged Neighbourhoods and Improving Community Safety**

This chapter will consider:
- Policies in relation to neighbourhood regeneration and community safety.
- Evidence from evaluations of ecologically-informed community programmes.
- The potential of family group conferences to contribute to improving community safety.
- Some of the difficulties of successfully translating ecological theory into practice in relation to large-scale community programmes.

Introduction

The issues of neighbourhood regeneration and community safety have been of central concern to successive governments and a wide range of agencies and professionals, including child and family welfare practitioners, in the UK and elsewhere, for many years now. Whilst we would not claim to have a fully developed model of ecological practice in relation to these areas of concern, it is possible to provide information about a number of community programmes and other practice approaches that have their origins in ecological theory. In particular, we will consider a range of individual, group and community programmes designed to regenerate disadvantaged communities and reduce crime, which have been introduced and, at least to some extent, evaluated in the UK over recent years.

In the foreword to the New Labour government's strategy for neighbourhood renewal the Prime Minister, Tony Blair, wrote about neighbourhoods '. . . scarred by unemployment, educational failure and crime . . . (which had) . . . become progressively more cut off from the prosperity and opportunities that most of us take for granted' (SEU, 2001). The increasing concentration of deprivation in particular locations, that was considered in Chapter 2, was also highlighted in this document, with 82 per cent of the most deprived wards located in just over half of the total number of local authorities in England. The North West, North East, Yorkshire and Humberside, and London regions were the worst affected, with particularly high concentrations of deprived wards. The government's strategy for addressing the problems found in these neighbourhoods focused on tackling a number of inter-related problems, including reducing unemployment and crime, as well as improving health, education, skills, housing and the physical environment, with the aim of ensuring that 'within ten to twenty years, no one should be seriously disadvantaged by where they live'.

Surveys of the views and perceptions of children and adults living in disadvantaged neighbourhoods make it clear that one of their main worries is the high levels of crime and anti-social behaviour, especially involving teenagers, which tends to be associated with these particularly disadvantaged areas (Camina, 2004). Partly in response to these concerns, alongside its neighbourhood regeneration programmes, the government introduced a wide range of interventions designed to reduce crime and anti-social behaviour and improve community safety. As we will go on to see, many of these new initiatives contain elements of what can be identified as ecological practice, directed at individuals, groups or whole communities. National and local evaluations of the main government and non-government initiatives in this area of practice not only provide evidence of the impact of different programmes to date, but also enable us to identify some of the ecological processes at work and to highlight the main messages for ecological practice.

Ecological processes and practice within neighbourhood renewal programmes

The Single Regeneration Budget

By the late 1990s, when the study by Ruth Lupton (considered in Chapter 4) was undertaken, the *Single Regeneration Budget* (SRB) programme was providing funds for a wide range of neighbourhood renewal and community safety activities in most of the neighbourhoods studied, including improvements to their housing stock, economic infrastructure and community facilities, as well as contributing to skills training, crime reduction and youth work programmes (Lupton, 2003).

However, despite the valuable work that Lupton found was being undertaken with SRB funding, the professionals and residents involved identified a number of significant problems with the programme. First of all, despite the SRB programme's requirement that all schemes had to be based on partnerships including local residents, a genuine sense of local ownership and inclusion had proved difficult to achieve. Residents, who had often seen previous regeneration programmes come and go whilst their neighbourhoods continued to decline, were understandably cynical and difficult to engage. The key components of programmes where good partnership relationships with residents had been achieved included the provision of training for all those involved, giving local people positions of responsibility, and actively promoting inclusion through employment and the provision of locally-based services.

The second problem concerned the funding process, which was based on competitive bids for time-limited projects. Not only was bidding against other equally deprived areas for funding distasteful for many of the people involved, but it also resulted in a rather fragmented approach to what were, after all, closely inter-related problems.

Thirdly, and arguably most importantly, many respondents considered that SRB projects could not overcome some of the main causes of neighbourhood decline, which stemmed more from the wider economic and social structures of society than from factors at the neighbourhood level. As a result, local SRB projects often adopted more limited (but realistic) goals than overall neighbourhood regeneration, seeking to slow down the rate of decline, or to build a platform for future recovery (Lupton, 2003: 124–39).

The interim report of the national evaluation of the SRB programme found that there had been only modest improvements in the lives of some residents, which were largely offset by a similar proportion who experienced a slight deterioration in their circumstances. Like Lupton's study, the evaluation also identified community involvement and capacity building as problematic in the early stages, and noted that good community practice requires time, strategic planning and the involvement of local people from all sectors of the community from the very start (Rhodes et al., 2002). No blueprint was identified for successful partnership working, but the key issues included: an inclusive approach to membership, with adequate support for community representatives; effective monitoring and review processes that keep partners fully informed of progress and facilitate strategic planning; and the identification of key partnership objectives, at an early stage, including how they fit with the goals of mainstream services.

More generally, the factors associated with successful schemes at this interim stage included accurate analysis of the area's problems, appropriate service responses, and recognition of the potential for helpful interactions between different initiatives. Project managers with the necessary vision and skills to successfully lead partnerships were also a crucial component.

New Deal for Communities and the National Strategy for Neighbourhood Renewal

The *New Deal for Communities* (NDC) programme, launched in 1998, was designed to overcome some of the shortcomings of previous area-based regeneration schemes. Not only was there to be greatly increased funding (of about £50m for each area) concentrated on a more limited number of smaller neighbourhoods (39 in total), but the funding was also to be provided over a longer time-scale (10 years rather than seven), and local people were to be given the lead role in the partnerships that had to be established in each NDC area.

The NDC programme was followed by the announcement of the wider, *National Strategy for Neighbourhood Renewal* in 2001, which placed an emphasis on establishing comprehensive and long-term mainstream regeneration mechanisms. As already noted, the strategy paid particular attention to the 88 most deprived local authority districts, and was intended to work alongside other area-based initiatives, such as 'action zones' for health, education and employment, and Sure Start areas in which multi-agency centres provide integrated services for families with young children. It was also intended to complement other national anti-poverty and social inclusion policies, such as significant increases in the funding of public services, the re-introduction of a national minimum wage, and the development of a range of tax credits to increase the household income of low-paid workers and to help parents joining the labour market with the costs of childcare.

The NDC programme, like its SRB predecessor, is also being independently evaluated. The interim evaluation report, covering the first four years of the programme, found that, although local residents were well represented on NDC partnership boards, this was not replicated in the staff teams employed by local schemes, or in their direct involvement in NDC activities (ODPM, 2005). A number of mechanisms that encouraged community involvement were identified in the report, including positive responses to consultation processes, the provision of easily accessible projects that met local needs, and regular communication about plans, progress and funding. However, it also identified some familiar barriers, including the existence of cliques, difficulties in engaging with some groups, transience, community tensions, limited infrastructure, and overload on key figures, most of which were also highlighted as difficulties in relation to community capacity building in the previous chapter.

Over the period 2002 to 2004, the report identified some progress in NDC areas, including improving relationships between partnerships and local authorities, the introduction of neighbourhood management schemes, improvements to the environment and housing, and local agency support for a range of different initiatives and projects. However, other aspects of NDC programmes did not show improvements during this period with, for example, little increase in resident participation in voluntary and community groups or improvements in their attitudes towards neighbourliness, and tensions between different groups such as existing and new residents.

Comparing the responses of residents in NDC areas with those in comparable non-intervention areas over this two-year period, the evaluation team found that there had been relatively bigger improvements in the NDC areas in relation to subjective measures, such as resident satisfaction with the area and perceptions that the area had improved. However, on more objective outcome measures there were few signs of significant improvements, with measures of employment, crime, health and education showing little, if any, change over and above those found in similar areas without NDC programmes (ODPM, 2005).

Part of the explanation for the limited measurable impact of the NDC programme undoubtedly lies in the short time-period over which the projects had been in existence at the time of the interim evaluation. Although, even when these policies have had more of a chance to make a difference, the failure of successive governments to target the reduction of the UK's chronically high levels of inequality in the distribution of income and wealth, that were discussed in Chapter 2, mean that the potential contribution of area-based initiatives like the NDC will inevitably be compromised. In particular, the spatial dimensions of the UK economy mean that many deprived neighbourhoods simply do not fit with existing or future patterns of demand for employment (Begg et al., 2002), making the wholesale regeneration or renewal of many deprived neighbourhoods an unrealistic goal (Lupton, 2003: 219–20).

However, this rather gloomy conclusion should not deter ecological practitioners from working with the residents in disadvantaged neighbourhoods in ways that are designed to address some of the negative impact of inequalities on their day-to-day lives. At the same time, ecological practitioners should support the representatives of disadvantaged neighbourhoods in applying pressure on national and local politicians and other decision makers to tackle the structural causes of individual and area inequalities.

Furthermore, no matter what the shortcomings of area-based community pro-grammes, all of the evaluations have noted the benefits that these programmes have produced for significant numbers of people living in disadvantaged areas. For example, Lupton found that they were providing new investment in all of the 12 deprived neighbourhoods that she studied, including improvements in childcare services and facilities, as well as early years and adult education (Lupton, 2003). Similarly, the interim evaluation of the NDC programme found that virtually all partnerships had introduced improved neighbourhood management arrangements, as well as community policing and other measures to improve safety and associated factors affecting the quality of life in public places, such as reducing litter and graffiti (ODPM, 2005). The community development, resident participation, and capacity building aspects of these area-based initiatives also have the potential to produce significant improvements in the confidence, capabilities, and skills of residents living in disadvantaged neighbourhoods.

In the current political context, therefore, it is important to be realistic about both the positive potential *and* the limitations of working with children and families within disadvantaged neighbourhoods. The comprehensive regeneration of some areas, whilst desirable, may be an unrealistic goal in the present UK context of continuing high levels of inequality. However, more limited objectives, such as the provision of improved facilities for young people, and the reduction of offending and anti-social behaviour by the same group, which contribute to improvements in the quality of life and future life chances of residents in these areas, are nonetheless worth pursuing. Ecologically-informed individual, group and community approaches to these issues are the subject of the second part of this chapter.

Individually and family oriented programmes to reduce youth offending and anti-social behaviour

On their own, none of the following programmes can be considered to constitute fully developed forms of ecological practice. However, when viewed as part of a range of responses, the combination of mentoring schemes, parenting programmes and community family group conferencing reviewed here can be seen to be addressing a number of inter-related issues at the interface between the internal and external worlds of children and their families.

Mentoring

Mentoring represents one of the main individually-oriented approaches to improving the lives of vulnerable or disadvantaged young people, offering them the opportunity to develop a one-to-one relationship with a more experienced person, who acts as a role model and tries to help them address a range of problems, including poor educational attainment, relationship issues, drug use, and homelessness. About £10m was invested in such schemes by the Youth Justice Board throughout England and Wales between 2001 and 2005.

Within the national evaluation period (2001–2004), mentoring projects recruited over 3,000 community volunteers, training many of them as mentors, and subsequently matching them with a similar number of young people. Although the schemes evaluated varied considerably in length and form, they appear to have had a beneficial impact for some participants, with a third of those involved either entering or re-entering education or training, and involvement in community activities also showing improvement. However, a smaller in-depth study, which compared a sample of mentored young people with a non-mentored comparison group, found no evidence of improvements in other outcomes, including behaviour, literacy and numeracy. This is hardly a surprising finding, given the extent of the young people's problems and the limited nature of the intervention, which amounted to an average of just 20 hours of contact time between the young person and their mentor.

To compound these rather disappointing outcomes, the schemes also proved relatively expensive to run, and over half of the 5,000 or so young people referred to the projects either refused to take part altogether or did not engage with their mentors (YJB, 2005).

Parenting programmes

Although parenting programmes have been used to address a range of issues, the particular national programme that is reviewed here was specifically targeted at the parents of young offenders. Within this programme, the individual projects all adopted a groupwork approach, but their membership was determined by individual referrals, rather than being open to all parents living within a disadvantaged neighbourhood. The aim of the overall programme was to reduce the sort of family and parental risk factors associated with offending behaviour by young people that were discussed in Chapter 4, including harsh and erratic discipline, poor supervision, and family conflict.

The programme, which was funded by the Youth Justice Board, and consisted of 42 projects run by youth offending teams in partnership with local agencies across England, was independently evaluated by the Policy Research Bureau (Ghate and Ramella, 2002). Nearly 3,000 parents attended one of the 34 projects included in the national evaluation, two-thirds of them on a voluntary basis, with the others subject to court-imposed Parenting Orders. Most of the parents were identified as 'White British' (96%) and female (81%), and half were lone parents. As a group, the parents who attended programmes were characterised by very high levels of need, ranging from housing and debt problems, to problems with their health and personal relationships. The majority said they particularly wanted help in managing the difficult behaviour of the young person that had given rise to the referral, most of whom were aged between 14 and 15 years. Following their attendance, most parents reported significant positive changes in relation to the young people concerned, including improved communication, supervision and monitoring of their activities, handling the (less frequent) conflicts that arose, giving praise and approval (with less criticism and loss of temper), and influencing their behaviour. The overwhelming majority of participants were positive about their experience, with only six per cent giving either negative or indifferent ratings for the programme that they attended, and nine out of ten saying that they would recommend it to others in their situation.

The young people's behaviour also appeared to have been influenced for the better following their parents' participation in the programme. For example, in the year prior to their parents' involvement, 89 per cent of the young people concerned had been convicted of an offence, but this fell to 61.5 per cent in the year following the programme. Furthermore, the average number of recorded offences committed by the young people concerned fell by over 50 per cent, from 4.4 in the year prior to the programme, to 2.1 in the following year (Ghate and Ramella, 2002).

Community family group conferencing

Community family group conferencing (CFGC), like the Youth Justice Board parenting programme discussed above, is another approach which combines individual and family level components, but this time with an added community dimension, making it a more rounded form of ecological intervention. Family group conferences were originally developed in New Zealand, in relation to child protection concerns within families (Jackson and Nixon, 1999). They have subsequently been developed in the UK and elsewhere to address these issues, as well as being adapted to deal with offending and anti-social behaviour by young people in the community. The following extended practice example concerns a case dealt with by a local housing department which had established a Family Support Project to work with households failing to comply with their tenancy agreements. The project works with families by defining boundaries for acceptable behaviour, clarifying potential enforcement action, and using community family group conferences to help families to identify what help they need to improve their situation and maintain their tenancy. The CFGC component of the project is optional, but there is pressure on families to accept it, as the likely consequence of refusing to engage is a move towards more formal and punitive interventions.

This example of ecological practice has the following elements:

- Giving all the members of the family the chance to say what would improve their situation, both within the family and in their relations with local people.
- Facilitating the involvement of members of the wider family, friends and neighbours in finding solutions to the family's difficulties and the problems that they presented to the local community.
- Supporting family members to identify positive action for change that they themselves could take, as well as action that friends, neighbours and agencies could take to help them.
- Agencies responding to the family's problems by addressing the issues identified by them in the FGC plans.

The Samuels are a white, two-parent family living on a large post-war estate. They have four children, Jason, Kerry, Matty and Lianne, aged between 10 and 15 years. The family have a lengthy history of involvement with social workers, education welfare officers, the police, Connexions staff, and housing, youth offending, and mental health workers. There were serious concerns about Mr and Mrs Samuels' ability to provide adequate care for their children, two of whom had not been to school for an extended period of time and had been refused home tuition because of the perceived risk to the teachers. Jason was also the subject of an Anti-Social Behaviour Order (ASBO).

If the family situation deteriorated further, there was a strong chance that drastic (and very expensive) action, such as taking the children into local authority care, might have to be considered. The family also presented major difficulties for their neighbours and the local community, with a history of complaints about the family's behaviour going back at least five years. The 15 year old boy had been part of a group that had brought stolen cars back onto the estate, and there had been many complaints about general anti-social behaviour, including fighting and shouting in the street and playing very loud music in the house. There had also been complaints about criminal damage, such as scratching cars belonging to neighbours, and the children had also been involved in the intimidation and harassment of other local children. Neighbours living on the estate had recently organised a petition demanding that the family be moved elsewhere.

The Samuels agreed to engage with the Family Support Project and work with an independent co-ordinator from Barnardo's to set up their community family group conference. A decision was taken to hold two conferences – the first about Jason and

Matty, followed two weeks later by a meeting about Kerry and Lianne – because each of the children had so many professionals involved with them that having everybody there on the same day would have been overwhelming. All of the immediate family also attended the family group conferences, along with their maternal grandfather, two sets of aunts and uncles, and an adult cousin.

In each of the meetings there was a dual emphasis, not only focusing on the needs of the children, but also on the difficulties they were causing for the local community. Each of the children had independent advocates to help them present their wishes and feelings to the meetings, and a worker from the Family Support Project negotiated an 'acceptable behaviour contract' with each child that had to form part of their plan, covering specific behaviours, such as throwing stones, which had to stop.

The family were asked to make a plan in relation to the following questions:
- *How can the family improve their behaviour in the community and secure their tenancy?*
- *How can Jason, Kerry and Lianne be supported to get back into education?*
- *How can Jason be helped to keep the conditions of his ASBO?*
- *What support do Mr and Mrs Samuels need to regain control of their children and live as a family together?*

At the beginning of the conference the professionals outlined the concerns they had about the children, the impact of their behaviour on the community, the enforcement action that would follow if things did not improve, and the kind of services they could provide that might be helpful. The parents and the children (and their advocates) gave their views to the meetings, and the other family members had the opportunity to ask questions. Then the family were left on their own to make a plan for their future. The message given to the family was 'you're the experts on what is happening in your family and how things could change'.

At their conferences, the two children who were not attending school identified the support that they thought would help them to return to school. They wanted someone to help them get to school for the first few days, as they were afraid of the reactions to their long absence from both fellow pupils and teachers. They also negotiated with the Head of Year, who came to the meetings, to come in early on their first day back, and she agreed to a part-time return for one of the girls, initially, and to share some of their anxieties with the teachers involved.

The parents described how difficult their lives had become and the mother, in particular, identified the kind of help she felt would make a difference to her. Mrs Samuels said that the children overwhelmed her and that, most of all, she wanted the family to stop shouting at each other. The children also commented on how they hated all the shouting. This subsequently became one of the issues addressed in the parenting group that Mrs Samuels agreed to attend. Mrs Samuels also said that she could not cope with the chaos of the mornings, trying to get the children up and ready for school which she said was one of the main reasons they didn't go to school. As a result, it was arranged that a family support worker would help Mrs Samuels to get the children ready for school, and to make sure they got there on time.

There were also positive outcomes from the conferences for members of the local community. For example, in response to the complaints of very loud music, two of the children said that they didn't know 'how loud loud is'. This led to one of the housing agency workers, after getting agreement from the neighbour involved, arranging for the children to go next door and listen to their music at different volumes. A simple contract was set up, identifying acceptable volume levels at different times of the day. The contract also covered other areas, including the children not throwing stones outside the house. There had also been complaints about one of the girls using a play area that was designated for younger children. The Samuels children agreed to keep away from this area, but asked if the community police officer could talk to two families that chased them off another play area that they were entitled to use.

It would be naïve to suggest that the family group conference approach outlined in this example can produce complete solutions, either to all of the difficulties identified, or for all members of the family and the community. It is also important to note that the families that become involved in community family group conferencing through this project realise that things have to change if they want to keep their tenancy. In this case, a review conference, held six months after the initial meetings, identified several positive outcomes for both the family and the community. A key aspect of the success of this ecological method of working, linking internal (family) and external (community) factors, appeared to be that the family had been given the central role in defining the nature of the support they needed and a chance to say what would make a difference to their conflicts with neighbours, and that the various agencies acted on the family's views of what would make a difference, providing resources identified in the family plan.

When asked at the review what they thought about the intervention, one of the two children who had returned to full-time education and maintained her attendance thereafter referred back to the original conference and said *'because I said I would do it'*. Mrs Samuels reported that she benefited from the practical support she had received, including the home visits by the family support worker and the parenting programme that she successfully completed. Jason had not breached his ASBO in those six months either, and complaints to the police about the family had dropped by over 75 per cent, with neighbours also reporting that they felt more positive about the family's behaviour.

Community-oriented programmes to reduce youth offending and anti-social behaviour

There are two different types of community-oriented interventions directed at reducing offending and anti-social behaviour by young people that we have not yet considered. The first of these involves interventions targeted at young people identified as being at 'high-risk' for future offending, examples of which include the On Track, Youth Inclusion and Summer Plus programmes. Secondly, there are community-focused initiatives which aim to promote social inclusion, attempting to involve all young people living in 'high-risk' areas. The main examples of this latter type of programme are the Positive Activities for Young People, and Communities That Care programmes. Some young people's consultation and participation projects may also fall within this category, although there is less information about their impact, since evaluations have tended to focus on process issues and participant satisfaction surveys (e.g. Combe, 2002; Doy et al., 2001; Pain et al., 2002). Although studies of this nature have helped to identify important elements of successful strategies to involve young people at risk of social exclusion in decision-making and service development processes, most have yet to produce reliable evidence about any lasting impact that different approaches may have with different groups of young people (Jack, 2006).

The Youth Service can also be considered as a community-oriented national programme, providing youth clubs and other forms of group and individual interventions which often have, as one of their main aims, the reduction of youth offending and anti-social behaviour. Although, historically, youth services adopted a universal approach to their remit, government policy now requires that a clear emphasis is placed on work with specific groups, such as disadvantaged, 'at-risk', and socially excluded young people (DfES, 2001). There are, however, a great number of other clubs providing educational, leisure and support services and opportunities to young people, often from a wider range of backgrounds, including uniformed, church-based, sporting, arts, and other activity-based groups. Whilst evaluation evidence in relation to most of these clubs and activities is very limited, a recent research study has compared the impact of more structured leisure activities on relative life chances in adulthood with that of less structured youth clubs. The findings of this piece of research, which are discussed in more detail at the end of this chapter, are important because they have had a significant impact on current government youth policy.

On Track

The *On Track* programme was launched by the Home Office in 2000, with £30m of funding aimed at children and young people living in 24 'high crime, high deprivation communities'. It was intended to be an evidence-based prevention programme that adopted a community approach, targeting children aged 4–12 years identified as being at high risk of offending and anti-social behaviour. The aim was to develop programmes which would act as models of best practice in the early prevention of offending and the promotion of the health, education and behaviour of children and young people (Home Office, 1999).

Unfortunately, as one of the members of the national evaluation team has pointed out, there are some serious difficulties associated with using risk and protection factors as the basis for targeted interventions to reduce offending by young people (Hine, 2005). Perhaps the most significant of these problems is that the associations between risk factors and offending behaviour by young people are well established only at group levels. This does not mean, therefore, that they can be used as a reliable screening tool for identifying high-risk *individuals* in the way that the On Track and Youth Inclusion programmes have attempted to do. It has been acknowledged for many years now that any approach to social problems based on aggregated lists of risk factors is likely to lead to problems of false negatives and false positives (Parton, 1985). Not only is it likely that many young people who will subsequently go on to offend will not be identified by such screening processes (false negatives) but others, who would not have gone on to become offenders, are likely to be wrongly identified and included in interventions (false positives). Being falsely identified in this way may not only have damaging consequences for the individuals concerned, but their inclusion in offending prevention schemes also tend to confound the conclusions of programme evaluations (Armstrong et al., 2005).

Another problem facing these programmes is the difficulty of consistently implementing a nationally devised programme in a large number of local sites. Each locality, whilst sharing certain characteristics, will have its own unique combination of social, economic and organisational characteristics (Camina, 2004). This was an issue identified in an early report by the On Track national evaluation programme (Harrington et al., 2004). Factors such as the local employment market, community make-up and history of partnership working were all found to influence the implementation process in the first 18 months of the programme. Furthermore, local projects faced real problems in basing their interventions on evidence of 'what works', with tensions between local and national interpretations of what constituted 'evidence-based' practice (Hine, 2005).

Despite these problems, some early signs of positive impact were evident in the national evaluation, with over a third of participants showing improvements in relation to their offending and anti-social behaviour. Similar or slightly higher proportions of participants also showed improvements in relation to a range of family and environmental risk factors such as parental supervision and discipline, family conflict, and violent and aggressive behaviour. Between one third and one half of participants also showed signs of improvement in school-related areas, including attainment, attendance and exclusions after On Track interventions (France et al., 2004). However, at this early stage in the evaluation process, it was not possible to say whether or not these improvements are likely to be maintained in the longer-term.

Youth Inclusion Programme and Summer Plus

The other targeted community-focused initiatives to have been independently evaluated so far are the Youth Inclusion and Summer Plus programmes. The *Youth Inclusion Programme* provides services for the 50 young people, aged 13–16 years, identified by a range of local agencies as the most high-risk offenders in their area. It has been operating since 2000 in 72 of the most deprived, high crime estates in England and Wales. The main focus of the programme is the provision of activities designed to help the targeted young people to learn new skills and receive education and careers help and advice from paid workers and volunteer mentors.

The evaluation of the programme's first three years of operation was reasonably encouraging, with the arrest rates of the participants in each area having fallen by an average of 65 per cent. Nearly three-quarters of the targeted young people who were previous offenders had lower levels of arrest after the YIP intervention, whilst a similar proportion of those who had not previously offended before their participation had not subsequently offended within the evaluation period (MHB, 2003). On the back of this encouraging start, a Junior Youth Inclusion Programme for 8–12 year-olds has also been introduced which, like its counterpart for teenagers, is jointly funded by the Youth Justice Board and local agencies.

The *Summer Plus* programme, which was designed to reduce street crime by 'high-risk' 8–19 year-olds, ran in 34 local education authorities across England during the summer of 2002, providing a range of 'purposeful activities' and access to key worker support. The programmes engaged over 10,000 young people in a range of activities that were either entirely new or that were extensions of existing activities.

A small-scale qualitative study by independent evaluators noted that developmental activities, usually including an explicit educational component, had more beneficial impact on participants than purely diversionary activities. The evaluators also found that crime by young people in the study areas had fallen significantly more than in the rest of England, but they were not able to say that these differences were attributable to Summer Plus because of the possible effects of other initiatives operating simultaneously in these areas. In interviews, participants in Summer Plus thought that the scheme had helped to reduce their negative behaviour, as well as increasing their self confidence, empathy towards others, respect for authority figures, and motivation to make positive changes in their lives. The report went on to recommend that this one-off initiative should become an on-going programme, running throughout the year rather than just in the summer months, and adopting a more inclusive approach by involving a wider range of young people (CRG, 2003). In this respect, the conclusions support the views of many experienced practitioners who highlight the stigmatising potential of targeted services and advocate the benefits of more universal approaches, wherever possible (for example, see Holman, 2000).

Positive Activities for Young People

The recommendation that Summer Plus should become an on-going programme paved the way for *Positive Activities for Young People*, launched in 2003 as a cross-departmental initiative, and again aimed at 8–19 year-olds at risk of social exclusion or involvement in crime. A range of constructive sports, arts and educational activities were to be provided during school holidays and out of school hours throughout the year, with additional support and guidance from a key worker allocated to the youngsters identified as most at risk. Participation in these activities was intended to increase the opportunities for children and young people to develop new skills and interests, passing their leisure time in an enjoyable and rewarding way and broadening their outlook and social networks by mixing with others from different geographical and ethnic communities. All of this was designed to help them either to return to, or engage more productively with education, training or employment, to reduce offending and anti-social behaviour, and to encourage volunteering and active citizenship in their communities.

Approximately 290,000 young people participated in PAYP between 2003 and 2006, the majority of whom were considered to be 'at risk' because of concerns about where they lived, who they were associating with, or their individual behaviour. Nearly four in ten participants received key worker support, which the national evaluation identified as of central importance to their engagement with the PAYP programme (CRG, 2006).

Unfortunately, once again, the evaluators were not able to utilise the sort of comparative approach that would have enabled any impact of the PAYP programme to be isolated from the influence of other initiatives operating at the same time. However, from the management information available to them they concluded that participation in the PAYP programme contributed both to reductions in the criminal and anti-social behaviour of the young people involved, and in supporting them back into education and training (CRG, 2006: vi). By the end of year two of the programme, for example, three-quarters of young people whose views were surveyed said that they had learned new things from the programme, and only slightly smaller proportions said that they had made new friends, got on better with adults, and felt better about themselves. At the same stage of the evaluation, anecdotal evidence from shopkeepers and community wardens in areas running PAYP schemes suggested that the activities provided were having a positive influence on the levels of 'nuisance' caused by groups of young people in their communities (CRG, 2006).

Communities That Care

Finally, we come to what is arguably the most comprehensive ecologically-based community prevention programme for young people to have been implemented in the UK to date. This is the *Communities That Care* (CTC) programme, which was originally developed in the USA but has now been piloted in a number of projects around Britain. In addition to targeting the reduction of youth crime, CTC is also designed to reduce school failure, drug abuse and pregnancy among young people.

Like *On Track*, this programme uses the known risk and protective factors for social problems affecting young people, but it does not use them as a screening tool to identify 'high-risk' children and young people for special attention. Instead, it adopts a community-level approach, aiming to reduce the risk factors, as well as to increase the protective factors associated with these problems in particular neighbourhoods, on the assumption that this will lead to lower overall levels of criminal and anti-social behaviour by young people in those locations (Catalano and Hawkins, 1996). The collection and analysis of data about the particular combinations of risk and protective factors that exist in specific locations is used as the basis for discussions between local professionals, residents, and business people, to establish what is really going on in those locations. Involving the community in this way is also intended to amplify the impact of interventions by increasing the level of social organisation of the areas in which they are based, promoting stronger pro-social norms and a sense of ownership and investment in prevention activities (France and Crow, 2001). The CTC programme also promotes an evidence-based approach to effective interventions, as well as the importance of adults as positive role models and mentors for young people.

Independent evaluations of CTC pilot projects in different parts of the UK found that they were proving to be reasonably successful in engaging and maintaining a degree of active community involvement. However, the numbers of people, especially young people, directly involved in each area were relatively small, and many of the adults were already involved in preventive activities with young people in the locality in some way. As in other community programmes, the role of programme co-ordinator was identified as crucial in achieving and maintaining community participation (France and Crow, 2001; Bannister and Dillane, 2005).

In the three pilot projects evaluated in England and Wales, situated in Barnsley, Coventry and Swansea, self-report surveys of young people's behaviour and other sources of local data were used as the basis for analysis of local conditions and shared decision-making about resources and services between professionals and local people. However, in an interim report after the projects had been in operation for approximately two years, the evaluators questioned the degree to which these processes were truly evidence-based, because of problems with such things as data collection, the production of 'risk-audits', and assessing the effectiveness of existing local services (France and Crow,

2001). Evaluators of the three CTC programmes piloted in Scotland also noted the problems caused by the fact that the areas were markedly different from the original CTC criteria, both in terms of the size and the structure of the neighbourhoods involved (Bannister and Dillane, 2005).

These three pilot areas in England, Scotland and Wales, also started from very different points, in terms of their histories of partnership working and general 'community readiness' for a programme like CTC, as well as the resources made available by local agencies to help to implement the programme. For example, one programme was without a co-ordinator for nearly 18 months, and the agencies in this area failed to provide any new resources, resulting in cynicism among the local people involved. By way of contrast, the pilot area that was judged to be most successful had engaged a wide range of partners, crossing both agency and hierarchical boundaries. From the very start, it also involved local people and those who would later be responsible for delivering services. These processes enabled participants in the CTC process to build up shared knowledge about prevention theory and practice. However, even this project only managed to produce what this final evaluation report called 'promising but inconclusive' evidence of any positive impact on the behaviour of young people in the area. The other two pilot projects included in the final evaluation were judged, overall, to have had little impact (Crow et al., 2004).

Given the implementation problems experienced by the majority of the CTC projects that have been evaluated so far, and the relatively short period of time that most of them have been in operation, coupled with the ambitious community-level goals of the CTC programme, this conclusion is not really surprising. Ideally, all of the pilot projects need a much longer period of time to elapse, after successful implementation, before their potential effectiveness is judged. If they are allowed this time, they will also be able to benefit from the improved guidance and assessment tools that CTC (UK) has been able to develop in the light of the early teething problems experienced in implementing the model in the UK, including an improved risk audit tool and more comprehensive guidance on effective interventions. Furthermore, as the final evaluation report for the England and Wales pilot programmes points out, CTC projects need to be able to draw upon more reliable community-level data (provided by central and local government) to supplement the self-report surveys on which they have largely depended so far (Crow et al., 2004).

The role of structure in leisure activities

Before concluding this chapter, it is worth reflecting on the government's interest in the development of more structured leisure activities for young people, such as those upon which the Summer Plus and PAYP programmes are based. This has arisen because of national and international research evidence that 'how and where young people spend their free time is ... significant in influencing their life chances' (HM Treasury and Department for Education and Skills, 2007: 38). It seems that it may be better for some young people not to be involved in community activities with their peers at all than to participate in unstructured activities (Mahoney and Stattin, 2000). For example, a research study used in formulating the *Youth Matters* Green Paper (DfES, 2005b), concluded that the contexts in which young people congregate carry risks as well as opportunities (Feinstein et al., 2005). The study examined the effects of participation of young people in leisure activities at the age of 16 on a wide range of measures of social exclusion when they were 30 years of age, using a number of control variables to deal with any selection bias problems. It found that young people who participated in youth clubs, which typically lack any formal structure, tended to have personal and family characteristics associated with adult social exclusion. Conversely, young people who engaged in the more highly structured activities offered by uniformed or church-based clubs shared the opposite tendencies, whilst those involved in sports or community centre activities were a more heterogeneous group, showing no clear association with any particular personal or family characteristics. Crucially the study found that, for young people with similar behaviour and levels of success and aspiration at age 16 (as well as comparable cognitive skills and other factors at age 10), those who attended youth clubs were less likely to achieve educationally and more likely to be offenders than those who did not. This led the researchers to conclude that the provision of structured activities at age 16 can make a big difference to the life paths of adolescents (Feinstein et al., 2005: iii).

The policy review of children and young people, used to inform the 2007 Comprehensive Spending Review for the period 2008–2011, acknowledges that its findings about the unstructured activities traditionally provided by youth centres and clubs have been challenged by practitioners and commentators defending these services. However, although it accepts that the effects of this type of provision are not intrinsically negative, it is also clear that not every activity or setting can be considered as having positive effects on different groups of young people. Whilst the review, therefore, considers that unstructured settings have an important role to play in attracting disadvantaged young people, it concludes that the main challenge lies in finding ways of engaging them in leisure activities that will have a positive impact on their future life chances (HM Treasury and DfES, 2007). This is likely to require the development of specific initiatives and programmes, including a significant role for outreach approaches and local community activities, which can successfully engage young people within their local environments in an appropriate range of structured activities. As the evaluation of the national mentoring scheme discussed earlier illustrated, this is a difficult trick to pull off, depending both on engaging young people in the designated activities in the first place, and then on the ability of workers and volunteers to gain the trust and co-operation of marginalised groups of young people living in some of the most deprived neighbourhoods across the country.

Conclusion

Neighbourhood prevention programmes, such as Communities That Care, ultimately face the same problems as those experienced by the community regeneration programmes discussed at the beginning of this chapter. Namely, that it will require national social and economic policies to bring about significant reductions in the inequalities between individuals and neighbourhoods before even well designed and generously resourced local interventions can play an effective role in further improving the circumstances and future prospects of the many millions of people currently living in seriously disadvantaged communities in the UK.

Unless and until such changes occur, ecological practitioners and their employing agencies need to set themselves realistic goals that focus on facilitating achievable improvements in the quality of life of children and families living in disadvantaged circumstances. This is where the full range of individual, family and community social inclusion programmes, reviewed in this chapter, have an important role to play in the development of prevention and early intervention strategies designed to reduce youth offending and anti-social behaviour.

Chapter 10. **Developing Practitioner-Participant Evaluation of Ecological Practice**

This chapter will consider:
- The importance of developing practitioner-participant evaluation of ecological practice.
- Evaluation issues connected with inter-agency working.
- The key characteristics and challenges of evaluating ecological practice.
- Baselines, processes and outcomes.
- Learning and empowering through evaluation.
- Children's voices in evaluation.

Introduction

One of the key changes in child welfare work over recent years has been an increasing emphasis on measuring outcomes (Tunstill, 2003). Evaluation and monitoring, informed by appropriate theoretical concepts and frameworks (Katz and Pinkerton, 2003) now plays a central role in judging the effectiveness of interventions, and the direction of future policy, with its associated funding and practice implications.

In this chapter, we are not so much concerned with the external evaluations of large-scale community programmes that are now a common feature of national initiatives, such as the Sure Start and On Track programmes, since the methods and outcomes of these evaluations have already been well documented and reviewed, both earlier in this book and elsewhere (see, for example, Jack, 2005; Jack, 2006). Rather, in line with our aim of developing ecological practice, we will concentrate on evaluation which can be achieved by agencies and practitioners as a *routine* part of their work, and which can contribute to the development of everyday practice. We do, however, refer to some of the principles established through large-scale evaluations, and the issues that they highlight, when they are also relevant for smaller-scale agency and practitioner level evaluations.

As already indicated above, one of the major differences between these two approaches is that most evaluations of large-scale programmes are undertaken by independent, external researchers who have not been directly involved in planning or delivering the service that they are evaluating. This has obvious potential advantages, in that it minimises any possible bias and dependence on the outcomes of the evaluation, thereby increasing the validity and reliability of the data produced (Ghate, 2001). However, even within large-scale programmes, there are usually significant deficits in evaluation skills and resources which mean that these potential advantages can easily become compromised. For instance, the experience of one of the authors, as an 'independent' researcher in several large-scale evaluations, reflects that of others, who have found that the boundaries between 'independent' evaluation and more direct involvement in programme planning, delivery and review can quickly become blurred (Coote et al., 2004; France, 2001; Freeman et al., 2005). Not only are evaluators' interim reports often influential in the subsequent development and delivery of programmes, but evaluators themselves are also frequently drawn in to the roles of educator and consultant, in order to develop the capacity of programme staff.

In practice, these difficulties are not ones that often confront the smaller-scale projects and interventions that are the main focus of this chapter, because they are usually unable to provide the resources necessary to employ independent evaluators in the first place. Furthermore, it can be argued that the managers and practitioners directly responsible for such smaller-scale interventions are often in the best position to develop evaluation for ecological practice, alongside the participants, because of their detailed knowledge about the children and families involved, and the neighbourhood and community contexts in which the work is taking place.

Inter-agency working and the evaluation of ecological practice

The independence of evaluators, and, therefore, the validity and reliability of the data they produce, can be enhanced if agencies working together in the provision of children's services share staff resources in their evaluation work, with any limitations of the information produced being critically examined and honestly acknowledged. In fact, one of the principles of ecological practice is that agencies should link together whenever it is necessary to develop more holistic approaches to safeguarding children and promoting their welfare, which has obvious implications for the evaluation of that practice as well. On a very local scale, the following hypothetical example developed to aid working between two different types of agency (Barnardo's and a housing association), illustrates the possibility of developing joint outcomes and a joint language:

> There are serious tensions between the children and parents in two families living alongside one another on a local disadvantaged housing estate. The workers employed by the housing association responsible for the estate express their concerns about this situation primarily in terms of anti-social behaviour, and the effect that it may have on the security of the two families' tenancies, as well as other residents, and the reputation/stability of the overall estate. By way of contrast, the Barnardo's staff working on the estate frame their concerns primarily in terms of the effects on the well-being of the children involved in the two families, who they consider to be less likely to achieve and less likely to be safe, if the problems between the two families cannot be successfully resolved.
>
> Although the two agencies begin their dialogue by using different language and frameworks for expressing their concerns, it doesn't take long for the workers to realise that, in essence, they are talking about similar issues, pointing to the need for an inter-agency strategy (perhaps including some form of community family group conferencing), and a joint approach to the evaluation of its effectiveness.

Key characteristics and challenges in evaluating ecological practice

The kind of evaluation appropriate to the practice approach that we are advocating in this book has a number of characteristics. These include:

- Working alongside communities, to identify what are the important issues that impact on children's lives at a local level.
- Directly involving children and young people in evaluations.
- Recognising that children's lives are affected by the interactions between factors that are internal to the family (e.g. characteristics of relationships, ability of family to safeguard children, family's resources) and those that are external to the family (e.g. housing, schools, community resources), and incorporating this understanding into programmes of evaluation.
- Using evaluation to assist the processes involved in different elements of ecological practice.

These characteristics clearly present a number of challenges. Perhaps most significant among them is the development of methods that can successfully integrate understanding of the impact of interventions on the different areas of children's lives, at individual, family and community levels.

Evaluation of ecological practice needs to include a focus on all of these different elements. Just as ecological practice itself involves adopting a holistic approach, drawing on different ways of working with children, families and communities, so its evaluation must incorporate methods that can capture the impact of individual and groupwork with children and families, alongside that of broader community-focused initiatives, and the connections between these different levels of intervention. In addition, ecological practice, as we have demonstrated earlier in the book, is often multi-layered. Children and parents can be involved at different levels and stages of interventions, often simultaneously, with the child or parent frequently moving into and out of different 'service user' roles. For instance, a parent may be a resident, benefiting from general community-level initiatives designed to improve the overall social environment, whilst at the same time being involved in a targeted groupwork programme which addresses the links between community and family issues, perhaps because of particular concerns about their parenting capacity. In what follows, we outline some of the strategies that we (and others) have developed to address the main challenges involved in evaluating all of these inter-connected facets of ecological practice.

Developing a baseline: establishing the capacity of communities to meet the needs of children and families

The first task in evaluation for ecological practice is to develop reliable and up-to-date community profiles, which provide information about the capacity of different communities to meet the needs of children and parents, providing a baseline for assessing any subsequent developments and changes (Smalle and Henderson, 2003). Here, we can draw upon a growing literature that provides guidance about the collection and presentation of information, from a variety of sources, including the perceptions of local residents and other community members, both adults and children, as well as socio-economic and demographic data, and audits of local services (see, for instance, Green, 2000; Hawtin et al., 1994; Murtagh, 1999; Nelson and Baldwin, 2002; Skinner and Wilson, 2002). A number of ecologically-based initiatives have specifically set out to develop community baselines related to children's experiences, including the Communities That Care (CTC) programme, referred to in Chapter 9.

In an earlier publication (Jack and Gill, 2003) we provided a framework for analysing the impact of community factors on the safety and well-being of children and parents. This framework, which offered a way of assessing the strengths and pressures within local communities, along a number of different dimensions, was designed to help practitioners to develop ecological assessments. The six dimensions included in framework were:

1. Practical resources in the community.
2. Natural networks in the community.
3. Child and family safety in the community.
4. Community norms around children and childcare.
5. The individual family and child in the community.
6. The cumulative impact of the above factors.

In the full model, we identified the different components of each dimension. For instance, under 'natural networks in the community' (for parents) we included such strengths as 'reciprocal helping relationships in the community', 'long term residence of families', 'non-threatening relations with immediate neighbours', and 'a balanced community with a mixed age structure'. We acknowledged that the framework was not fully developed, and invited practitioners to add to it and modify it, in the light of their experience in the communities in which they were working. However, even in its present form, the framework offers a starting point for looking at the needs of children and families within their community contexts. It also provides a useful framework for developing a baseline of the circumstances of children and families who belong to particular communities, as well as for direct work with communities, helping to identify their particular strengths and pressures in relation to local children and their families, thereby facilitating one of the basic aims of ecological practice – to share information and ways of thinking with members of the communities concerned.

The above provide some examples of different approaches to the development of comprehensive community baselines and audits, that attempt to look at all of the important characteristics associated with children's well-being in their community contexts. However, we recognise that such comprehensive approaches may not always be practicable. It should, though, always be possible to select from children's experiences, within their community settings, particular issues on which to focus, and then to work to establish appropriate baselines. This was the approach taken by workers in developing a baseline for the development of ecological practice in the seaside town that was described in Chapter 6, which is briefly outlined below (Gill and Sharps, 2004):

The task in this piece of work was to obtain information about children's experience in a context that had three key characteristics: pockets of deprivation linked to small developments of social housing; high rates of transience into and out of the area; and a low child density.

No potential sampling frame of children in the area existed, and it was necessary to build up a baseline of children's experiences by talking to children, in their community settings. It was considered important to talk to children directly, rather than to go through formal agencies such as schools, because this allowed the workers to see the children and listen to their views in their natural settings, and to explore the social networks that existed in the community.

Using the 2001 Census, workers identified an area of the town where significant numbers of children were living and then 'door knocked', to identify families with children in the target age range (5–13 years). A strict protocol of signed permissions was used to talk to the parents we identified in this way and, once they had been interviewed, the workers asked if they would give their permission for the workers to talk to their children.

This way of working produced a valuable picture of the current problems in the area, and information about the kind of changes parents and children wanted to see in their community. It also produced information about the social networks and levels of social isolation in the area, and it enabled the workers to identify clusters of families with young children, which proved to be valuable in the subsequent work of the project.

In particular, this approach got at the children's own perspectives on what was happening in their community and some of the ways that local conditions impacted on their sense of well-being, as the following examples illustrate:

People bang our door. Once they pulled it open . . . They bang the windows . . . often in the day. It makes me feel horrible. (nine year-old boy).

I don't feel fairly safe by the road. Cause there's strangers and the strangers tripped mummy up by the legs. I'm scared at night when there's shadows. Every time I face each way I see monsters. I'm worried about that man. (six year-old girl, following recent sex attacks in the area)

The sequence of evaluation

Once appropriate community baselines have been established, that incorporate children's and parents' direct experiences, the task of evaluation is to identify changes in the well-being of children and their families, and to attempt to analyse the contribution of particular services and interventions to these changes. This means that the relevant characteristics and circumstances of service recipients must be identified, before the intervention to be evaluated has started. It also means that, wherever possible, a comparison group of similar people, perhaps in a neighbouring location, or held on a waiting list for a particular service, is constructed to enable the evaluation to establish what *additional* effects the intervention may have had (Ghate, 2001).

The assessment of change, leading to the achievement of outcomes, is now central to the way that agencies work in all settings which involve children and families. For these purposes, it is important to understand the basic sequence of analysis for evaluating the production of outcomes. Barr (2003: 140) defines this sequence as a four stage process, involving:

1. *Inputs* – the resources used to formulate or execute a policy, programme or project, including people, buildings, equipment, and funding.
2. *Processes* – the manner in which inputs are applied to achieve the intended outputs (how we go about it).
3. *Outputs* – the specific products of the process activities involved in a programme or project (what we actually do).
4. *Outcomes* – the effects of the outputs (the difference we make).

Looking at this in a little more detail, this means that practitioners and managers need to think clearly about the *inputs* that are necessary to achieve their aims, and the *processes* whereby these inputs impact on children's lives, as well as the *outputs*, in the sense of what workers actually do or set up, and the *outcomes*, in terms of the differences that are made to different groups of children, through what mechanisms, and in what contexts (Pawson and Tilley, 1997). Because social welfare interventions involve human understandings and interactions, and are subject to differing interpretations and perspectives, their evaluation needs to focus, in particular, on *process* issues, and to include the views of participants, practitioners and other stakeholders about *why* things have happened in the way that they have (Hughes and Traynor, 2000; Newburn, 2001).

A practical and apparently straightforward example can be used to illustrate the four-stage sequence outlined above, although it is important to realise that, underlying even 'straightforward' events, there are usually more complex social processes at work. Under the broad objective of *achieving economic well-being, enjoying* and *staying safe*, the market town project introduced in Chapter 6 was established with the aim of reducing the impact of poverty and disadvantage on children's lives. One of the summertime activities that was set up involved trips to the seaside for families who had very limited financial resources, and no access to transport to get them away from their housing estate on days out. Without these trips, many of the children would have done very little in the summer holidays except 'hanging about'.

The purpose of these outings was twofold. Firstly, they offered a chance for children and families to have a good time together. They targeted families who, in addition to having insufficient money and access to transport, also perhaps lacked the confidence or the motivation to organise enjoyable and stimulating experiences for their children. Secondly, they aimed to cut down the social isolation that parents living in family poverty in disadvantaged communities can experience by developing the networks of support, in the local neighbourhood, that have been shown to be so important for families in coping successfully with living in such circumstances (Jack and Gill, 2003). The following is a summary of the inputs, processes, outputs and outcomes involved in this piece of work.

Inputs: The provision of resources, including transport; staff and volunteer time to talk to vulnerable parents, encouraging them to participate and reassuring them that additional adult support would be available, to ensure that their children had a good time.

Processes: The staff and volunteer skills involved in supporting children and parents, including supporting vulnerable parents to organise, as well as take part in, these outings. For instance, addressing the particular difficulties of a parent experiencing agoraphobia in order to enable the parent and her child to participate.

Outputs: The successful completion of the trip, ensuring that nobody was excluded and that everybody came back safely.

Outcomes: The children said they had a great time ('enjoying' and 'staying safe') and the parents reported having developed confidence in their ability to provide enjoyable experiences for their children. The parents also said they had made new social contacts in their neighbourhood which will, potentially, carry over into other areas of their lives. Some also reported that they felt good about themselves, as parents, for having taken part in the outing for the benefit of their children.

Also through these kinds of social activities some parents develop confidence, contacts and information useful in accessing help for other difficulties in the family.

Evaluating outcomes for the individual child and family in the community

As we have stressed throughout this book, ecological practice is not only about working with communities to make general changes for the benefit of all children and families. It is, equally importantly, about individual children and families, working so that they can access the benefits and resources of their communities, and avoid the main dangers and difficulties that may exist there.

Whilst there are well established processes and methods for recording outcomes, both for individual children within their families and for groups of children in their communities, there is currently very little information on evaluations which focus on the links between these two sets of outcomes (Axford et al., 2005). This is a central challenge for the development of ecological practice and its evaluation. In this, the notion of community profiling or community auditing again is central – but this time in relation to the individual child. The starting point for ecological practice with individual children and families involves mapping the neighbourhood and community resources that exist, *from the particular child's and family's perspective*, to provide the basis for planning individual pieces of ecological practice. In working with a child from this perspective, it is essential to understand what formal and informal resources they perceive are available to them in their local area, including their views on any particular difficulties and dangers that they face.

Again, we can return to the model of the strengths and pressures of the community that was considered earlier, but this time as a tool for mapping the world of the individual child and family, and assessing any changes that take place over time. We can, for instance, focus on networks of support and networks of danger, gathering information about a number of issues, including the presence or absence of:

- Adults outside the family who will look after the child in an emergency.
- Wider family members (grandparents, uncles, aunts) who are involved with the child and concerned about their safety and development.
- Role models available to the child, as they move through the different stages of childhood and adolescence.
- Children, young people, or adults in the community who are either important sources of support, or present a potential threat to the child.

This is the sort of information that is often represented on eco-maps and, again, the framework of inputs, process, outputs and outcomes can be used to explore the way in which interventions may impact on children's and families' access to local resources.

In the following (hypothetical) example, based on a number of real cases, we look at the way in which a piece of individual work with a child may be viewed, using an outcomes framework that explicitly links what is happening within the family, with community factors and resources. The case described is of a 13 year-old girl who we call Maria, who is 'hanging around' with a group of local males aged 19 and 20 in a block of flats in another part of the estate on which she lives. There have been reports by neighbours, to the social services, that Maria is spending time in the flats and is not only in danger of sexual abuse, but also of becoming involved in drug taking.

Table 5 Evaluating outcomes for the individual child and family in the community

Aims	Inputs	Process	Output	Outcomes
Individual children staying safe in their local community.	(a) Work with Maria's parent and with Maria. (b) Work to identify alternative, pro-social and age appropriate activities in the neighbourhood. (c) Making practical and financial assistance available.	(a) Work with Maria and Maria's parent to map the social characteristics of the local area. (b) Work with Maria's parent to identify protective factors and resources in the neighbourhood (e.g. extended school activities, play activities) (c) Supporting Maria to get involved.	(a) Maria spends more time in the safer settings of organised activities. (b) Maria's parent is more aware of the dangers Maria is facing. (c) Maria's parent feels more supported in dealing with the challenges that Maria presents to her parenting capacity.	(a) Maria is safer (b) Some of the community's resources are brought into play for Maria's benefit. (c) Maria's parent feels her capacity to keep Maria safe is enhanced.

Learning from the process, contexts and individual workers

Within the practitioner-participant approaches to evaluation that we are discussing in this chapter, there is not only an emphasis on achieving outcomes, but also on learning from the *process* of the work. Barr accurately pinpoints the role of evaluating process when he says that 'It is not that attention to process becomes an end in itself (a not uncommon criticism of community practitioners) but that it is needed to enhance the probability of successful outcomes' (Barr, 2003: 144). In other words, although we might be able to establish that things have changed for a community, or for an individual child or family in a community, it is also crucial to understand *how* and *why* they have changed. This is where it is important to identify the theoretical basis for interventions and their evaluation, like the 'theory of change' (Weiss, 1995) which underpins a number of recent community programmes, and is based on detailed discussions with all stakeholders, that help to identify *how* services are expected to work and *why* they might be expected to make a difference to the service recipients involved (Axford et al., 2005). It is only through such understanding that learning is developed, and the lessons of one setting can become incorporated into interventions in other settings.

Evaluation of ecological practice must also take into account the local contexts of different settings, exploring the structure and dynamics of particular communities, and how these influence the children and families who belong to them. As Squires and Measor have noted 'If evaluation remains oblivious to contextual factors and fails to draw upon practical and experiential insights we will never discover why any given project 'works' or not, why it is successful for some and not others and which features of it might be translated elsewhere' (Squires and Measor, 2005: 27). This is the basis of the 'realistic evaluation' approach developed by Pawson and Tilley (1997), which represents the process in terms of particular outcomes being produced by different mechanisms acting in specific contexts.

Evaluations may also need to acknowledge the particular contribution made to interventions by key workers, who possess certain attributes and skills. It is not just the methods that individual workers adopt which may be important; it is also who they are, and what they bring to their contact with children, families and communities, which will need to be understood. In the search for lessons of general applicability in evaluation work, these individual characteristics are easily overlooked. This is a point also made by Squires and Measor, in the context of national evaluations of youth justice schemes:

> *Often where projects succeeded in engaging effectively with young people it could be almost entirely attributable to the commitment, experience, skill, personal charisma and hard work of the youth justice practitioners themselves. That is to say factors that the national evaluation did not acknowledge.*

(Squires and Measor, 2005: 24)

These personal attributes and ways of working are an important aspect of evaluation which are particularly relevant in small-scale, practitioner-participant evaluations of ecological practice.

Evaluation and empowerment

In the evaluation of ecological practice, as in the work itself, it is important to acknowledge issues of power, and to move towards sharing power with the people and communities directly involved in the work. The principle of empowerment through shared learning needs to be embedded, not only at the level of the community, but also at the level of the individual child and family. The importance of empowerment through learning, and the attendant capacity building, is captured in the evaluation of the *Communities That Care* programme:

> *Being involved in the process is also educational for participants, in that as people become more involved in the programme of assessment, they also become more*

knowledgeable about risk and protection. CTC offers a route into developing local capacity and knowledge about local levels of risk.

(Crow et al., 2004: 77)

In any piece of practice there are always a number of different stakeholders involved, each of whom is likely to have different priorities and viewpoints (Coote et al., 2004; Glass, 2001). Therefore, in setting up and carrying out evaluations, it is important to recognise that there may well be tensions between the perspectives of different stakeholders. Rather than being regarded as a sign of particular problems, recognition of the tensions that inevitably exist demonstrates that the process of evaluation is actively engaging with the perspectives of different stakeholders. In fact, the apparent absence of such tensions might be a more worrying sign in an evaluation, since it may point to the fact that one group is in a controlling position, perhaps through academic authority, professional control, or self-definition as sole representatives of what are actually heterogeneous communities.

Local communities must always be recognised as key stakeholders. This is a fundamental principle of mainstream community development, and it is important that the same principle is built into the evaluation of ecological practice. Communities are key stakeholders, not only in the sense that resources are being spent on their behalf, but also because they need to learn about the interventions so that the information produced can become part of what constitutes 'community knowledge', and contribute to building the capacity of local communities (Coote et al., 2004). The *Framework for Community Development*, developed by the Standing Conference for Community Development (2001: 13) states this principle succinctly:

Evaluation and dissemination are about learning from practice and sharing this with others. They are fundamental to community development because of the role they can play in empowering communities and contributing to change.

The logical extension of this emphasis on empowerment is that members of the communities involved should, themselves, be involved in generating information about their own community and in evaluating 'what works'. Such an approach has been strongly advocated by Beresford (2005) amongst others, who has noted the important constituents of community-led research which, he suggests, should:

• Originate from service users.
• Involve them in some or all of its different stages.
• Consider including service users as researchers.
• Aim to advance the rights, needs, and interest of service users.

This approach has also been strongly recommended for use with communities where there may be significant cultural differences between community members and those carrying out the work. For instance, Dyson and Harrison (1996) writing about Black community members as researchers, have stressed the benefits of working alongside members of Black communities, both in terms of carrying out research, and in terms of members of those communities influencing the content of research, taking responsibility for some of its organisational aspects and reflecting on the results.

To illustrate the benefits of involving communities directly in research and evaluation, we return to our example of working with Bristol's Somali community. Descriptions of this work have appeared earlier in this book, but here we concentrate on the methodological aspects of developing a collaborative community profile.

As previously discussed, Bristol has a quickly changing demography in relation to its Black and minority ethnic (BME) communities. By 2005 there were more Somali children in Bristol's schools than children from any other BME group in the city. Although information was available on the children's levels of achievement in school, and associated factors, there was only very limited information available on more general community factors relevant to the five *Every Child Matters* outcomes. What follows provides an outline of the collaborative approach taken to rectifying this important gap in local knowledge:

A partnership was developed between local Barnardo's staff and representatives of the main Somali supplementary school in the city (see Awad et al., 2006). The main aims of the partnership were: (a) to look at the situation of the children within an ecological framework; (b) to identify the links between individual outcomes, such as educational 'underachievement', and the structural position of Somali children in Bristol; and (c) to encourage the direct involvement of local Somali people in evaluation, generating information about what was happening in relation to children in their community.

Each partner brought different skills to the partnership. Barnardo's brought skills in community research, knowledge of local childcare resources and policy, and familiarity with current funding and project development opportunities. The Somali volunteers, active in their community, brought knowledge of the community, bilingual language skills, a knowledge of 'what works ' in their community, sensitivity and culturally-based skills in talking to families from their community, and strong networks with Somali families in the city.

Questions that the research would cover were developed through detailed discussions with representatives of the Somali community, who were also trained and paid to carry out the interviewing. The training included research practicalities, issues in talking with children and child protection. The interviewers then reflected on the results of the interviewing with the Barnardo's staff, and jointly produced the conclusions of the study.

This collaborative approach was seen as particularly beneficial for the following reasons:

- *Significant questions were formulated by members of the community, based on their immediate and personal knowledge of the community and its strengths and difficulties. The planning of the research could also incorporate cross cultural issues such as different understandings around play and children's mental health.*
- *The community researchers were able to make contacts, for the purposes of constructing a sample, where no immediate sampling frame was available.*
- *The levels of participation in the research were relatively high because it was respected members of the community who were making contact, rather than external interviewers.*
- *The interviewers could talk to people in their own language, and with an intimate knowledge of the cultural issues affecting their community.*

- *The community researchers were able to feedback to participants, explaining particular findings from the research, and putting those findings into context.*
  Apart from generating more reliable and culturally sensitive information, this approach also had the advantage of playing a part in empowering local Somali people to be fully involved in influencing the responses of statutory and voluntary organisations to the strengths and pressures found in their developing community.

  The results of the research were presented at a large community event attended by senior agency and political representatives and at least 70 Somali children and parents. Somali community members and Barnardo's staff jointly presented the findings of the research, and there was an emphasis on structural and poverty issues and the links between health, safety and enjoying and achieving.

Children's voices in evaluation

The main beneficiaries of the ecological practice initiatives discussed throughout this book are, of course, intended to be children and young people. It should, therefore, be self-evident that their voices are central to any evaluation process, with the product of the evaluation also being accessible to them.

As we have noted earlier in this volume, children's voices, perspectives, and priorities are likely to differ from those of their parents and other adults in some important respects. Agencies and practitioners must be constantly alert to what children are telling them, both in their words and actions. Within ecological practice and its evaluation, practitioners need to listen very carefully to children talking about their lives, especially in relation to the connections that they make, either explicitly or implicitly, between different aspects of their experiences and circumstances.

Another important aspect of listening to children, for evaluation purposes, will be to acknowledge that children's views of 'seriousness' may sometimes differ from those of adults (for example, see Butler and Williamson, 1994). In our practice, we are aware that children will often regard as 'serious' something that adults, with their administratively-determined agendas, will be more ready to discount, as illustrated by the following case example:

Evidence emerged from consultation work with children that they were anxious about crime and anti-social behaviour. When asked to respond to this, a local councillor for the area commented along the lines that the 'fear of crime only bears a limited relationship to the actual level of crime'. To the practitioners involved this seemed to be, in part, missing the point. The important point was what was impacting on children's lives and, in this, the fear of crime and anti-social behaviour was important in its own right, directly affecting their quality of life and sense of personal safety.

Practitioners and evaluators will, however, also need to engage in processes of interpretation and analysis, using their knowledge, experience and imagination, to draw appropriate conclusions from what they have heard or observed. Again, a case illustration, this time from the Bristol Somali work, helps to illustrate the point:

Children were asked to say whether there were 'good places to play' where they lived. One ten year old boy, who lived in a large block of flats, answered 'yes'. When he was asked where these good places were he said 'the corridor and the car park'. The interviewer involved in this was left wondering whether there was, in fact, something special about the corridor and the car park that made them good places to play, or whether the child's response was more an indication of a lack of alternative play areas in this neighbourhood.

Finally, it is important to recognise that there may be other ways of recording the views of children and young people than including them in written reports. Methods such as getting children to draw maps of their routes to favourite locations within their local areas, or to produce drawings and photographs of their favourite places for playing and socialising in the neighbourhood, or the use of video, drama and storytelling, may all be useful ways of capturing important aspects of children's social networks and local environments, and the impact of their life experiences and interventions on their self-image and well-being (Graham and Harris, 2005; Morrow, 2001).

Conclusion

This chapter has mapped out ways of developing forms of practitioner-participant evaluation suitable for ecological practice, which we have argued needs to be an integral part of that practice. Central to our thesis, here, is that the forms of evaluation developed and employed must be congruent with the content and values of ecological practice itself. This necessarily involves focusing evaluations on the links between the individual child and family, and the community context to which they belong, as well as involving the subjects of interventions directly in the evaluation of their own circumstances and the effectiveness of particular efforts to improve the quality of their lives.

Chapter 11. **Conclusion: The Challenges of Ecological Practice for Organisations and Practitioners**

This chapter will consider:
- The organisational context for ecological practice, focusing on children's centres and extended schools.
- The integration of community and individual approaches to safeguarding children and promoting their well-being.
- Some of the incremental steps involved in developing ecological practice.
- Taking steps to 'poverty-proof' children's services.

Introduction

In this concluding chapter we will consider the implications of developing ecological practice for child welfare organisations and practitioners. As noted in the introductory chapter, the UK has a long history of favouring individual over community-oriented approaches to child welfare. There have been few attempts to systematically integrate these perspectives into a form of practice, capable of addressing the needs of the whole child and family within the community contexts in which they are living, in the way that the ecological practice described in this book attempts to do.

However, major reforms to the way in which children's services are organised and delivered, under the *Every Child Matters* agenda in England and similar developments in the other countries of the UK, present an important opportunity to develop a more holistic approach to promoting children's welfare. Under these reforms, it is envisaged that there will be a much greater emphasis on prevention and early intervention than there has been in the past, with multi-agency services delivered increasingly via integrated children's centres and extended schools located either within or close to the communities that they are designed to serve. We therefore begin by examining some of the main implications of these new organisational arrangements for the development of ecological practice.

Organisational contexts for ecological practice: children's centres and extended schools

As we noted in the introductory chapter, structural changes of the magnitude involved in developing the sort of integrated, multi-agency children's services, that focus more of their resources on prevention and early intervention, carry with them major implications for changes in organisational and professional cultures (Mackian, 2002). This is an issue that has been acknowledged by the UK government, both in relation to their overall proposals for reform (HM Treasury, 2003), and in relation to the development of the main vehicles for the delivery of the new services envisaged – integrated children's centres and extended schools (DfES, 2006).

Building on the foundations of the earlier Sure Start programme, children's centres are multi-purpose, multi-agency centres designed to bring together childcare, early education, health, employment and support services for pre-school children and their families. The first 800 centres were located in the most disadvantaged areas of England, but it is planned that there will eventually be a centre in every community, with funding already earmarked for 3,500 centres by 2010. Extended schools are intended to provide continuing access to the services and resources that the government consider all families are likely to need as children progress through their school years. Through the development and wider use of school facilities, as well as partnerships arrangements with other agencies, it is proposed that, by 2010, every school in England should provide access to childcare, study and parenting support, sports, arts and ICT activities, and referral to wider services, often beyond the school day, to help to meet the needs of children and young people, their families and communities.

Unfortunately, the early evidence from the national evaluation of Sure Start has revealed just how difficult it is, in the present UK context of continuing high levels of inequality and social exclusion, to deliver services experienced as beneficial to the families who are in the greatest need of support. For example, in a study of the effects of the programme on parents and their children, between the ages of 9 and 36 months, the research team found that, despite funding amounting to some £3 billion, local Sure Start services had provided only 'small and limited' benefits for relatively less socially deprived parents and their children, and had actually produced *adverse effects* on the most disadvantaged children (Belsky et al., 2006: 1). The main explanation offered for this finding was that socially deprived families with greater personal resources may have been better able to take advantage of the services available in their local area, leaving the most deprived families with less access to services than if they had not lived in a Sure Start area. The researchers also suggested that more socially deprived parents, such as young mothers and lone parents, may have found the extra attention of service providers in Sure Start areas 'stressful and intrusive' (p. 4). What this evaluation evidence appears to indicate is that, particularly in such an unequal society as the UK, even universal children's services like Sure Start are liable to be taken over by more able families, and avoided by more disadvantaged families.

One of the other major challenges presented by these reforms has been highlighted in a study of the perceptions and attitudes of education professionals and their partners in other agencies in relation to the proposals for extended schooling (Cummings et al., 2006). Drawing on interviews with over 350 professionals, the researchers identified two broad understandings about the proposed reforms which, in the absence of clear and specific central government guidelines, are likely to significantly shape the way that they develop in practice. The first form of understanding was characterised as 'school-oriented' because it was based on the belief that the best way for schools to contribute to the overall well-being of children (and the communities they come from) is to maximise their individual level of educational attainment. This contrasted with the 'community-orientation', which viewed the role of schools in much broader terms, including addressing some of the problems and priorities of the local communities they serve.

Predictably enough, the education professionals interviewed were more likely to hold school-oriented understandings, whilst partner agency professionals tended to display more 'community-oriented' perspectives. Nevertheless, the researchers stress that these were only broad tendencies, with considerable individual diversity. Both positions appeared to be based largely on individual beliefs and assumptions, rather than generated by common professional backgrounds or rational debate. Perhaps the most worrying aspect of this study for the development of the sort of ecological approach to children's services that we have advocated in this book, was the 'widespread perception that local families and communities were mired in problems (that) originated in part from their own deficits' (Cummings et al., 2006: 9). This meant that some professionals were disinclined to consider local people as equal partners in shaping the development of the services to be provided by extended schools.

What both of these examples illustrate is the central importance of working in partnership with children, families and communities, a theme that we have highlighted throughout this book, and to which we will return later in this concluding chapter.

Integrating individual and community approaches to safeguarding children and promoting their well-being

As we have seen earlier in this volume, the integration of individual and community approaches to addressing some social problems affecting children and families in the UK, such as youth crime and community safety, is now well established. However, we have also discovered that it is not something that has been successfully developed in relation to other aspects of child and family welfare, including the safeguarding of children and support services for families of children in need, in any widespread or consistent fashion. For example, both the police and local authorities now routinely collate information about 'hot spots' of criminal and anti-social behaviour on which to base strategies that involve the deployment of resources for preventive action at the community level, as well as the development of early interventions targeted at individuals considered to be at high risk of offending. By way of contrast, the history of mainstream children's services in the UK indicates that the development and maintenance of partnership-based, community-focused prevention policies (and ecological practice) alongside more targeted and formal individual strategies, has been difficult to achieve (Parton, 1997; Wattam, 1999; Jack, 2000, 2004). The following example, described by Liz Davies (2004: 431) provides an illustration of the problems of establishing a community orientation to safeguarding children in one local authority in England:

> A community involvement strategy was begun in 1995, aimed at increasing the awareness of the general public about the role that they could play in safeguarding children. Various forms of publicity were used by local child welfare agencies to raise the community's awareness of child protection issues, and a training programme was developed for a wide range of statutory and voluntary organisations in the area which had some involvement in children's lives. These agencies were also assisted to develop their child protection procedures and protocols, with identified advisers in voluntary agencies and community groups acting as communication bridges between local residents and mainstream child welfare agencies. The network of 'protective adults' that was established through this initiative subsequently played an important role in managing the risks posed by known child sexual offenders in the area, as well as identifying vulnerable children. However, this community involvement strategy came

to an abrupt end in 2000, not because of any inherent failings, but due to a change in management which adopted a more 'top-down' approach to child protection issues, emphasising individual case management and target setting.

A similar pattern to that described above, in which the development of a partnership-based community-oriented preventive initiative, with positive influences on services to promote children's welfare, is followed by changes in personnel, funding, or organisational priorities that result in a return to prioritising individual case approaches, has been repeated across the UK ever since child abuse was 'rediscovered' during the 1960s.

Some of the reasons for this phenomenon were considered by Bill Jordan (1997) following his involvement in an initiative designed to increase partnership working with service users in the delivery of children's services in a local authority in South Wales. He found that the attempt to shift the balance in the authority's work away from individual child protection strategies towards partnership and family support approaches 'challenged assumptions about power, responsibility, ownership and the nature of the services themselves' (Jordan, 1997: 213). In particular, he found that many social workers and their managers were resistant to these changes because they had an investment in a style of work that he described as 'power-laden, formal and individualised'. They demonstrated considerable resistance and adopted strategies that effectively sabotaged a move towards approaches that involved greater sharing of power, based on more negotiated, informal styles of work (Jordan, 1997: 219) which are the basis of the model of ecological practice that we are promoting here.

Although these examples concern only two local authorities, they correspond with our own wider and more recent experience of working with social workers and other child welfare workers, from a broad range of different authorities and employing agencies across the Northern and South West regions of England. Typically, these practitioners work within organisations that operate according to a hierarchy of priorities and professional status largely based upon the extent to which activities are perceived to be related to what is commonly termed 'heavy-end child protection work'. Roughly translated this means fieldwork staff and their managers involved in formal child protection investigations, usually involving 'new cases', which are likely to result in applications for court orders. Other child welfare professionals, working in a wide range of different agencies and settings, tend to be excluded from this definition despite the fact that many of them are dealing with on-going child protection issues every day of their working lives. For example, one very experienced local authority social worker, employed in a team for children with disabilities, told us that she and her colleagues were not considered by other staff in their department to be dealing with child protection issues because they didn't have any open cases on the child protection register, thereby ignoring the extensive and long-term preventive and early intervention 'child protection' work that was the basis for this desirable outcome.

The majority of workers are therefore confronted by a culture that tends to underplay the real significance of their work and which operates on the basis of priorities determined by questionable assumptions about who is doing 'real' child welfare work. What is actually being afforded higher status, within this prevailing culture, is a formal and power-laden style of work with 'high-risk' individuals, undertaken by a minority of staff, reinforced by entrenched organisational priorities that are very resistant to change.

Steps along the road to developing ecological practice

The above examples highlight some of the difficulties likely to be involved in developing ecological practice within mainstream child welfare agencies. However, as we have shown elsewhere in this volume, there is now enough research and practice evidence to confirm the central importance of an ecological approach to work with children and families living in disadvantaged communities. Although it may be difficult to achieve, and may depend on small incremental steps being taken over a period of time, we believe that this approach is of fundamental importance to current government policies for safeguarding children and promoting their well-being. It is to some of the incremental steps involved in developing ecological practice within mainstream services that we now turn.

Developing appropriate services

One of the implications of ecological practice is that services need to be developed which link the internal and external worlds of children and young people, their families and carers.

Within present organisational and professional arrangements, there are many occasions when the issues and difficulties experienced by families, which have their origins in the *external* world of the child or family (such as inadequate housing, unemployment, lack of transport, or lack of other community resources) are redefined in terms of the internal dynamics of family life, to fit in with existing agency expertise and accustomed ways of working. For instance, a parent may approach a local agency experiencing high levels of stress as a result of her housing situation, having to cope with the demanding behaviour of her children in accommodation which is clearly inappropriate for family life. However, it is not uncommon for these problems to be reinterpreted in terms of personal, relationship or 'parenting' difficulties, with interventions planned accordingly. Alternatively, parents may approach an agency because of difficulties with their children in the school holidays, which may be redefined as difficulties in parent-child relationships rather than being the consequence of a lack of suitable activities for children from low income families during the long, stressful and often empty school holiday period.

However, not all of the difficulties experienced by children and families seeking the support of child welfare agencies will be related to the redefinition of external pressures as personal or family problems. Experienced practitioners will, for instance, be familiar with the family that wants to make a 'fresh start' in a new area, identifying their difficulties as being generated by factors in the local community, when many of their problems are actually internal to the family, with the consequence that a move of house will have little impact.

Locating the real sources of a family's difficulties will not, of course, immediately produce new resources, but it is a prerequisite of ecological practice that the combination of individual, family and community factors responsible for family difficulties need to be accurately assessed.

Following on from this, a key requirement for agencies is that the voices of children and families are at the centre of both policy and practice issues. Participation and listening to children, parents and communities is at the heart of ecological practice.

At times this will be challenging and uncomfortable for agencies, often requiring that they rethink their existing policies and approaches. For example, children will often have different views about what is important in some aspects of their lives to the views of professionals. Practitioners therefore need to listen carefully to what children, in particular, consider important. This also requires that a joint language is developed which is equally accessible to children, parents, other agencies and the communities involved. One of the real strengths of the five *Every Child Matters* outcomes is that they provide the basis for the development of such a joint language.

Developing interagency collaboration

Ecological practice is about seeing the links between different aspects of the lives of children and families. This not only involves individual agencies and workers listening and being responsive to what children and families are saying, but also that there is improved liaison and co-operation between all of them. For example, the group developed in Devon to provide integrated leisure activities for disabled and non-disabled teenagers, already discussed in Chapter 7, involved collaboration between many professionals from several different agencies in the local area. These included social workers and occupational therapists from the care management team, a community worker and a welfare officer from the education authority, a support worker from the youth offending team, a member of staff from the local volunteer bureau, and teachers and other staff from the school in which the group met. When so many organisations and professionals are involved, the development of codes of practice and inter-agency protocols, covering issues such as information sharing, confidentiality, and the extent of professional responsibility and control, will be of particular importance.

The successful development of ecological practice also requires clarity about the balance between influencing the decisions of other agencies, for the benefit of particular children and families, and adherence to equal opportunities policies which uphold the right of all children and families to equitable treatment. The following practice notes illustrate the tensions that can arise between these two positions:

An inter-agency meeting was set up in the community centre to bring agencies together to focus on their responses to children and families living in a relatively small geographical area characterised by high rates of child poverty. The meeting was attended by a number of agencies, including representatives from the housing and health visiting services.

A discussion developed between representatives of these two services about the potential benefits of formalising an arrangement whereby health visitors could recommend families for transfer on the basis of their perceptions of the stress the families were under and the extent to which this was related to their housing circumstances.

However, it was apparent to other members of the meeting that such an arrangement could potentially be against the interests of other families on the estate and to the equitable distribution of resources in the area.

Understanding community

As we discussed earlier in the book, community characteristics are the result of complex interactions between a wide range of factors and processes, including local economic circumstances, policy decisions about the structure of the built environment (including facilities for children and families), and the allocation of publicly controlled housing. The structure and composition of the local community will also, in part, be the result of the links with the wider area and region in which it is located, with access to work and other opportunities also of crucial importance. In addition, the historical development of local cultures and the way in which these relate to the wider culture will be key factors, and the eventual form of 'community' will also be the result of what people come to believe about the places where they live and the 'kind of people' who live there.

These broad forms of analysis of the structure of local communities may be beyond the scope of many individual agencies and workers. However, for the development of ecological practice, with its emphasis on linking up family and community level factors, it is important that agencies and workers develop an understanding of the communities in which they work. Typically agencies and workers are more adept and practised at understanding the internal dynamics of family life than they are at recording and focusing on what is happening within different communities. Many organisations use forms and frameworks for assessing things like the quality of parenting and other family relationships, but far fewer are available to assist workers in understanding important aspects of the communities in which children and families are living, which often play such a crucial part in determining the quality of their lives. This was abundantly clear when the *Framework for the Assessment of Children in Need and their Families* was produced (DoH, 2000) with none of the resources provided to accompany the framework helping practitioners to assess the impact on children's lives of factors such as wider family relationships, community resources, social integration, income, employment and housing.

At the very least, agencies and workers need to understand their local communities in terms of some of the main strengths and pressures that they present to children and families. Building on our earlier analysis of these strengths and pressures (Jack and Gill, 2003) we consider that agencies and workers need to develop understanding of the following types of strengths for children and parents in the local community:

- Community resources that benefit children and parents, including those provided via children's centres and extended schools.
- Opportunities for network development in the local community.
- Natural support networks in the community.
- Positive community norms about children's development and well-being.

Equally, child welfare organisations and practitioners need to be aware of the pressures and dangers that parents and children may face in the local community. These can include:

- A culture of people 'keeping themselves to themselves'.
- High rates of mobility into and out of the neighbourhood, producing an unstable social environment.
- Harassment (including racial harassment) from neighbours.
- Potentially dangerous people living in the community.
- Physical dangers in the community.
- Negative perceptions of minority groups of children and parents in the community.

Local and up-to-date perspectives are needed about all of these potential sources of community strengths and pressures. We know from practice experience how neighbourhoods can change markedly in their social resources or dangers within the space of a few hundred metres or within a period of a few weeks or months. Equally, we know from research into children's lives in their communities just how small in scale the significant local environment for children can be.

Understanding the parent and child in the context of their community

It is important to emphasise, once again, that ecological practice involves not only understanding the impact of communities on children, but also how individual children and families respond to the particular strengths and pressures of their local communities. Agencies and workers need to build this into their work, not only in terms of assessing children but also in terms of planning interventions.

Again, developing our earlier analysis of the strengths and pressures that exist within communities, we contend that ecological practice involves working with parents to help them to develop:

- Personal resources and knowledge which enable them to access available facilities.
- Personal resources to develop and maintain supportive networks.
- Personal resources, knowledge and networks which assist their children to access available resources.

It also involves working with children to help them to develop:

- Confidence in using available facilities.
- Access to positive and safe role models in the community.
- Confidence and ability to access local networks involving other children.

Equally, ecological practice involves supporting parents and children to avoid some of the problematic aspects of their community settings. For parents this may involve helping them to avoid alienating potential sources of support and to avoid networks that make demands upon them, without offering any reciprocal support. For children, it will involve helping them to avoid networks that produce difficulties rather than strengths.

All of the above involves better education and training of practitioners, to help them develop skills in ecological practice, including advocacy work on behalf of disadvantaged groups in the community and capacity building work with community groups, networks and individuals. It also involves developing training resources for work with children and parents that enable them to benefit from the strengths of their communities through informal support networks, and the development of improved knowledge and skills.

Understanding the impact of organisational policies on communities

A related aspect of the challenge facing agencies in developing ecological practice is that they need to be aware of the impact that they, themselves, can have on the communities they serve and hence on the welfare of the children and families living there. All decisions about the location of community facilities, and where different people live, through the allocation of publicly controlled housing, will have an impact on the lives of children and families. For instance, focusing on the impact of large scale planning decisions on the lives of children, Freeman and colleagues (1999: 117) have talked about the increasing concentration of facilities located away from where children live, noting that:

Decentralisation processes that particularly affect children include the trend towards closing local cinemas and swimming pools while opening large cinema and leisure complexes at motorway junctions or on peripheral retail sites which can only be reached by car.

A major and obvious example of the way that organisational and political decisions can influence the structure of communities is the way in which many of the large estates, characteristic of the second half of the twentieth century, were developed. The enthusiasm and optimism of their designers were, in many cases, misplaced, resulting in some very unbalanced communities being created. The large peripheral estate from which some of the practice examples used earlier in the book are drawn exemplifies this issue. It was developed in the 1950s and 1960s, and became a key housing resource for allocation to the young families that were being moved out of deteriorating and apparently unviable inner-city accommodation. But the consequence of this was that, not only were there a large number of families brought together in a geographical location lacking adequate community facilities, but also a community was created which had a very uneven age structure. Because the estate was used for the families in most urgent need of new housing, it became overwhelmingly a place where young, sometimes large families were placed. It is little surprise, then, that by the mid-1970s, when the demographic 'bulge' of young children was moving through to their teenage years, the area became synonymous with juvenile delinquency and vandalism.

The full implications of these large-scale changes in communities, in part driven by policies such as those outlined above, and in part by fluctuating economic fortunes and employment opportunities, are beyond the scope of the present book. Our purpose in referring to them, however, is to highlight the fact that public agencies not only respond to community 'needs', they also often play a critical role in creating community characteristics.

In some situations the impact of the built environment and policy decisions on the development of communities will be recognised and attempts will be made to influence their future development. For instance, one of the contributory factors in the 2001 race disturbances in Oldham was seen to be housing segregation between Asian and white communities. Part of the resulting local strategy to tackle this problem therefore involved encouraging people to move into homes across the racial divide, redesigning and changing the roads and parks that separated the two communities, and developing 'shared spaces' where members of both communities could mix.

In other situations, the policy decisions of certain agencies will have an impact on the actions and effectiveness of other agencies. A clear example of this is the interaction between housing policy and educational provision illustrated in research by Clark and colleagues, which found that the policies pursued by social landlords may have significant impacts on local schools. Housing families on the basis of need can mean that more children with difficulties enter local schools which, in turn, can have a significant impact on the nature of the school and the tasks faced by parents (Clark et al., 1999).

The key point from all of this is that agency decisions and actions inevitably have some impact on their local communities and, therefore, on the experiences of children and families, and it is an important aspect of ecological practice that this should be recognised. Planning for the welfare of children and parents means not only responding to needs as they are presented to agencies, but also anticipating the consequences of policy decisions on the structure of communities and neighbourhoods, and hence on the welfare of children.

Engagement with the local community

As we have stressed at different stages of this book, although there is much talk about the desirability of building the capacity of local communities, there is often little information about how this should happen, and few resources to put it into practice. Different practitioners who we have talked to in the course of writing this book have identified that resources tend to be put into working with existing groups which are seen, in one way or another, to represent the views of the community. Typically, much less time is put into establishing or working with less visible or well organised groups of people in local communities so that, in the course of time, they may become actively involved in influencing agencies for the benefit of their community.

This initial capacity building in local communities has traditionally been seen as one of the main activities of community development workers but, in our experience, it now tends to be given less prominence. One of the reasons may be that this initial capacity building can be resource intensive, and it can take longer than the short time-scales of many regeneration and community engagement initiatives. However, for the welfare of children, this initial basic capacity building with less visible groups of children and parents may be just as important as working with larger, more powerful community organisations. The child's world is highly localised and the support networks of children and families living in disadvantaged communities often have to be built up at a very immediate and small-scale level.

As we noted in Chapter 8, it is also important to stress that the potential of developing local community capacity can only be fully realised if agencies are prepared to make changes as well. Agencies need to build their own capacity to engage with their local communities. This is a point well made by Henderson and Thomas (2002: 6): 'Usually it has been applied to the less powerful side of any partnership. Until recently, there have been few examples of building up the capacity of the powerful to listen to the weak'.

In broad terms, this capacity to respond on the part of agencies will involve:

- Being open and listening to what local communities are saying.
- Being able to 'let go' of some of their professional power.
- Putting resources into local capacity building.
- Developing increased understanding of the complexity of whether local groups 'represent' the community or only sectional interests within it.
- Facilitating the involvement of communities and community representatives in different ways by, for instance, scheduling meetings to fit in with the routines of local people, and providing adequate childcare cover and expenses so parents can attend community meetings.

Although this list is relatively short, in itself, nonetheless it is likely to present both organisations and practitioners with many challenges. As we have previously noted, the impact of being asked to share some elements of power with local communities should not be underestimated, both in terms of established ways of working and in terms of workers' sense of professional competence. Honest and reflective practitioners who, in theory at least, support the empowerment of communities, might also admit to being reluctant or unwilling to genuinely move towards sharing power when it relates to the welfare of children, either because of genuine doubts about children's safety, or because of (often unspoken) fears about the perceived challenge that this way of working presents to their accustomed professional authority and discretion (Jordan, 1997).

The challenge of the structural context for ecological practice in the UK: engaging with child poverty and inequality

We started this book with an analysis of child poverty and inequality in the UK, linking this with area disadvantage and the development of increasingly polarised communities. An underlying challenge facing agencies attempting to develop ecological practice in their local communities is therefore to develop a locally-based awareness of the impact of child poverty and inequality on the children and families with whom they come into contact. This is particularly important at the present time when, although there are a plethora of new initiatives for the benefit of children, they are taking place against a backdrop of persistently high rates of child poverty and other forms of inequality affecting families.

The worker who, for instance, sees the connection between the economic circumstances and housing conditions that a family has to endure and at least some of the tensions that are experienced within the family, cannot justifiably avoid considering issues of social inequality and housing poverty. Similarly, the practitioner who recognises the connection between the fear and anxiety experienced by a lone parent as a result of mounting debts and the quality of childcare that they are able to provide, is inexorably drawn to considering issues of income maintenance. And the worker who sees the connection between the lack of safe supervised play activities in a neighbourhood and the bullying and fear that children experience in their communities, is unavoidably drawn to considering issues of the resource available to those communities.

We fully recognise that such awareness can produce feelings of impotence on the part of practitioners when faced, day in and day out, with the personal pressures and consequences of child poverty (Dowling, 1999). We also recognise that, although recent Labour governments have emphasised the importance of ending child poverty, it is unclear how many of the key child welfare policies and strategies that agencies are currently implementing are likely to contribute to achieving this aim. Child welfare agencies may sign up to national anti-poverty agendas but, at a local level, they often adopt priorities that do not necessarily improve the resources to which poor people have access (Munro, 2004).

We can offer nothing that approaches a comprehensive solution for practitioners in this respect. We can, however, make some limited suggestions to assist agencies and practitioners who recognise that much of their work takes place in the context of high rates of child poverty and inequality:

- *Poverty Challenge One.* Working with parents and children within their own communities and developing ecological practice involves being open to children and parents in a different way, being willing to hear the connections they make about the different pressures on their lives. Often these pressures will have their origins in inequality and disadvantage and the social policies being implemented by the government of the day.
- *Poverty Challenge Two.* Related to 'poverty challenge one' is the responsibility of agencies and practitioners to engage in a discourse with politicians, funders, other agencies and the media about issues of child poverty and inequality, and their impact on the children and families with whom they are working. In spite of the emphasis in current government policies on reducing poverty and social exclusion, often little of this gets transferred into the discourse of agencies and workers engaging with very disadvantaged children and families on a daily basis. In child poverty campaigning, nationally, it is recognised that two broad approaches are necessary. One is the technical campaigning around detailed changes to policies and benefit rates that will assist in the eradication of child poverty. The other is to raise awareness of the extent and impact of child poverty. In a divided and segregated world, in which the majority of the population may not come into contact with people living in poverty, and are fed a daily media diet of profligacy and benefit fraud, it is crucial that child welfare agencies and practitioners work to redress the balance by describing the very real impact of structurally determined poverty on the children and families with whom they are working.
- *Poverty Challenge Three.* Agencies and practitioners working from an ecological perspective with children and families living in poverty should all, without exception, have a basic awareness of benefit entitlement and the potential resources available through the tax and benefit systems, as well as through more local provision. This does not mean that all practitioners should be experts, or that all agencies should offer detailed advice on income support issues, but it does mean that they should be aware of the basic entitlements, enabling them to identify when more specialist help is required.
- *Poverty Challenge Four.* Throughout this book we have stressed that poverty and disadvantage have an immediate and tangible impact on children's everyday lives, as well as their future life chances. It therefore follows that practitioners and agencies should strive to put in place resources that help to counteract the effects of poverty, even if only in small ways, in the 'here and now', as well as looking to the longer-term. For instance, developing more of a community perspective can alert practitioners to the benefits for children 'enjoying' their life of developing their range of community activities and social networks.
- *Poverty Challenge Five.* Agencies and practitioners who work from an ecological perspective with families where children are living in poverty should also, in a wider sense, attempt to 'poverty proof' their services. As in other areas of the development of ecological practice, the five *Every Child Matters* outcomes offer an effective way of working towards this objective. In terms of an anti-poverty perspective we might, for instance, look at the responsibilities of agencies and workers in the following way (Table 6).

Table 6 Poverty proofing services

Staying healthy	What economic factors impact on the children we work with that mean they cannot stay healthy? What local actions are we able to take to address these?
Staying safe	What economic factors impact on the children we work with that mean they cannot stay safe? What local actions are we able to take that address these?
Enjoying and achieving	What economic factors impact on the children we work with that mean they cannot enjoy and achieve? What local actions are we able to take that address these?
Making a positive contribution	What economic factors impact on the children we work with that mean they cannot make a positive contribution? What local actions are we able to take to address these?
Achieving economic wellbeing	What local actions can we take that increase the likelihood of the children we work with achieving economic well-being?

If the ecological approach, in part, focuses on the impact of community resources on the lives of individual children, it follows that its adoption requires workers to confront the adequacy of that provision. Ultimately, ecological practice may therefore require workers to be involved in challenging resource allocations. It may require workers to be more 'political' as well as 'professional' in their approach to the welfare of children. These tensions, and the fact that child welfare practice inevitably involves operating in a contested arena, are not new in child and family welfare over recent decades. They have elements of the tensions that existed between individual caseworkers and community workers apparent in the 1970s, as well as those around the development of 'community social work' in the early 1980s, and of the more recent tensions between 'control' and 'support' approaches to work with children and families.

Conclusions

We started this final chapter by stating that, too often, agencies define themselves as being 'community-based', but with little attempt made to think clearly about the community contexts in which they are operating. We therefore finish by identifying what we regard as being some of the prerequisites for any 'community-based' agency wishing to develop ecological practice with children and families.

First of all, agencies need to be accessible to the local communities that they are set up to serve. Accessibility has a number of aspects, including physical accessibility for disabled children and their parents, accessibility for people living in poverty who may not have their own transport, and accessibility in terms of how the agency is perceived by the community. Accessibility also requires that agencies are highly visible, locally. It is little use if an agency acknowledges the importance of working with the community but no one in the community knows what it does. Organisations and practitioners who wish to develop ecological practice also need to support parents and children to access the beneficial aspects of the communities in which they live, and to cope with their main dangers and pressures.

Ecological practice also requires that agencies make a real effort to understand and record, in a systematic way, what is happening in their local communities. At the very least, agencies should monitor demographic, cultural and network patterns in their local communities on a regular basis, as well as making use of the existing local and national indices of deprivation and the emerging data about children's well being discussed in the first chapter. Beyond this, child welfare agencies need to understand and attempt to engage with the specific issues of child poverty and other forms of inequality and disadvantage that families are experiencing, being alive and sensitive to local conditions which are especially important to children, such as opportunities for contact with positive role models within disadvantaged communities.

However, perhaps most fundamental of all, organisations and workers need to ensure that they are genuinely open to community involvement in their work, developing decision-making processes and patterns of service delivery that are directly influenced by the communities that they have been established and are funded to serve.

References

Abel-Smith, B. and Townsend, P. (1965) *The Poor and The Poorest*, Occasional Papers in Social Administration 17. London: Bell.

Allen, C. (2003) Why Living in a Deprived Area is a (Hidden) Disability Issue: Some Housing Policy and Practice Implications. *Journal of Integrated Care*, 11(1): 28–32.

Anderson, B. et al. (2001) *Risk and Protective Factors Associated With Youth Crime and Effective Interventions to Prevent It.* London: Youth Justice Board.

Armstrong, D. et al. (2005) *Children, Risk and Crime: The on Track Youth Lifestyles Surveys.* Home Office Research Study 278. London: Home Office.

Atkar, S. et al. (2002) Promoting Effective Family Support and Child Protection for Asian Children. In Baldwin, N. (Ed.) *Protecting Children. Promoting Their Rights.* London: Whiting Birch.

Atkinson, A.B. (2000) Distribution of Income and Wealth. In Halsey, A.H. and Webb, J. (Eds.) *Twentieth-Century British Social Trends.* Basingstoke: Macmillan.

Awad, A., Gill, O., Thomas, R., Hussein, Y., Noor, K. and Wiltshire, P. (2006) *Somali Children in Bristol: Achieving The Five Outcomes From Every Child Matters.* Bristol: Barnardo's Amana Partnership.

Axford, N. et al. (2005) Evaluating Children's Services: Recent Conceptual and Methodological Developments. *British Journal of Social Work*, 35: 73–88.

Baldwin, J. and Bottoms, A.E. (1976) *The Urban Criminal.* London: Tavistock.

Baldwin, N. and Carruthers, L. (1998) *Developing Neighbourhood Support and Child Protection Strategies.* Aldershot: Ashgate.

Banks, S. et al. (Eds.) (2003) *Managing Community Practice: Principles, Policies and Programmes.* Bristol: The Policy Press.

Bannister, J. and Dillane, J. (2005) *Communities That Care: an Evaluation of The Scottish Pilot Programme.* Research Findings No. 79. Edinburgh: Scottish Executive Social Research.

Barnardo's (2005) *Carrickfergus Parent and Child Project. Interim Evaluation Report: September 2003–June 2005.* Belfast: Barnardo's.

Barnes, J. (2004) *Place and Parenting: A Study of Four Communities.* London: Institute for The Study of Children, Families and Social Issues, Birkbeck, University of London.

Barr, A. (2003) Participative Planning and Evaluation Skills. In Banks, S. et al. (Eds.) *Managing Community Practice; Principles, Policies and Programmes.* Bristol: The Policy Press.

Bartley, M. (2006) *Capability and Resilience: Beating The Odds.* London: UCL Department of Epidemiology and Public Health.

Becker, S. (1997) *Responding to Poverty. The Politics of Cash and Care.* Harlow: Addison Wesley Longman Ltd.

Begg, I., Lever, W. and Boddy, M. (2002) *Urban Competitiveness: Policies for Dynamic Cities.* Bristol: The Policy Press.

Beinart, S. et al. (2002) *Youth at Risk? A National Survey of Risk Factors and Problem Behaviour Among Young People in England, Scotland and Wales.* London: Communities That Care.

Belsky, J. (1993) Etiology of Child Maltreatment: A Developmental Ecological Analysis. *Psychological Bulletin*, 114: 3, 413–34.

Belsky, J. et al. (2006) Effects of Sure Start Local Programmes on Children and Families: Early Findings From A Quasi-Experimental, Cross-Sectional Study. *British Medical Journal*, 332: 1476–81.

Ben-Arieh, A. and Goerge, R.M. (2006) *Indicators of Children's Well-Being. Understanding Their Role, Usage and Policy Influences.* (www.Springer.Com).

Beresford, B. et al. (1996) *What Works in Services for Families with a Disabled Child?* Basingstoke: Barnardo's.

Beresford, P. (2005) Service User Involvement in Evaluation and Research; Issues, Dilemmas and Destinations. In Taylor, D. and Balloch, S. (Eds) *The Politics of Evaluation.* Bristol: The Policy Press.

Berthoud, R. (2002) Poverty and Prosperity Among Britain's Ethnic Minorities, *Benefits 33*, 10 (1): 3–8.

Blanden, J., Gregg, P. and Machin, S. (2005) *Intergenerational Mobility in Europe and N. America.* London: Centre for Economic Performance, London School of Economics.

Bottoms, A.E. and Wiles, P. (1997) Environmental Criminology. In Maguire, M., Morgan, R. and Reiner, R. (Eds.) *The Oxford Handbook of Criminology.* 2nd edn. Oxford: Clarendon Press.

Bottoms, A.E., Claytor, A. and Wiles, P. (1992) Housing Markets and Residential Community Crime Careers: A Case Study From Sheffield. In Evans, D.J., Fyfe, N.R. and Herbert, D.T. (Eds.) *Crime, Policing and Place: Essays in Environmental Criminology.* London: Routledge.

Bradshaw, J. (2002) Child Poverty and Child Outcomes. *Children in Society*, 16: 131–40.

Bradshaw, J. (2005) Child Poverty in Larger Families. In Preston, G. (Ed.) *At Greatest Risk; The Children Most Likely to Be Poor.* London: Child Poverty Action Group.

Bradshaw, J., Hoelscher, P. and Richardson, D. (2006) An Index of Child Well-Being in The European Union. *Social Indicators Research*, 80: 1, 133–77.

Brickell, P. (2000) *People Before Structures: Engaging Communities Effectively in Regeneration.* Demos, London.

Bronfenbrenner, U. (1979) *The Ecology of Human Development.* Cambridge: Harvard University Press.

Bronfenbrenner, U. and Morris, P. (1998) The Ecology of Developmental Processes. In Damon, W. and Lerner, R. (Eds.) *Handbook of Child Psychology. Volume 1: Theoretical Methods of Human Development.* 5th edn. New York: Wiley.

Brooks-Gunn, J. et al. (1993) Do Neighborhoods Influence Child and Adolescent Development? *American Journal of Sociology*, 2: 353–95.

Burns, D., Williams, C. and Windebank, J. (2004) *Community Self Help.* Basingstoke: Macmillan.

Burrows, R. (1997) *Contemporary Patterns of Residential Mobility in Relation to Social Housing in England.* York: University of York, Centre for Housing Policy.

Burrows, R., Ellison, N. and Woods, B. (2005) *Neighbourhoods on the Net: The Nature and Impact of Internet-Based Neighbourhood Information Systems.* Bristol: The Policy Press.

Butler, I. and Williamson, H. (1994) *Children Speak: Children, Trauma and Social Work.* Harlow: Longman.

Camina, M. (2004) *Understanding and Engaging Deprived Communities*. London: Home Office.

Catalano, R. and Hawkins, J. D. (1996) The Social Development Model: A Theory of Antisocial Behaviour. In Hawkins, J.D. (Ed.) *Delinquency and Crime*. Cambridge: Cambridge University Press.

Cebello, R. and McLoyd, V.C. (2002) Social Support and Parenting in Poor, Dangerous Neighborhoods. *Child Development*, 73: 1310–21.

Chanan, G., West, A. et al. (1999) *Regeneration and Sustainable Communities*. London: CDF Publications.

Cicchetti, D. and Lynch, M. (1993) Towards an Ecological/Transactional Model of Community Violence and Child Maltreatment. Consequences for Children's Development. *Psychiatry*, 56: 96–118.

Clark, B. and Davis, A. (1997) When Money's Too Tight to Mention. *Professional Social Work*, March: 12–13.

Clark, J., Dyson, A. and Millward, A. (1999) *Housing and Schooling: A Case Study in Joined-Up Problems*. York: Joseph Rowntree Foundation.

Cole, I. et al. (1996) *Creating Communities or Welfare Housing?* Coventry: Chartered Institute of Housing.

Combe, V. (2002) *Up for It: Getting Young People Involved in Local Government.* Leicester: NYA.

Commission of The European Communities (1994) *The Demographic Situation of The European Union*, Document No. COM (94) 595. Luxemburg: Office for Official Publications of The European Communities.

Coote, A., Allen, J. and Woodhead, D. (2004) *Finding Out What Works: Building Knowledge About Complex Community-Based Initiatives*. London: The King's Fund.

Cote, S. and Healy, T. (2001) *The Well-Being of Nations. The Role of Human and Social Capital.* Paris: Organisation for Economic Co-Operation and Development.

Coulthard, M., Walker, A. and Morgan, A. (2002) *People's Perceptions of Their Neighbourhood and Community Involvement*. London: The Stationery Office.

Coulton, C. et al. (1995) Community Level Factors and Child Maltreatment Rates. *Child Development*, 66, 1262–76.

Coulton, C., Korbin, J.E. and Su, M. (1999) Neighborhoods and Child Maltreatment. A Multi-Level Analysis. *Child Abuse and Neglect*, 23: 1019–40.

Craig, G. (2005) Poverty Among Black and Minority Ethnic Children. In Preston, G. (Ed.) *At Greatest Risk: The Children Most Likely to Be Poor*. London: Child Poverty Action Group.

CRG (2003) *An Evaluation of Summer Plus: A Cross-Departmental Approach to Preventing Youth Crime*. DfES Brief No. 392. London: DfES.

CRG (2006) *Positive Activities for Young People: National Evaluation*. Cardiff: CRG Research Limited.

Crow, I. et al. (2004) *Does Communities That Care Work? An Evaluation of a Community-Based Risk Prevention Programme in Three Neighbourhoods*. York: Joseph Rowntree Foundation.

Cummings, C., Todd, L. and Dyson, A. (2006) Towards Extended Schools? How Education and Other Professionals Understand Community-oriented Schooling. *Children and Society* (Online 28 July).

Cummins, S. et al. (2005) Neighbourhood Environment and its Association with Self-Rated Health: Evidence From Scotland and England. *Journal of Epidemiological Community Health*, 59: 207–13.

Davies, L. (2004) The Difference Between Child Abuse and Child Protection Could Be You: Creating a Community Network of Protective Adults. *Child Abuse Review*, 13: 426–32.

Davis, J. and Ridge T. (1997) *Same Scenery, Different Lifestyles: Rural Children on a Low Income*. London: The Children's Society.

Department for Work and Pensions (2004) *Opportunity for All*. (www.Dwp.Gov.Uk/Ofa/Reports/2004/Summary).

Department for Work and Pensions (2005) *Households Below Average Income 2004*. (www.Dwp.Gov.Uk/Asd/Hbai/Hbai2004/Contents.Asp).

DfEE (2001) *Children's Fund: Part One Guidance*. London: DfEE.

DfES (2001) *Transforming Youth Work: Resourcing Excellent Youth Services*. London: DfES.

DfES (2005a) *Common Core of Skills and Knowledge for The Children's Workforce*. London: DfES.

DfES (2005b) *Youth Matters*. London: DfES.

DfES (2006) *The Governance and Management of Extended Schools and Sure Start Children's Centres*. London: DfES.

DfES /DoH/Home Office (2003) *Keeping Children Safe: The Government's Response to The Victoria Climbié Report and The Joint Chief Inspector's Report Safeguarding Children*. London: HMSO.

DoH (2000) *Framework for The Assessment of Children in Need and Their Families*. London: The Stationery Office.

DoH (2002) *Safeguarding Children: A Summary of the Joint Chief Inspectors Report on Arrangements to Safeguard Children*. London: DH Publications.

Dorling, D. and Rees, P. (2004) A Nation Dividing? Some Interpretations of the Question. *Environment and Planning*, 36: 369–73.

Dowling, M. (1999) *Social Work and Poverty: Attitudes and Actions*. Aldershot: Ashgate.

Doy, E., Gilbert, D. and Aitland, L. (2001) *Empowering Young People in Rural Suffolk: an Evaluation Report for The Home Office*. London: Home Office.

Dyson, S. and Harrison, M. (1996) Black Community Members as Researchers. Working With Community Groups in the Research Process. *Groupwork*, 9: 2, 203–20.

Eastham, D. (1990) Plan it or Suck it and See. In Darvill, G. and Smale, G. (Eds.) *Partners in Empowerment: Networks of Innovations in Social Work*. London: NISW.

Ellen, I. and Turner, M. (1997) Does Neighbourhood Matter? Assessing Recent Evidence. *Housing Policy Debate*, 8, 833–66.

European Union (2001) *Draft Report on Social Exclusion*. European Commission: British.

Evans, M. and Scarborough, J. (2006) *Can Current Policy End Child Poverty in Britain in 2020?* York: Joseph Rowntree Foundation.

Farmer, C. (2005) *2003 Home Office Citizenship Survey: Top-Level Findings from the Children's and Young People's Survey*. London: Office for National Statistics.

Farnell, R. et al. *Faith in Urban Regeneration? Engaging Faith Communities in Urban Regeneration*. Bristol: Policy Press.

Farrington, D. (1996) *Understanding and Preventing Youth Crime*. York: Joseph Rowntree Foundation.

Feinstein, L., Bynner, J. and Duckworth, K. (2005) *Leisure Contexts in Adolescence and Their Effects on Adult Outcomes*. London: Centre for Research on The Wider Benefits of Learning, Institute of Education.

Fitzpatrick, S. (2004) *Poverty of Place*. Keynote Address to The Joseph Rowntree Foundation Centenary Conference 'Poverty and Place: Policies for Tomorrow', University of York.

France, A. (2001) Involving Communities in the Evaluation of Programmes with 'At Risk' Children and Young People. *Children and Society*, 15, 39–45.

France, A. and Crow, I. (2001) *Communities That Care – The Story So Far: an Interim Evaluation of Communities That Care*. York: Joseph Rowntree Foundation.

France, A. and Utting, D. (2005) The Paradigm of 'Risk and Protection-Focused Prevention' and Its Impact on Services for Children and Families. *Children and Society*, 19: 77–90.

France, A. et al. (2004) *The on Track Early Intervention and Prevention Programme: From Theory to Action*. Home Office Online Report 10/04. London: Home Office.

Fraser, M.W. (Ed) (1997) *Risk and Resilience in Childhood: an Ecological Perspective*. Washington, DC: National Association of Social Work Press.

Freeman, C., Henderson P. and Kettle J. (1999) *Planning With Children for Better Communities: The Challenge to Professionals*. Bristol: Community Development Foundation/The Policy Press.

Freeman, P., Kelly, N., Proykov, T., Norwich, B., Burden, B. and Jack, G. (2005) *An Evaluation of the Devon Children's Fund*. Exeter: University of Exeter.

Furstenberg, F.F. and Hughes, M.E. (1995) Social Capital and Successful Development among At-Risk Youth. *Journal of Marriage and The Family*, 57: 580–92.

Furstenberg, F.F. et al. (1999) *Managing to Make It. Urban Families and Adolescent Success*. Chicago: University of Chicago Press.

Garbarino, J. (1976) A Preliminary Study of Some Ecological Correlates of Child Abuse: The Impact of Socioeconomic Stress on Mothers. *Child Development*, 47: 178–85.

Garbarino, J. and Crouter, A. (1978) Defining the Community Context for Parent-Child Relations: The Correlates of Child Maltreatment. *Child Development*, 49: 604–16.

Garbarino, J. and Kostelny, K. (1992) Neighbourhood and Community Influences on Parenting. In Luster, T. and Okagaki, L. (Eds.) *Parenting: an Ecological Perspective*. Hillsdale, NJ: Lawrence Erlbaum.

Garbarino, J. and Sherman, D. (1980) High-Risk Neighborhoods and High-Risk Families: The Human Ecology of Child Maltreatment. *Child Development*, 51: 188–98.

Gattrell, A. et al. (2000) Understanding Health Inequalities: Locating People in Geographical and Social Spaces. In Graham, H. (Ed.) *Understanding Health Inequalities*. Buckingham: Open University Press.

Ghate, D. (2001) Community-Based Evaluations in the UK: Scientific Concerns and Practical Constraints. *Children and Society*, 15, 23–32.

Ghate, D. and Hazel, N. (2002) *Parenting in Poor Environments: Stress, Support and Coping*. London: Jessica Kingsley Publishers.

Ghate, D. and Ramella, M. (2002) *Positive Parenting: The National Evaluation of The Youth Justice Board's Parenting Programme*. London: YJB.

Gilchrist, A. (2003) Linking Partnerships and Networks. In Banks, S. et al. (Eds.) *Managing Community Practice: Principles, Policies and Programmes*. Bristol: The Policy Press.

Gilchrist, A. (2000) The Well-Connected Community: Networking to the Edge of Chaos. *Community Development Journal*, 35: 3, 265–75.

Gill O. (2001) *Invisible Children; Child and Family Poverty in Bristol, Bath, Gloucestershire, Somerset and Wiltshire*. Barkingside: Barnardo's.

Gill, O. (1996) Child Protection and Neighbourhood Work. Dilemmas for Practice. *Practice* 8: 2, 33–45.

Gill, O. and Sharps, S. (2004) *Children and Community in Central Weston-Super-Mare*. Bristol: Barnardo's.

Gill, O., Tanner, C., and Bland, L. (2000) *Family Support: Strengths and Pressures in a 'High Risk' Neighbourhood*. Barkingside: Barnardo's.

Gilligan, R. (1998) The Importance of Schools and Teachers in Child Welfare. *Child and Family Social Work*, 3: 1, 13–25.

Ginsberg, N. (2005) The Privatisation of Council Housing. *Critical Social Policy*, 25: 1, 115–35.

Glass, N. (2001) What Works for Children: The Political Issues. *Children and Society*, 15: 14–20.

Glennerster, H. et al. (2004) *One Hundred Years of Poverty and Policy*. York: Joseph Rowntree Foundation.

Gordon, D. et al. (2000) *Poverty and Social Exclusion in Britain*. York: Joseph Rowntree Foundation.

Graham, K. and Harris, A. (2005) New Deal for Communities as a Participatory Public Policy: The Challenges of Evaluation. In Taylor, I. and Balloch, S. (Eds.) *The Politics of Evaluation*. Bristol: The Policy Press

Green, R. (2000) Applying a Community Needs Profiling Approach to Tackling Service User Poverty. *British Journal of Social Work*, 30: 3, 287–303.

Gregg, P., Hansen, K. and Wadsworth, J. (2000) *Measuring the Polarisation of Work Across Households* (Working Paper) Essex: Department of Economics, University of Essex.

Guardian (2005) Ministers Warned Over 'Dumped Children' *The Guardian* July 5th p10.

Harper, R. (2001) *Social Capital: A Review of the Literature*. London: Office for National Statistics.

Harrington, V., Trikha, S. and France, A. (Eds.) (2004) *Process and Early Implementation Issues: Emerging Findings from the on Track Evaluation*. Online Report. London: Home Office.

Hawtin, M., Hughes, G. and Percy-Smith, J. (1994) *Community Profiling: Auditing Social Needs*. Buckingham: Open University Press.

Heenan, D. and Birrell, D. (2002) Re-Evaluating the Relationship Between Social Work and Community Development. The Northern Ireland Experience. *Social Work and Social Sciences Review*, 9: 2, 42–57.

Henderson, P. and Thomas, D. (2002) *Skills in Neighbourhood Work* (3rd Edn.) London: Routledge.

Herbert, G.W. and Wilson, H. (1978) *Parents and Children in the Inner City*. London: Routledge.

Hill, M.S. and Jenkins, S.P. (2001) Poverty Among British Children: Chronic or Transitory? In Bradbury, B., Jenkins, S.P. and Micklewright, J. (Eds.) *The Dynamics of Child Poverty in Industrialised Countries* (UNICEF) Cambridge: University of Cambridge Press.

Hills, J. (1995) *Inquiry Into Income and Wealth (Vol. 2)* York: Joseph Rowntree Foundation.

Hills, J. (2004) *Inequality and the State.* Oxford: Oxford University Press.

Hine, J. (2005) Early Multiple Intervention: A View from on Track. *Children and Society,* 19: 117–30.

Hirsch, D. (2004) *Strategies Against Poverty: A Shared Road Map.* York: Joseph Rowntree Foundation.

Hirsch, D. (2006) *What Will It Take to End Child Poverty? Firing on all Cylinders.* York: Joseph Rowntree Foundation.

HM Treasury (2003) *Every Child Matters.* London: The Stationery Office.

Hoggett, P. (1997) *Contested Communities: Experiences, Struggles, Policies.* Bristol: The Policy Press.

Holman, B. (1981) *Kids at The Door.* Oxford: Blackwell.

Holman, B. (2000) *Kids at The Door Revisited.* Lyme Regis: Russell House Publishing.

Holman, B. (2003) A Different World. *Community Care, 18–24 Sept.* (11–12)

Home Office (1999) *On Track Programme: Invitations to Bid.* London: Home Office Family Policy Unit.

Home Office (2001) *Children's Fund Guidance.* Children and Young People's Unit. London: HMSO.

Home Office (2003) *Building Civil Renewal. Government Support for Community Capacity Building and Proposals for Change.* London: The Stationery Office.

Hope, T. and Foster, J. (1992) Conflicting Forces: Changing The Dynamics of Crime and Community on A Problem Estate. *British Journal of Criminology,* 32: 488–504.

Hughes, M. and Traynor, T. (2000) Reconciling Process and Outcome in Evaluating Community Initiatives. *Evaluation,* 6: 1, 37–49.

Jack, G. (1997) An Ecological Approach to Social Work With Children and Families. *Child and Family Social Work,* 2: 2, 109–20.

Jack, G. (2000) Ecological Influences on Parenting and Child Development. *British Journal of Social Work,* 30, 703–20.

Jack, G. (2004) Child Protection at The Community Level. *Child Abuse Review,* 13: 368–83.

Jack, G. (2005) Assessing the Impact of Community Programmes Working With Children and Families in Disadvantaged Areas, *Child and Family Social Work,* 10: 293–304.

Jack, G. (2006) The Area and Community Components of Children's Well-Being. *Children and Society,* 20: 334–47.

Jack, G. and Gill, O. (2003) *The Missing Side of The Triangle: Assessing The Importance of Family and Environmental Factors in The Lives of Children.* Barkingside: Barnardo's.

Jack, G. and Jack, D. (2000) Ecological Social Work: The Application of a Systems Model of Development in Context. In Stepney, P. and Ford, D. (Eds.) *Social Work Models, Methods and Theories: A Framework for Practice.* Lyme Regis: Russell House Publishing.

Jack, G. and Jordan, B. (1999) Social Capital and Child Welfare. *Children and Society,* 13, 242–56.

Jackson, S. and Nixon, P. (1999) Family Group Conferences: A Challenge to The Old Order? In Dominelli, L. (Ed.) *Community Approaches to Child Welfare: International Perspectives.* Aldershot: Ashgate.

Jones, T., Gill, O. and Lewis, J. (2002) Children in the Round. *Community Care, 18–24 April* (9–10).

Jones, L., Davis, A. and Eyers, T. (2000) Young People, Transport and Risk: Comparing Access and Independent Mobility in Urban, Suburban and Rural Environments. *Health Education Journal*, 59: 315–28.

Jordan, B., Redley, M. and James, S. (1994) *Putting the Family First: Identities, Decisions, Citizenship*. London: UBL Press.

Jordan, B. (1997) Partnership With Service Users in Child Protection and Family Support. In Parton, N. (Ed.) *Child Protection and Family Support: Tensions, Contradictions and Possibilities*. London: Routledge.

Joshi, H. et al. (2000) Putting Health Inequalities on the Map: Does Where You Live Matter? In Graham, H. (Ed.) *Understanding Health Inequalities*. Buckingham: Open University Press.

Katz, I. and Pinkerton, J. (Eds.) (2003) *Evaluating Family Support: Thinking Internationally, Thinking Critically*. Chichester. Wiley.

Katz, L., Kling, J. and Liebman, J. (2001) Moving to Opportunity in Boston: Early Results of A Randomized Mobility Experiment. *Quarterly Journal of Economics*, 116: 2, 607–54.

Kemp, P. et al. (2004) *Routes Out of Poverty: A Research Review*. York: Joseph Rowntree Foundation.

Kohen, D.E. et al. (2002) Neighborhood Income and Physical and Social Disorder in Canada; Associations With Young Children's Competencies. *Child Development*, 73: 1844–60.

Korbin, J.E. (1989) Fatal Maltreatment by Mothers: A Proposed Framework. *Child Abuse and Neglect*, 13: 481–9.

Laming, Lord (2003) *The Victoria Climbié Inquiry Report*. London: The Stationery Office.

Land, H. (2002) *Meeting The Child Poverty Challenge: Why Universal Childcare is Key to Ending Child Poverty*. London: Daycare Trust.

Lee, P. and Murie, A. (1997) *Poverty, Housing Tenure and Social Exclusion*. Bristol: The Policy Press.

Lupton, R. (2003) *Poverty Street: The Dynamics of Neighbourhood Decline and Renewal*. Bristol: The Policy Press.

Mack, J. and Lansley, S. (1985) *Poor Britain*. London: Allen and Unwin.

Mack, J. and Lansley, S. (1991) *Breadline Britain*. London, Unwin Hyman.

Mackian, S. (2002) Complex Cultures: Rereading The Story About Health and Social Capital. *Critical Social Policy*, 22: 203–25.

Mahoney, J.L. and Stattin, H. (2000) Leisure Activities and Adolescent Antisocial Behaviour: The Role of Structure and Social Context. *Journal of Adolescence*, 23: 113–27.

Margo, J. and Dixon, M. et al. (2006) *Freedom's Orphans. Raising Youth in A Changing World*. London: Institute for Public Policy Research.

Marsh, A. and Perry, J. (2003) Ethnic Minority Families: Poverty and Disadvantage. In Kober, C. (Ed.) *Black and Ethnic Minority Children and Poverty: Exploring The Issues*. London: NCB.

Masten, A.S. and Coatsworth, J.D. (1998) The Development of Competence in Favourable and Unfavourable Environments. *American Psychologist*, 53: 2, 205–20.

Matthews, H. (2001) *Children and Community Regeneration. Creating Better Neighbourhoods*. London: Save The Children.

MHB (2003) *Evaluation of The Youth Inclusion Programme: End of Phase One Report.* London: Morgan Harris Burrows.

Millward, A. and Wheway, R. (1997) *Child's Play: Facilitating Play on Housing Estates.* Coventry: Chartered Institute of Housing.

Monk, D. (2004) *The Use of Genograms in The Child Abuse Investigative Process.* Exeter: Unpublished Mphil Thesis, University of Exeter.

Morrow, V. (2001) *Networks and Neighbourhoods: Children's and Young People's Perspectives.* London: Health Development Agency.

Morrow, V. (2002) Children's Rights to Public Space: Environment and Curfews. In Franklin, B. (Ed.) *The New Handbook of Children's Rights.* London: Routledge.

Moss, P. and Petrie, P. (2002) *From Children's Services to Children's Spaces: Public Policy, Children and Childhood.* London: Routledge Falmer.

Mumford, K. and Power, A. (2003) *East Enders; Family and Community in East London.* Bristol: The Policy Press.

Munro, E. (2004) Can Tracking Children Reduce the Harm of Poverty? *Poverty,* 119: 7–10.

Murie, A. (1997) Linking Housing Changes to Crime. *Social Policy and Administration,* 31: 5, 22–36.

Murtagh, B. (1999) Listening to Communities: Locality Research and Planning. *Urban Studies,* 36: 7, 1181–93.

Nelson, S. and Baldwin, N. (2002) Comprehensive Neighbourhood Mapping: Developing A Powerful Tool for Child Protection. *Child Abuse Review,* 11, 214–29.

Nelson, S. and Baldwin, N. (2004) The Craigmillar Project: Neighbourhood Mapping to Improve Children's Safety From Sexual Crime. *Child Abuse Review,* 13, 415–25.

Newburn, T. (2001) What Do We Mean by Evaluation? *Children and Society,* 15, 5–13.

Newman, T. (2004) *What Works in Building Resilience?* Barkingside: Barnardo's.

NISW (1982) *Social Workers: Their Role and Tasks (Barclay Report)* London: Bedford Square Press.

NYA (1994) *Nothing Ever Happens Around Here. Developing Work With Young People in Rural Areas.* Leicester: NYA.

ODPM (2004a) *The English Indices of Deprivation 2004.* London: Her Majesty's Stationery Office.

ODPM (2004b) *Housing Statistics 2004.* London: The Stationery Office.

ODPM (2005) *New Deal for Communities 2001–2005: an Interim Evaluation.* Research Report 17. London: ODPM.

Office for National Statistics (2002) *People's Perceptions of Their Neighbourhoods and Community Involvement.* London: The Stationery Office.

Office for National Statistics (2004) *Focus on Social Inequalities.* London: Office for National Statistics.

Oxley, H. et al. (2003) Income Inequalities and Poverty Among Children and Households With Children in Selected OECD Countries. In Vleminckx, K. and Smeeding, T.M. (Eds.) *Child Well-Being, Child Poverty and Child Policy in Modern Nations* (Revised Edition) Bristol: The Policy Press.

Packman, J., with Randall, J. and Jacques, N. (1986) *Who Needs Care? Social Work Decisions About Children.* Oxford: Blackwell.

Pain, R. et al. (2002) *'Hard to Reach' Young People and Community Safety: A Model for Participatory Research and Consultation.* London: Home Office.

Palmer, G., Carr, J. and Kenway, P. (2004) *Monitoring Poverty and Social Exclusion*. York: Joseph Rowntree Foundation.

Parton, N. (1985) *The Politics of Child Abuse*. Basingstoke: Macmillan.

Parton, N. (Ed.) (1997) *Child Protection and Family Support. Tensions, Contradictions and Possibilities*. London: Routledge.

Pawson, R. and Tilley, N. (1997) *Realistic Evaluation*. London: Sage.

Pevalin, D.J. and Rose, D. (2003) *Social Capital for Health: Investigating The Links Between Social Capital and Health Using The British Household Panel Survey*. London: Health Development Agency.

Power, A. (1997) *Estates on the Edge. The Social Consequences of Mass Housing in Northern Europe*. London: Macmillan.

Power, A. (1989) Housing, Community and Crime. In Downes, D. (Ed.) *Crime and The City: Essays in Memory of John Barron Mays*. Basingstoke: Macmillan.

Putnam, R. (2000) *Bowling Alone: The Collapse and Revival of American Community*. New York: Simon and Schuster.

Rhodes, J. et al. (2002) *Lessons and Evaluation Evidence From Ten Single Regeneration Budget Case Studies*. London: Department for Transport, Local Government and The Regions.

Rock, P. (1988) Crime Reduction Initiatives on Problem Estates. In Hope, T. and Shaw, M. (Eds.) *Communities and Crime Reduction*. Home Office Planning Unit, HMSO, London.

Rowntree, B.S. (1941) *Poverty and Progress: A Second Social Survey of York*. London: Longmans.

Rowntree, B.S. and Lavers, G.R. (1950) *Poverty and the Welfare State: A Third Social Survey of York Dealing only with Economic Questions*. London: Longmans.

Rutter, M. (1980) *Changing Youth in a Changing Society*. Cambridge, MA: Harvard University Press.

Rutter, M. (1985) Resilience in the Face of Adversity: Protective Factors and Resistance to Psychiatric Disorder. *British Journal of Psychiatry*, 147: 598–611.

Rutter, M., Giller, H. and Hagell, A. (1998) *Antisocial Behaviour by Young People*. Cambridge: Cambridge University Press.

Sampson, R.J. and Groves, W.B. (1989) Community Structure and Crime: Testing Social Disorganisation Theory. *American Journal of Sociology*, 94: 4, 774–802.

Sampson, R.J., Morenoff, J.D. and Earls, F. (1999) Beyond Social Capital: Spatial Dynamics of Collective Efficacy for Children. *American Psychological Review*, 64: 633–60.

Sampson, R.J., Raudenbush, S.W. and Earls, F. (1997) Neighbourhoods and Violent Crime: A Multi-Level Study of Collective Efficacy. *Science*, 277, 1–7.

Seaman, P. et al. (2006) *Parenting and Children's Resilience in Disadvantaged Communities*. London: NCB.

Shelter (2002) *Where's Home? Children and Homelessness in Bristol*. London: Shelter.

Shera, W. and Wells, L.M. (Eds) (1999) *Empowerment Practice in Social Work*. Toronto: Canadian Scholars Press.

Sidebotham, P. and The ALSPAC Study Team (2000) Patterns of Child Abuse in Early Childhood, A Cohort Study of the 'Children of The Nineties'. *Child Abuse Review*, 9: 311–20.

Sidebotham, P. and The ALSPAC Study Team (2002) Child Maltreatment in The 'Children of The Nineties': Deprivation, Class and Social Networks in a UK Sample. *Child Abuse and Neglect*, 26: 1243–59.

Simon, B.L. (1994) *The Empowerment Tradition in American Social Work. A History.* Columbia: Columbia University Press.

Skinner, S. and Wilson, M. (2002) *Assessing Community Strengths: A Practical Handbook for Planning Capacity Building.* London: Community Development Foundation.

Smalle, Y. and Henderson, P. (2003) The Manager's Role in Community Auditing. In Banks, S. et al. (Eds.) *Managing Community Practice, Principles, Policies and Programmes.* Bristol: The Policy Press.

Social Exclusion Unit (1998) *Bringing Britain Together: A National Strategy for Neighbourhood Renewal.* London: The Cabinet Office.

Social Exclusion Unit (2001) *A New Commitment to Neighbourhood Renewal: National Strategy Action Plan.* London: Social Exclusion Unit.

Spencer, N. (1996) Reducing Child Health Inequalities. In Bywaters, P. and McLeod, E. (Eds.) *Working for Equality in Health.* London: Routledge.

Squires, P. and Measor, L. (2005) Below Decks on the Youth Justice Flagship. The Politics of Evaluation. In Taylor, D. and Balloch, S. (Eds.) *The Politics of Evaluation.* Bristol: The Policy Press.

Standing Conference for Community Development (2001) *A Strategic Framework for Community Development.* Sheffield: SCCD.

Stewart, K. (2005) Towards an Equal Start? Addressing Childhood Poverty and Deprivation. In Hills, J. and Stewart, K. (Eds.) *A More Equal Society? New Labour, Poverty, Inequality and Exclusion.* Bristol: The Policy Press.

Stones, C. (1994) *Focus on Families: Family Centres in Action.* Basingstoke: Macmillan.

Thomas, B. and Dorling, D. (2004) *Know Your Place. Housing Wealth and Inequality in Great Britain 1980–2003 and Beyond.* London: Shelter.

Thomas, G. and Thompson, G. (2004) *A Child's Place: Why Environment Matters to Children.* London: Green Alliance/DEMOS.

Thompson, R.A. (1995) *Preventing Child Maltreatment Through Social Support.* Sage: London.

Townsend, P. (1962) The Meaning of Poverty. *British Journal of Sociology,* 13: 3, 210–27.

Townsend, P. (1979) *Poverty in The United Kingdom: A Survey of Household Resources and Standards of Living.* Harmandsworth: Penguin.

Tunstall, R. and Lupton, R. (2003) *Is Targeting Deprived Areas an Effective Means to Reach Poor People? An Assessment of One Rationale for Area-Based Funding Programmes.* CASE Paper 70. London: London School of Economics.

Tunstill, J. (2003) Political and Technical Issues Facing Evaluators of Family Support. In Katz, I. and Pinkerton, J. (Eds.) *Evaluating Family Support: Thinking Internationally, Thinking Critically.* Chichester: Wiley.

Vinson, T., Baldry, E. and Hargreaves, J. (1996) Neighbourhoods, Networks and Child Abuse. *British Journal of Social Work,* 26, 523–43.

Walklate, S. (1998) Crime and Community: Fear or Trust? *British Journal of Sociology,* 49: 550–69.

Wattam, C. (1999) The Prevention of Child Abuse. *Children and Society,* 13: 317–29.

Wedderburn, D. (1962) Poverty in Britain Today: The Evidence. *Sociological Review,* 10: 3, 257–82.

Weil, M. (1996) Community Building. Building Community Practice. *Social Work* 4: 5, 482–99.

Weiss, C.H. (1995) Nothing as Practical as Good Theory: Exploring Theory-Based Evaluation for Comprehensive Community Initiatives for Children and Families. In Connell, J.P. et al. (Eds.) *New Approaches to Evaluating Community Initiatives: Concepts, Methods and Contexts.* Washington, DC: Aspen Institute.

Westcott, H. and Cross, M. (1996) *This Far and No Further: Towards Ending The Abuse of Disabled Children.* Birmingham: Venture Press.

Wikström, P-O.H. (1991) *Urban Crime, Criminals and Victims: The Swedish Experience in an Anglo-American Comparative Perspective.* New York: Springer-Verlag.

Wilkins, H. (2004) Fancy Using This Subway? *Regeneration and Renewal,* 5th March: 19.

Williamson, H. (2006) Opinion: Find Structure in the Unstructured Work. *Young People Now,* 8 Nov. (13).

Wilkinson, R. (2005) *The Impact of Inequality: How to Make Sick Societies Healthier.* London: The New Press.

Winnicott, D.W. (1964) *The Child, The Family, and The Outside World.* Harmondsworth: Penguin Books.

Wright, S. (2004) Child Protection in The Community. *Child Abuse Review,* 13, 384–98.

Yates, T. and Masten, A. (2004) The Promise of Resilience Research for Practice and Policy. In Newman, T. *What Works in Building Resilience?* Barkingside: Barnardo's.

Youth Justice Board (2005) *Mentoring Schemes 2001 to 2004.* London: YJB.

Index

Russell House Publishing Ltd

We publish a wide range of professional, reference and educational books including:

Social work and well-being
By Bill Jordan   2007   ISBN 978-1-905541-13-3

Using practice examples, up-to-date survey evidence, historical analysis, and ideas from several disciplines, Jordan's compelling voice adds to those already challenging the assumption that happiness is affected more by people's material circumstances than by their physical and mental health, and their relationships with others.

Kids at the door revisited
By Bob Holman   2000   ISBN 978-1-898924-58-6

This book tells the story of a community youth work project in Bath through interviews with young people who were involved. It also tells their stories over the decade that followed.

Its core message must not be overlooked: effective support for young people at risk cannot be built in a vacuum and must be developed organically in the context of the cultures and communities to which they belong.

Young People Now

Don't shoot! I'm a detached youth worker
By Mike and Inez Burgess   2006   ISBN 978-1-903855-95-9

Flexible and responsive, detached youth work works – in a wide variety of social settings – providing focused support for young people within communities, in places where they congregate.

His accounts of successful project work are both lively and informative.

Young People Now

Working with Black young people
Edited by Momodou Sallah and Carlton Howson   2007   ISBN 978-1-905541-14-0

Bringing together this work's different dimensions and perspectives, this book seeks to challenge both the accepted status quo of Black young people's negative over-representation in most aspects of life – including education, criminal justice, housing and health – and their under-representation in empiric literature. It seeks to help find ways forward.

Having their say
Young people and participation
Edited by David Crimmens and Andrew West   2004   ISBN 978-1-898924-78-4

An interesting and informative read for policy makers, professional and young people themselves, and indeed anyone interested in developing children and young people's participation in political life, citizenship and social inclusion.

Children & Society

Secret lives: growing with substance
Working with children and young people affected by familial substance misuse
Edited by Fiona Harbin and Michael Murphy   2006   ISBN 978-1-903855-66-9

Most books of this genre discuss either how to assess the issue or how to work with it: this book does both, leaving the reader with a sense of confidence as to how they might go about working with this group of service users, as well as why they are working with them in this way . . . I recommend this book for all concerned about substance misuse.

Community Care

Safeguarding children and young people
A guide to integrated practice
By Steven Walker and Christina Thurston   2007   ISBN 978-1-903855-90-4

In homes, schools, clubs, communities . . . affirms it is everyone's responsibility to work together to safeguard children.

Rostrum

An excellent reference book and packed with resources, case studies and examples to inform and help you train and equip others.

Youthwork

A valuable guiding resource.

Community Practitioner

An outstanding and comprehensive book.

The Teacher

Respect in the neighbourhood
Why neighbourliness matters
Edited by Kevin Harris   2007   ISBN 978-1-905541-02-7

Offers an astute analysis of the nature and effects of 'respect', as it is lived out in the day to day lives of ordinary people, but also points to ways in which it might be sustained and, even more ambitiously, restored.

Professor John Pitts, Editor of the *Community Safety Journal*

It shows how the weakening of communities is related to the weakening of respect.

Bob Holman

For more details on specific books, please visit our website:
www.russellhouse.co.uk
Or we can send you our catalogue if you contact us at:
Russell House Publishing, 4 St George's House, The Business Park, Uplyme Road, Lyme Regis, DT7 3LS
Tel: 01297 443948
Fax: 01297 442722
Email: help@russellhouse.co.uk